EA

FRIENDS
OF ACPL

D1236101

STOLEN!

A History of Base Stealing

by

RUSSELL ROBERTS

McFarland & Company, Inc., Publishers
Jefferson, North Carolina, and London

Cover: Pepper Martin displays the speed that enabled him to lead the
National League in steals three times (1933, 1934, and 1936). (Courtesy
of the National Baseball Hall of Fame Library, Cooperstown, New York.)

British Library Cataloguing-in-Publication data are available

Library of Congress Cataloguing-in-Publication Data

Roberts, Russell, 1953–
    Stolen! : a history of base stealing / by Russell Roberts.
        p.   cm.
    Includes bibliographical references (p.) and index.
    ISBN 0-7864-0650-X (sewn softcover : 50# alkaline paper) ∞
    1. Base running (Baseball)—History.   2. Baseball players—United
States—History.   I. Title.
    GV868.R63   1999
    796.357'27—dc21   98-53595
                                                                            CIP

Manufactured in the United States of America

McFarland & Company, Inc., Publishers
    Box 611, Jefferson, North Carolina 28640

To My Father

Who always played catch with me
when he got home from work,
just because I asked him to.

Acknowledgments

Any book is much more than the work of just one person. I would like especially to acknowledge Larry Lester for pointing me in the direction of an invaluable source of Negro League information, and all the other writers and editors of the many baseball books that were used in the preparation of this volume.

I would also like to thank the staff at the National Baseball Hall of Fame Library and Archives for continually searching out player files for me. A special mention goes to Darci Harrington and Pat Kelly for their help with photos.

Table of Contents

Introduction

It's a long way to Cooperstown. That wasn't meant literally, although it happens to be true. No interstate highway or modern multilane roadway leads directly to the little town in New York where the National Baseball Hall of Fame is located. Sure, I-88 brings you within the general vicinity of Cooperstown, but once you leave the comfort of this wide-lane feather bed it's a long trip down a winding, narrow country road until at last you reach the town. In the winter, with the rain coming down and freezing on the road and your car's steering wheel spinning like the ship's wheel on *Gilligan's Island* before the *Minnow* crashed, the trip becomes longer still.

Yet, despite the difficulty involved in actually arriving at Cooperstown, it's that much harder to get to when you're a baseball player. Putting aside the question of whether or not the Hall of Fame has lowered its induction standards, the fact remains that just a small fraction of those who played the game ever make it there. Lowered standards or not, the Hall of Fame is still one of the most exclusive clubs in the country.

It becomes even more restrictive if you're a base stealer. Think about it. The next time you visit the Hall, sweep your eyes along the rows of golden plaques glistening in the sunlight that streams in through the skylight in the Hall of Fame Gallery; how many of those immortalized heroes are in there because they were base stealers?

The simple answer: not many. There's Sliding Billy Hamilton, the nineteenth century speedster; King Kelly, the first great superstar; Max Carey, Cool Papa Bell, Lou Brock, and Luis Aparicio. Others, such as Ty Cobb, Honus Wagner, Eddie Collins, and Joe Morgan, were great base stealers but are in the Hall more for the overall excellence of their play than for their skill at swiping sacks.

That means it's six; just six ballplayers out of the more than 230 who are enshrined in the Hall of Fame are there mainly because they were the best at stealing bases. That's not a lot.

Certainly, other player categories have a much greater representation. There are sluggers galore, great pitchers by the dozens, and outstanding managers peeking around nearly every corner. But as for the base stealers, well, you have to look long and hard to find them.

Some folks believe that's probably the way it should be. To them, the stolen base is a relatively minor movement in the grand ballet of baseball. While it occasionally causes excitement and sometimes is even a critical part of the game, in general (say these folks) the steal has little or no effect on the outcome of the game, and in fact, more often than not, it costs the stealer's team more than it gains.

There might be some truth to that, although some of those who make their living by the stolen base take umbrage at that type of thinking, as Rickey Henderson does in Chapter 10 of this book. It is also true that historically it is the big slugger or the great pitcher, rather than the consummate base stealer, who brings fans out to the park. Anticipation of an offensive onslaught can lure fans for an entire season. As talented as Cobb and his other dead ball, base-stealing cronies were, the moment Babe Ruth started belting balls into the seats in record numbers Cobb could have swiped bases while running on his hands, and no one would have cared; the home run was all anyone wanted to see.

There is, nevertheless, something about the stolen base that appeals to most baseball fans. Certainly, the lack of a running game renders a team, and by extension any game they play, more one-dimensional. Eventually, sitting around and waiting for Harry Homer or Lou Long Ball to hit one out gets boring and stagnates the game, as happened in the 1950s. Baseball needs the steal, or at least the threat of the steal, to interject the unexpected into the game.

What's interesting about the steal is that, once a runner gets on first, he can use it to advance himself around the bases without any help from the batter. Each base that he steals gets the crowd a little more excited. Each time he breaks for the next bag, the crowd turns as one to watch him, momentarily forgetting the pitcher, catcher, hitter, hot dog vendor, and everyone else in the ballpark. Whether or not it makes sense, mathematically or otherwise, the steal is one of the most exciting plays in baseball.

Unfortunately, both in the Hall of Fame and the volumes of literature that have sprung up around the great game of baseball, stolen bases and the men who steal them have been noticeably absent. This book is meant to change that. It examines both the evolution of the steal throughout the years and the men who raised base thievery to a high art.

This book is not meant to be the ultimate word on the stolen base so much as the beginning of a dialogue on stealing. It's intended to be the written equivalent of two fans talking across the backyard fence about stealing and great base stealers, swapping stories, telling anecdotes, and trading information. Left to others is the exhausting but ultimately necessary task of producing a work covering every single aspect of stealing, including formulas that measure and rate all the base stealers.

This book, as might be ascertained from the comments above, is not a "numbers" book, full of ratios, percentages, and the like. Groups such as the very able Society for American Baseball Research are far more capable than I of crunching the numbers and producing a volume that measures, for instance, base stealing effectiveness.

What this book contains, instead, are the words of the base stealers and the stories about them. What does Rickey Henderson say is important to be a successful base stealer? What were Max Carey's views on stealing, and how did he get such a great jump? What method did Joe Morgan use to become one of the game's great stolen base artists? What were some of the antics that King Kelly used to pull to become such a memorable character? This is what can be found in these pages.

However, even a baseball book that isn't overly concerned with numbers needs to have *some*. After all, like all other sports, baseball does measure itself and its players by statistics. Most of the statistics in this volume have come from *The Baseball Encyclopedia*. Others were obtained from *The Sporting News Complete Baseball Record Book*. If some of the numbers provided in this book don't agree with those printed in other sources, it's not surprising. During the research and writing of this book it became apparent that different sources present different numbers for the same year, for player statistics, and for other measures of player performance.

But again, this is not a book about numbers. Instead, it is meant as the first step of a journey—a journey that with luck will someday shorten the distance to Cooperstown for those to whom there is nothing so honorable as stealing.

1

Diamond Delights
and Disasters

The way we think of stealing in baseball is highly romanticized: the runner's spikes flashing in the sun as he streaks toward the bag, the catcher throwing a laser strike to the base, both ball and runner arriving simultaneously while the umpire peers through a cloud of dust to make the call.

Unfortunately, reality is often just a bit different. More than likely the runner stumbles coming off the base, the catcher's throw goes into the next county, the cloud of dust is more like a puff, and the outcome is so obvious that the umpire could have made the call from the comfort of a luxury box.

Some steals are a delight to watch; others are Titanic-style disasters. With that in mind, what follow are some of the most notable examples of stolen bases in baseball history.

Of all the bases, home is the toughest to steal. One way to make it easier is if neither the runner nor the other team knows that it's being stolen. During a 1906 game between the Chicago Cubs and Pittsburgh Pirates, the Bucs loaded the bases. On third was future Hall-of-Famer Fred Clarke, Pittsburgh's player-manager. At the plate was first baseman Jim Nealon.

With the count three and one, Cubs' pitcher Mordecai "Three-Finger" Brown whipped a letter-high fastball past Nealon. It was a borderline pitch, but when umpire Hank O'Day didn't say a word, both Clarke and Nealon assumed it was ball four. Accordingly, Clarke trotted home from third, Nealon went to first, and the other runners moved up. Cubs' catcher Johnny Kling casually tossed the ball back to Brown.

Just as Clarke touched the plate, however, O'Day cried out, "Strike two!" Players from both teams stared at O'Day. "There was a frog in my throat," explained the embarrassed umpire. "I couldn't say a word."

Nealon had to return to the plate. However, since Clarke had crossed home at his own risk, without time being called, his run counted. The only way to credit it was as a steal of home.

Another momentous (or dubious) base-stealing milestone occurred in a 1905 game. Outfielder John Anderson of the Washington Senators (who was nicknamed the Terrible Swede, even though he was born in Norway) was on first, and decided to steal second. Since Anderson was a legitimate base-stealing threat (he would tie for the American League lead in steals in 1906 with 39), the play seemed to make sense. What Anderson had failed to consider, however, was that the bases were loaded, and so second base was already occupied. He broke for the bag and arrived there in short order, only to be quickly tagged out.

Making an out, however, was the least of the Terrible Swede's problems. The sheer stupidity of this play quickly circulated throughout baseball, with the result that every blockhead play was subsequently called a "John Anderson." Unfortunately for Anderson, the memory of his base-running gaffe lingered throughout the sport. The play was recounted year after year, like an old joke that can always be counted on to get a laugh. In 1911, a small article in the *New York Times* listed "John Anderson's slide as he stole second with the bases full" as one of the most notable "achievements" in the game's history—proof that even six years later, the play was still fresh in everyone's mind.

Anderson's reaction to his name's being synonymous with lamebrained play is not known. However, the Terrible Swede was "a man of peculiar disposition," according to contemporary newspaper reports, so it's likely that he was not particularly thrilled by the fact that pulling a "John Anderson" was about as far from a compliment as you could get on the diamond.

A few years later, a far more noteworthy base-stealing feat occurred. On June 20, 1912, the Boston Braves hosted the New York Giants. The Giants were on their way to their second straight pennant, while the Braves were heading for their fourth consecutive last-place finish.

Although it was only midseason, the teams were already playing as if it were late September, and their place in the standings had long since been determined. The Giants bombed a succession of hapless Boston pitchers, and by the top of the ninth New York led 14–2.

In the ninth, speedy Giants outfielder Josh Devore reached first safely. The previous year Devore had swiped 61 bases, which led the Giants and ranked him second in the National League in steals. However, in 1912 his pace had slowed radically; he would finish the year with just 27 steals. But on this day, Devore reached back for some of his old base-stealing magic. Despite the lopsided score, Devore decided to run, and stole second and third in rapid succession.

A hit drove the outfielder home. From his seat on the bench, Devore watched as the Giants continued to pound the ball. Before he knew it, he was up once again. Realizing a good thing when he saw one, Devore again singled, and again stole second and third.

Ultimately, the Giants poured across seven more runs in the inning, for a 21–2 lead. The Braves, not be outdone in a game that the next day's *New York Times* called a "farce comedy," answered back in the bottom of the ninth with 10 runs of their own. "Toward the end of the game," said the paper, "there was more or less demoralization on both sides and loose play, all of which excited the crowd to a high pitch of hilarity." The final score found the Giants on top by a touchdown and a safety, 21–12. The *Times* also noted that Devore had "distinguished himself by his base running." Indeed he had; four stolen bases in one inning set a record that has yet to be broken.

Getting thrown out while attempting to swipe a sack is one of the perils of being a base stealer. But getting thrown out twice in the same inning is something special.

It happened to Don Baylor of the Baltimore Orioles on June 15,

1974, in a game with the Chicago White Sox. With the score tied, the future manager of the Colorado Rockies entered the game in the ninth inning as a pinch runner. Baylor, who possessed better than average speed for a big man, promptly took off for second. Although catcher Ed Hermann's throw beat him to the bag, Baylor managed to kick the ball out of second baseman Ron Santo's glove. Though Baylor was safe, the rules required, however, that he be considered "caught stealing."

Baylor lost no time in stealing third. Then, with Andy Etchebarren at the plate, Orioles' skipper Earl Weaver called for the suicide squeeze. When Etchebarren missed the bunt the play became a straight steal and Baylor, running hard from third, was tagged out by Hermann—making it the second time he had been caught stealing in the same inning. Fortunately, the Orioles eventually won the game.

Winning was sometimes of secondary importance to some of baseball's early players. Detroit Tiger second baseman Germany Schaefer (his given name was Herman, but no one called him that) thought that baseball should be fun. To prove his point, he often entertained fans with a pregame juggling act.

One time, Schaefer, after telling the crowd that they were about to see "a demonstration of his great batting skill," clouted a home run. To celebrate, he slid into every base (including first), while announcing the results each time like a horse race: "The Prince leads at the quarter! It's the Prince at the halfway pole! It's the Prince by a mile!"

In Schaefer's somewhat unorthodox view of baseball, any play worth trying that did not work was worth trying again. Schaefer put this theory to the test in a 1908 game against Cleveland, when he was on first, outfielder Davy Jones was on third, and "Wahoo" Sam Crawford was at the plate.

Schaefer flashed Jones the sign for a delayed double steal. If all went according to plan, Schaefer would break for second, Cleveland catcher Nig Clarke would throw to the base trying to get him, and Jones would score. The first part of the scheme worked perfectly; Schaefer got a huge jump and slid safely into second base. Clarke, however, had figured out what was going on and held the ball. This left Schaefer at second, Jones at third, and Detroit still without a run scored.

This perturbed Schaefer. He had, after all, called the play, and he was determined to make it work. So, on the very next pitch, with a cry of "Let's try that again!" Schaefer took off once more—this time for first base. He arrived safely, in a cloud of dust, while the crowd roared and both teams wondered what was going on.

By this time Clarke had had enough. On the next pitch, Schaefer again bolted for second, but this time Clarke whipped the ball to the base, nailing him. Jones, however, broke for home after the throw to second. He scored, completing the double steal.

As daffy as stealing first base sounds, Schaefer did not originate the play. The 1903 *Reach Guide* recounted a similar incident that happened in a July 13, 1902, game between the Philadelphia A's and Detroit.

"It is customary to steal second and third, and even home sometimes, but here was a case where a player stole first," said the *Guide*. According to the book, the A's had Harry Davis on first and "Swarthy Dave" Fultz on third. Davis bluffed going to second, in hopes of drawing a throw, so that Fultz could break for home. Detroit, however, was wise to the scheme, and the catcher threw back to third, nearly picking Fultz off.

Here, however, is where it gets interesting. After being clever enough to foil the attempt at deception by the A's, the Detroit infield, without asking for time, decided to call a meeting, possibly to decide what to do against further Philadelphia trickery.

Unfortunately, they had neglected Davis, who was still standing benignly between first and second as a result of his aborted double steal attempt. Seeing his chance, Davis dashed back to first. The Detroit players went back to their positions, and pitcher George Mullin tried to settle down and concentrate on the batter.

But it was not to be. Suddenly Davis took off *again* for second. Mullin threw to shortstop Kid Eberfield, who had come over to cover second; however, since Davis had once again turned around and was heading back toward first, there was little Eberfield could do. Accordingly, he pegged the ball to first baseman Pete LePine. At that moment, just to complete the merry cycle, Fultz broke for home.

By this time, pandemonium reigned in the Detroit infield, especially for poor LePine, who, as the *Guide* put it, was "visibly rattled." His hurried throw to the plate was wide, and Fultz slid home for the well-earned run. "The audacity of Davis' play set the crowd wild," concluded the *Guide*.

Steals are rough on the opposing pitcher. Not only does he have to worry about the hitter—which is hard enough—but he also has to concentrate on keeping the base runner (or runners) pinned as close to the bag as possible, so that the catcher has at least a fighting chance of throwing him out should he try to steal. All of this can drive a pitcher to distraction.

In the late nineteenth century, legendary first baseman Adrian "Cap" Anson had a hard-throwing hurler on his staff who couldn't seem to remember to keep runners close at first. Naturally, the pitcher gave up stolen bases in bunches. Finally, Anson got tired of all this charity and admonished the pitcher to keep a closer eye on the runners. When the pitcher replied that he couldn't watch the plate and the base runners at the same time, Anson came up with a plan: he told the pitcher not to watch first, only home. Whenever the catcher took off his mask and spit tobacco juice, it was a signal for the hurler to whip the ball to Anson at first.

The next time the pitcher took the mound, Anson's words still rang in his ears. Just before the first batter stepped up, the catcher noticed that the plate was dirty. He took off his mask, spit some tobacco juice onto it, and cleaned it off.

Without hesitation the pitcher spun around and gunned the ball to Anson. Since there was nobody on base, this was the last thing that the first baseman expected, and the ball hit him squarely in the throat. As soon as he could eat solid food again, Anson cut the pitcher.

One of the most well-known stolen base episodes in baseball history involved a player who is more famous for hitting home runs than stealing bases: the immortal George Herman "Babe" Ruth.

Although no speed demon, the Babe stole 123 bases over the course of his 22-year career. Yet only his attempted steal in the seventh game of the 1926 World Series against the St. Louis Cardinals is remembered.

The Cardinals were clinging to a 3–2 lead against the New York Yankees when the ninth inning began. On the mound for the Redbirds was Grover Cleveland Alexander, who had already secured his place in baseball lore by fanning the dangerous Tony Lazzeri with the bases loaded in the seventh inning and the Cardinals ahead by that same 3–2 score. After getting the first two outs in the ninth, Alexander pitched carefully to Ruth—who had already belted four homers in the series—and walked him. Scornfully, the Babe flipped his bat high into the air and trotted down to first.

With hard-hitting Bob Meusel at bat and Lou Gehrig on deck, the Yankees were conceding nothing. But on Alexander's first pitch to Meusel, Ruth stunned the crowd by taking off for second. Cardinal catcher Bob O'Farrell gunned down the Babe, and the Cardinals were world champions for the first time in their history.

Most observers couldn't understand why Ruth tried to steal. "The only dumb play I ever saw Ruth make," Yankee general manager Ed Barrow said about it. But in the clubhouse after the game, Ruth explained that he thought Alexander was pitching so well that he felt compelled to do something to improve the Yankees' chances of scoring the tying run.

"I wasn't doing any good where I was [on first]," shrugged the Babe.

In 1974, staying on first was definitely *not* the idea for a unique new baseball specialist. Although, according to *The Baseball Encyclopedia*, Herb Washington played portions of two seasons for the Oakland Athletics, he never had an official at-bat. Yet this didn't stop him from stealing 29 bases in 1974 and igniting a charge of electrical excitement that surged through the crowd whenever he was on base. How did he do this? Simply by being Herb Washington—the major league's first "designated runner."

The designated runner was a brainstorm by A's owner Charles O. Finley, whose other bright ideas included orange baseballs, handlebar mustaches, and mule mascots. After all, he reasoned, baseball had introduced the designated hitter for those who couldn't hit; why not employ a designated runner for those who couldn't run?

The runner that Charlie O. selected was no slouch, either. Herb Washington was the fastest man in the world at that time, having run the 50-yard dash in 5.0 seconds while at Michigan State. The only problem was that Washington knew virtually nothing about base stealing, or even baseball. When Finley tracked him down, Washington was doing television sports. Undaunted, Charlie O. signed him, and brought in Maury Wills to tutor him.

Washington stole 29 bases in 45 attempts, including 17 out of 21 in one stretch, for a team that had won the World Series the previous two years and that included players such as Joe Rudi, Catfish Hunter, and Reggie Jackson. The A's won the American League pennant once again in 1974 and roared into their third straight World Series, this time against the Los Angeles Dodgers.

After dropping the first game, the Dodgers were ahead 3–0 in the ninth inning of the second contest. But the A's quickly struck for two runs, and with one out had the tying run on first base in the person of Rudi. What Oakland obviously needed was a way to get Rudi into scoring position without sacrificing an out. What the A's obviously needed was the designated runner, so out trotted Washington to run for Rudi.

On the mound for the Dodgers was ace reliever Mike Marshall, a man who had turned the pick-off into a science. Like everyone else in the ballpark, he knew precisely why Washington was out there. No sooner did Washington take his lead than Marshall stepped off the pitching rubber, driving the designated runner back to the bag.

Again Washington moved off first. This time, Marshall lobbed the ball over to first baseman Steve Garvey. Again Washington went back to the bag.

For the third time, Washington took his lead, and for the second time, Marshall stepped off the rubber. But this time, as Washington strolled back to first, expecting another soft toss, Marshall pegged a bullet to Garvey. Washington, who was so far off first base that he might have been in a different area code, was an easy out.

The Dodger Stadium crowd roared in delight at seeing the world's fastest man picked off. As the chagrined Washington returned to the dugout, the crowd on the first-base side of the field rose and let rip a resounding raspberry. (The last laugh, though, was on the Dodgers. Although they won the game, 3–2, the A's took the series, four games to one).

The next day, the *Philadelphia Inquirer* ran a photo of the play that showed the yawning gap between Washington and first base. "Washington Sleeps Here," read the caption.

The next season, Washington played only 13 games for the A's, and stole just two bases. Both Washington and the designated runner then disappeared from major league baseball.

Sadly, accounts of baseball's earliest—and greatest—base-stealing feats are also disappearing. Fans at the end of the nineteenth century knew it as the "$15,000 Slide." Although time has erased the memories, the play still stands as one of the most sensational endings ever to a World Series.

The year was 1886. The St. Louis Browns, champions of the American Association, were playing the Chicago White Sox, the top team in the National League, in the World Series.

Much was riding on the outcome of these games. Most significantly, it was a chance for the upstart American Association to prove that it was the equal of the older and more established National League. The National League, of course, wanted to confirm its superiority. Each team had the hopes of their respective league riding on their shoulders. For the players, victory came with an added incentive: whoever won the series got to keep all of the gate receipts. And with players still toiling under the restraints of the reserve clause, which allowed owners to blackball athletes refusing to sign low-wage contracts, surely few things motivated teams more than the prospect of a big payday.

Unlike other World Series during this era, the 1886 contest was a best-of-seven affair played at the home fields of each team. (Other World Series were played at various sites, including but not limited to the home parks of each team.) Each team had its stars. The Browns, considered one of the best teams of the nineteenth century, had Charles Comiskey, Bob Caruthers, Curt Welch, and Arlie "The Freshest Man on Earth" Latham. The White Sox countered with Cap Anson, Mike "King" Kelly, and ace pitcher John Clarkson.

Riding Clarkson's pitching, the White Sox jumped off to a 2–1 advantage in games. However, when the series switched to St. Louis, the rabid Browns rooters helped turn the tide for their team. By the time the deciding game began, the Browns were one win away from the championship.

For seven innings, however, the White Sox and Clarkson had other ideas. Behind their star hurler, Chicago built a 3–0 lead. Then, in the eighth inning, the roof caved in for the Sox, as the Browns scored three to tie the score.

At the end of nine the teams remained tied, and so the battle continued into extra innings. In the bottom of the tenth, speedy Browns outfielder Curt Welch was hit by a Clarkson pitch and started for first. After catcher King Kelly complained that Welch had deliberately tried to get hit, however, the umpire ordered the Browns player back to the plate. Angry, Welch promptly lashed a single to center. The next batter, Dave Foutz, hit a certain double-play grounder to short, but the ball was kicked around and everyone was safe. A sacrifice by Yank Robinson put Welch on third and Foutz on second.

With the frenzied St. Louis fans screaming, Welch began scampering up and down the third base line, bluffing a steal of home. The rattled Clarkson peered in for the sign from King Kelly. What happened next has been the object of debate for over a century.

Some say that Welch broke for the plate, stealing home in a classic cloud-of-dust slide that forever became known as the "$15,000 slide" (the approximate amount of the Browns' winnings). Others say that the pitch from Clarkson was wild and got past Kelly, enabling Welch to score standing up. Still another school of thought faults Kelly, declaring the pitch a passed ball. Perhaps the most reliable source is Kelly, who said: "I signaled Clarkson for a low ball on one side and when it came it was high upon the other. It struck my hand as I tried to get it and I would say it was a passed ball. You can give it to me if you want to. Clarkson told me that it slipped from his hands."

No matter how it happened, the play quickly became famous as a daring steal of home by Welch to win the World Series, and today the "$15,000 Slide" is part of the legend of baseball.

It's an insignificant play, one that has been obscured by the high drama of the entire game. But if not for this one seemingly trivial steal of second, the history of baseball might be different.

In the ninth inning of game four of the 1947 World Series between the Yankees and the Dodgers, New York's Bill Bevans was on the verge of doing what had never been done before in the Fall Classic: pitch a no-hitter. If Bevans could keep the Dodgers hitless in the bottom of the ninth and preserve his 2–1 lead, not only would he live forever in baseball lore, he would also give the Yankees a 3–1 stranglehold in games.

Pitching carefully in the ninth, Bevans walked Carl "The Reading Rifle" Furillo with one out. Following the second out, Al Gionfriddo went in to pinch-run for Furillo. With left-handed Pete Reiser up as a pinch hitter, Gionfriddo stole second.

Suddenly the entire complexion of the game changed. With the tying run now on second, Yankee skipper Bucky Harris ordered an intentional walk for Reiser, even though it was strictly against the book to put the potential winning run on base. But Harris knew that Reiser was the last left-handed bat on the Dodger bench. He wanted Bevans to take his chances with the next Brooklyn batter, the right-handed hitting Eddie Stanky, rather than with a dangerous lefty like Reiser.

Ironically, Reiser was at the plate with a broken ankle suffered in the previous game. He had asked that the injury just be taped to mask its severity, however, and so Harris had no way of knowing that the man he considered one of the most dangerous hitters for the Dodgers was severely hobbled.

So Reiser was walked, and Cookie Lavagetto was sent up to hit for Stanky. Any baseball fan knows what happened next: Lavagetto rattled a shot off the right field wall, and both runners scored. In an instant, both the no-hitter and the victory were snatched from Bevans' grasp.

Although it has never been singled out due to the dramatic circumstances surrounding it, Gionfriddo's steal of second was a pivotal play. Without it, Harris might have had Bevans pitch to Reiser. But with the Dodger outfielder on second representing the tying run, Harris went with the time-honored baseball axiom that a right-handed pitcher has a better chance against a right-handed hitter. That decision—caused by a steal of second base—doomed Bill Bevans' chance at immortality.

Sometimes steals are straightforward plays; sometimes they're more convoluted than a political speech. One of the most bizarre plays in Rickey Henderson's 1982 quest to break Lou Brock's season-high stolen base mark of 118 thefts might be called "the steal that didn't happen, thanks to the steal that didn't happen."

On August 24, 1982, the A's were playing Detroit in the last game of a long homestand. Henderson needed three steals to tie Brock and four to break the record. Both he and A's manager Billy Martin desperately wanted to set the record in Oakland as a reward for the hometown fans, who had strongly supported the team all season. Henderson stole two bases in the first inning, but didn't get another chance until the eighth.

Henderson was the second batter in the eighth. First up was last-place hitter Fred "Chicken" Stanley. Tiger pitcher Jerry Ujdur walked Stanley, prompting cries that he had done so just to clog up the bases and ruin any chance for Henderson to steal. When Rickey followed with a ringing single to left, it seemed like the Tigers' strategy had worked perfectly. Even the seemingly unstoppable Henderson couldn't steal second with the base already occupied. The hometown fans seemed destined to be disappointed.

But the Tigers had reckoned without Billy Martin. Dipping deep into his bag of tricks, the Oakland manager ordered Stanley to steal third. During his career, one thing that had never happened to Stanley was to be confused with Ty Cobb. Martin knew that Stanley, having stolen just 11 bases in his 13 years in the big leagues, had little chance of reaching third safely. The idea, then, was for him to be thrown out, thus clearing the bases for Henderson.

However, before the Chicken could unleash his lightning legs, Tigers' skipper Sparky Anderson figured the whole thing out. As Stanley inched further and further away from second, Anderson screamed at his infielders, "Do not tag him!"

Finally, Stanley wandered so far off second base that Ujdur was forced to throw to Tiger shortstop Alan Trammell, who had come over to cover the base. Obligingly, Chicken stopped between second and third, waiting to be tagged. Trammell, now faced with the curious situation of a runner trying to make an out and his manager telling him not to take the out, decided to pass the problem to third baseman Enos Cabell by throwing him the ball. Cabell, however, instantly whipped it to second baseman Lou Whitaker. Meanwhile, the Chicken remained rooted between second and third; if a hot dog vendor had wandered by Stanley would have had time for two franks and a beer. Finally, Whitaker mercifully ended the farce by tagging him out.

Martin's scheme had worked, although in a more circular fashion than he had anticipated, and the way was now clear for Henderson to reward the Oakland fans for their support. He immediately took off for second—only to get thrown out. Brock's record survived for a few more days, until Henderson tied and broke it in Milwaukee against the Brewers.

August 14, 1958, is a date that stands out in the long and sometimes odd history of the stolen base. That day, in a game between Cleveland and Detroit, yet another chapter was written in the story of stealing, by a player who stole just 45 bases in his entire career.

As a first baseman, Vic Power was a polished fielder, garnering seven Gold Gloves and consistently wowing the fans with his one-handed stabs at sizzling grounders and errant throws. At the plate Power wasn't too shabby either, posting a lifetime .284 average while striking out less than 250 times in over 6,000 at bats. On the bases, however, he was virtually a statue; he averaged just under four stolen bases per year during his career.

Yet on August 14, 1958, while a member of the Indians, Power stole home not once, but twice, in the same game. The first came in the eighth inning, against pitcher Frank Lary, and tied the score at 8–8. Then, in the tenth inning, the Indians loaded the bases, with Power again on third base. At the plate was slugger Rocky Colavito, who was on his way to a 41–home run season. With the count 2-and-1 on Colavito, Power amazed everyone by taking off for home again. He slid across the plate just ahead of the tag, and the Indians won the game 10–9, snapping a five-game losing streak.

In swiping home twice, Power became the first major leaguer since 1927 to accomplish the feat. Asked later to explain why he risked the out with the heavy-hitting Colavito at the plate, Power replied, "I'm black and it's a night game; no one saw me."

The response was typical Power. Originally signed by the Yankees, it was widely assumed that he would be the first black to play with New York. "Power Signing Sets Yankee Negro Policy," trumpeted a 1953 article that virtually guaranteed he would make the club, particularly after he had led the American Association in batting with a .349 mark.

But Power was too flamboyant and too exuberant for the prim-and-proper Yankees. As their first black player the team wanted a nice, inconspicuous Chevrolet, but Power was more like a flashy red Thunderbird, and he made the Yankees nervous. At one point he attempted to eat in an all-white restaurant in the South. Told that they didn't serve Negroes, Power responded, "I don't eat Negroes, I want rice and beans." He also sent Yankee blood pressure soaring when he asked a white waitress out on a date.

Convinced that Power didn't fit their conservative image, the Yankees traded the flashy first baseman to the Philadelphia A's prior to the 1954 season. Power went on to have a fine 12-year career.

In 1990, in an interview in *Sports Collectors Digest*, Power explained that he didn't steal home twice that day to get his name in the record book, but to get revenge on the Tigers. "I did it because those guys on Detroit used to hit me with pitches all the time," Power said. As always, Vic Power did things his own way.

The New York Yankees were also used to doing things their own way. Once, however, a steal changed all that.

The scene was the first game of the 1955 World Series. For the fifth time in nine years, the New York Yankees were playing the Brooklyn Dodgers. The Dodgers had never beaten the Yankees in the World Series. There was no reason to think that they ever would.

"We could play them ten times, and they'd still lose. They'd lose because they're the Dodgers," said Yankee second baseman Billy Martin, putting into words what many baseball fans felt.

So, when the first game of the 1955 series reached the eighth inning with the Yankees leading 6–4 behind ace southpaw Whitey Ford, it was, as Yogi Berra once so succinctly stated, "déjà vu all over again." Clearly the Bronx Bombers were on their way to beating the Dodgers in this game. The victory would inevitably be followed by three more wins, and, just as inevitably, by cries of "wait until next year" while the Dodgers retreated to lick the wounds of yet another defeat at the hands of the Yankees.

But Jackie Robinson had other ideas.

By now he was older and heavier than when he had come into the league in 1947 and terrorized opponents at bat and on the bases. His hair was graying, his waistline was expanding, and the magnificent, muscular legs that had once ruled the base paths were battered and scarred.

Maybe that's why Ford didn't pay particular attention to Robinson when he reached third base in the eighth inning of the first game. In another time, and another place, the idea of Robinson on third would have been enough to send a pitcher into apoplexy. But Ford could have been excused for thinking that this was now a different Robinson. The Old Lion was heading into winter; let him sleep in peace.

But the Old Lion was not sleeping—just feigning. All at once, he made a mad dash for the plate, his legs pumping with the youth and vigor of old. Ford, surprised, threw home, but it was too late. Robinson, in a scene so familiar to baseball fans, slid across the plate safely.

If this had been Hollywood, then the Dodgers, inspired by Robinson's bold gamble, would have risen up to smite the Yankees and storm to victory. But baseball was not Hollywood, and the Yankees held on to win 6–5. In fact, the Yankees won the second game as well, and for the Dodgers, it seemed as if déjà vu had indeed come again.

But then, improbably, Brooklyn took three in a row from the Yankees back in the cozy confines of Ebbetts Field. After the Bronx Bombers staved off elimination in Game Six, Johnny Podres sent the borough of Brooklyn into a delirium of delight by beating New York 2–0 in the seventh and final game.

And what of Robinson's steal of home, so seemingly inconsequential at the time? Many labeled it a turning point for the Dodgers—a signal that yes, the Yankees could be taken, and that this year things were going to be different. Robinson later said: "Maybe it [the steal] didn't make sense. We were two runs behind. But I didn't do it to win the ball game. I did it to lift us out of a rut—and it worked. That play, I suspect, shook up the Yankees."

2

Early Thefts and Thieves

Epic moments that shaped baseball in its formative years did not occur with a clap of thunder and the herald of trumpets from on high. Instead, like most things in life, they happened quietly and matter-of-factly, slipping by so unobtrusively that no one was aware of the significance until much later.

So it was with the first stolen base. Some sources identify Robert Addy as the pioneer base thief, while others give Ned Cuthbert the credit. It's likely that neither one was the originator of the stolen base, but rather that one or both of these men used the play very early on, and it was so unusual that special mention of it was made in a newspaper report of the game.

If Cuthbert was the first, however, it might have gone something like this:

The year was 1863. Although national attention was firmly fixed on the bloody Civil War now raging in its third year across the United States, baseball was at least able to provide a diversion from the endless causality lists that were making mourners out of a growing number of families. The sport had been slowly and steadily spreading across the country, from city to town to village. (Even Union and Confederate soldiers were playing baseball, to break the monotony of camp life.) Although the game was still evolving, more and more often the rules followed were those devised by Alexander Joy Cart-wright and Daniel Lucius "Doc" Adams on the pastoral greenbelt known as the Elysian Fields in Hoboken, New Jersey.

At this point baseball was still a casual outing, played by a loose confederation of teams primarily for fun and enjoyment. (The first completely professional team, the 1869 Cincinnati Red Stockings, was still six years away.)

Precisely because baseball was a work in progress, unexpected things could and did take place during a game that no one was quite certain how to handle. This is exactly what happened during a game in 1863, when young Ned Cuthbert of the Philadelphia Keystones ran from first to second without benefit of a hit.

Seeing Cuthbert, the crowd laughed; who did this cheeky teenager think he was? After all, everyone knew that you needed a hit in order to advance around the bases.

But Cuthbert knew exactly what he was doing. When the umpire tried to shoo him back to first, Cuthbert calmly informed him that there was nothing in the rules forbidding what he had just done. And indeed there wasn't. Cuthbert had stolen the first base in baseball history. (The term "stolen base," however, did not come into existence until 1871.)

Is this the story of the first stolen base in baseball history? Maybe… And maybe not. Failing the existence of any definitive evidence, however, it's as good a place as any to place the credit (although even if Cuthbert was the first base thief, some say that the event occurred two years later, in 1865).

One thing is certain: If Cuthbert was indeed the originator of the stolen base, then he apparently never sought credit for it. His file at the National Baseball Hall of Fame Reference Library in Cooperstown is slim and does not contain any documentation identifying him as the father of the stolen base.

Among the documents in the file is his death notice from 1905. The story states that he was "one of the most noted of the pioneer professionals," and also that he was "original and aggressive in his methods and aided a great deal in the development of the science of the game." Could those statements be allusions to the fact that Cuthbert actually did originate the stolen base? Unfortunately, it seems unlikely that anyone will ever know for sure.

Cuthbert was apparently an extremely skilled player. Although he compiled just a .219 lifetime batting average, an 1881 article describes him as occupying "a prominent position as a player, his magnificent outfielding, safe and sure batting and fast baserunning being each in turn deserving of commendation."

Yet despite Cuthbert's skill, neither he nor anyone else in the game apparently made much use of this new weapon that came to be called the stolen base. Innovation has always come hard to baseball, and new ideas are often treated as cautiously as cheese on a mousetrap. This was just as true in the early years of the game as it is today.

Although baseball was in its infancy in the late 1860s, traditionalists (yes, they were around even then) were already denouncing the recently-developed pitching innovation called the curveball as "deceitful." They also looked down their collective noses at another invention, the bunt, calling it a "baby" play.

"Somehow or other they don't play ball nowadays as they used to some eight or ten years ago," sighed a player in 1868, giving new meaning to the term "old-timer."

Thus, with many of the innovations in baseball getting the cold shoulder, it is likely that the stolen base was dismissed as well, its considerable offensive potential largely ignored. George Wright, who starred with the 1869 Red Stockings and played through the 1870s and 1880s, commented in 1915 that no one realized the value of the stolen base when he was playing.

Yet despite the protests, other new ideas were introduced, and remained part of baseball. Batting gloves, catcher's masks, and fielder's sunglasses were all introduced during the 1870s and 1880s. (This doesn't mean, however, that they were accepted without a struggle. In 1877, the Louisville *Courier-Journal* sniffed that "there is about as much sense in putting a lightning rod on a catcher as a mask.") The basic structure of the game was continually altered as well, as club owners repeatedly tinkered with the rules to try to strike a balance between offense and defense.

A major sign that base stealing would remain part of baseball came in 1876, when William Hulbert formed the National League, and base stealing was included as part of the rules for the new circuit.

Thus the stolen base must have been a more accepted part of the game at this time, although Bill James, in his *Historical Baseball Abstract*, points out that stealing was apparently not as common in the early years of the professional game as it was in the amateur game of the 1860s.

Possibly the value of stealing had begun to be appreciated more as the nature of the game changed. By the time the National League was founded, the leisurely and genteel contest of the 1860s had given way to a faster, more aggressive game. Instead of playing polite baseball, teams strove to win at all costs.

The changes in the game were mirrored by changes in the players. Rowdyism was becoming rampant throughout baseball, led by the St. Louis Browns of the American Association. Fights, umpire abuse, and verbal intimidation were common, as professional players, with more at stake than the amateurs, sought every edge. Clubs began coordinating their attacks, trying to fashion runs out of singles, doubles, and hard baserunning.

As teams and players became more aggressive, they sought plays that fit their style. By its very nature—attacking the defense without the ball—stealing is one of baseball's most aggressive plays. Teams looking for ways to jump-start their offense and shake up the defense seem to have slowly realized the value of stealing, and so the stolen base gradually became a more important offensive weapon.

Harold Seymour, in his comprehensive volume *Baseball: The Early Years*, reports that players from this era admired baserunning ability. In a refrain that would become all too common once Babe Ruth arrived on the scene, many baseball observers felt that anyone with half a brain could hit a home run, but that running and stealing required intelligence, cunning and an understanding of how the game was played. Certainly, this type of thinking helped spread the use and acceptance of stealing.

Another thing that helped the stolen base gain popularity was that catchers did not have an easy time of it during this era. In 1881, the pitching distance was set at 50 feet, and would remain there until 1893, when it was extended to the present 60 feet, 6 inches. A few years later, most of the restrictions were taken off a pitcher's motion. Thus catchers, working with either a small glove and mask, or possibly, no equipment at all, were forced to contend with balls thrown swiftly at them by a man standing 50 feet away. Needless to say, there were lots of passed and dropped balls, and base stealers were able to take advantage.

As if this weren't enough for catchers to contend with when trying to stop a steal, they also were not playing directly behind the batter. Instead, they remained at least ten feet behind home plate, out of harm's way of foul balls and swinging bats. Obviously, throwing a base stealer out from that distance was extremely difficult. It remained this way until catching equipment became more protective near the turn of the century, and back-stoppers moved closer to the hitter.

By 1886 stolen bases had become so prevalent that they were included among the game's official statistics for the first time. Unfortunately, records from that year are spotty. Some sources list the White Stocking's Cap Anson as the N.L. leader in steals with 29, while others give the credit to Ed Andrews of Philadelphia, who stole 56 bases that year. In 1887, however, most sources agree that the leading base stealer in the National League was John Montgomery Ward with 111.

But while such accomplishments sound impressive, they cannot be judged the same as stolen bases totals today. That's because at that time, a steal was awarded to a runner for each base he advanced on a batter's hit. Thus a player on first who made it to third on a single was credited with two thefts. This rule, which was not changed to the modern interpretation until 1898, is what makes it impossible to compare the merits of early base bandits against those who came later. On the other hand, while pre–1898 base stealers may have gotten a break on how a steal was scored, they also had to contend with a few obstacles that modern players do not. For example, a pitcher could feint a throw to first without being required to complete it. Then, after faking a pickoff, if a pitcher still came to a complete stop, he could throw home instead of to the base. The added protections that a base runner has today via the balk rule and other restrictions on pitchers trying to deke them might cancel out the more lenient scoring of steals before 1898.

Throughout its history, the stolen base has always been fortunate to have a champion—a talented, high-profile player, who steals bases by the barrelful, excites the crowd, and raises the overall awareness of stealing. This was especially true at the beginning, when the steal was a good play, but not one that necessarily drew crowds into ball parks, or sent youngsters home dreaming of achieving base-stealing glory. What the stolen base needed was someone to show precisely how devastating and effective a play it could be, while wowing the crowd. What it got was the King.

Mike "King" Kelly was a fleet catcher-outfielder who never met a lady or a saloon he didn't like. Kelly was the epitome of a nineteenth century ballplayer: thick mustache, dark hair combed rakishly to the side, and an intense expression that couldn't hide the rascal lurking inside. He played the game hard and he lived his life hard, and when he died in 1894 at age 36 from pneumonia, no one could say that he had been cheated at either endeavor.

Kelly starred for Cap Anson's White Stockings during the 1880s. He was a hard hitter who led the National League in doubles three times, runs three times, and batting average twice, including a gaudy .388 in 1886. The King was one of baseball's first superstars, with a charismatic presence both on and off the field that added to his value. His worth was so great that when Chicago management finally tired of Kelly's off-the-field antics in 1886, they sold him to the Boston Beaneaters for the then-staggering sum of $10,000. The transaction netted the King a new nickname—"The $10,000 Beauty"—as well as two white horses and a carriage from happy Boston fans to use for transportation back and forth from the park.

On the diamond Kelly was not only a skilled player, but an innovative one. He was one of the first catchers to use finger signals for his pitchers. In the outfield, he popularized the now-familiar practice of backing up infielders on plays.

His most storied invention, however, is the hook slide. No one had ever slid with such flair before, and it took the game by storm. Every appearance by Kelly on base became a thrill of anticipation for the fans, and a nightmare for opposing fielders. His slide was fifty percent guile, fifty percent terror, and one hundred percent unique. As one teammate described it:

"He would jump into the air ten feet from the sack, dive directly for it, dig one of his spiked shoes into the bag and then swerve clear over on his side. Few second basemen … had the nerve to block his hurricane dives."

Kelly's whirlwind slide was so popular that fans of both the home and visiting teams openly rooted for him to steal when he got on base. "Slide, Kelly, Slide," they pleaded from their seats, and the King, who was such a born ham it's surprising he wasn't covered in glaze, would often oblige.

Kelly's slide became so popular that it spawned a popular song, called *Slide, Kelly, Slide.* The lyrics can best be described as offbeat:

> Slide, Kelly, slide!
> Your running's a disgrace!
> Slide, Kelly, slide!
> Stay there, hold your base!
> If someone doesn't steal you,
> And if your batting doesn't fail you,
> They'll take you to Australia.
> Slide, Kelly, slide!

(The phrase "Slide, Kelly, Slide" remained so popular that in 1927, 33 years after Kelly's death, a movie was made with the same title. Thanks to Hollywood logic, the film had absolutely nothing to do with either sliding or Mike Kelly and is sometimes listed as one of the worst baseball movies ever made.)

Kelly's popularity influenced not only the music industry but the art world as well. Artist Frank O. Small immortalized the King's famous slide on canvas. Unfortunately, Small proved to be no baseball fan: he painted the hook-sliding King diving into a base headfirst!

During the early 1880s, while the King was sliding his way to stardom, stolen base records were not being kept, so it's impossible to know how many sacks he swiped. In 1887, the first year for which accurate stolen base statistics exist, Kelly is credited with pilfering 84 bases. Over the next three years, even though his skills were diminishing, he stole 56, 68, and 51 bases, many of them using his famous hook or "Chicago" slide, as it was also known. While other players have stolen more bases than the 315 Kelly is credited with from 1887 to 1893, no one did it with greater *élan* than the King.

As with many of the colorful early players, stories abound about Kelly. Once, while playing the outfield for Chicago in the gathering dusk, a ball was hit over his head in the top of the ninth with two outs. Kelly raced back, leaped into the air, stuck up his glove, then tumbled to the ground. Getting to his feet, he ran off the field as the suitably impressed umpire called the batter out. Later, manager Anson asked Kelly for the ball, so that it could be used for the next game.

"The ball?" said a quizzical Kelly. "It went a mile over my head."

Another famous incident took place during a period in baseball when the captain of a team could substitute one player for another by merely announcing it to the umpire. While with the Beaneaters, Kelly was on the bench, too ill (or hungover) to play, when a foul pop was hit close by. Seeing that catcher Charlie Ganzel could not make the catch, the King jumped up, announced, "Kelly now playing for Chicago," and caught the ball.

Unfortunately, the King's late-night antics finally caught up to his day job. Overweight, and with his skills drowned by alcohol, Kelly was a shadow of his former self by 1893, hitting just .269 in 20 games and stealing a meager three bases. That was his last year in baseball.

Like many a player back then, Kelly never believed that the gravy train would stop. When it did, he found himself without any means of support. He tried vaudeville, then opened a bar, but both failed. In November, 1894, he decided to return to Boston, but on his way there he caught a cold that turned into pneumonia. As death closed in on him, the King proved that he hadn't lost his touch; when he slipped off the stretcher bearing him to the hospital, Kelly supposedly gasped, "This is my last slide."

But although the King had indeed slid his last, the art of stealing that he had done so much to nourish remained strong and vibrant, thanks to numerous other base stealers who emerged in his wake.

One of the best of these was "Sliding" Billy Hamilton. He supplanted Kelly as the premier base stealer of the time, swiping 117, 102, and 111 bases in successive seasons (1889–1891).

Hamilton was the best leadoff hitter of the era. He hit .300 or better 12 years in a row, led the league in stolen bases four times, in

"Sliding" Billy Hamilton was the premier base stealer of the 1890s (courtesy of the Baseball Hall of Fame Library, Cooperstown, New York).

walks five times, and in runs scored three times. In 1894, with Philadelphia, he had one of the greatest seasons in major league history, hitting .399, stealing 99 bases and scoring 196 runs (a single season mark that still stands). He is one of a handful of players in baseball history to have more runs scored (1692) than games played (1593) in his career.

Although stolen bases were credited differently during much of

Hamilton's career than they are today, there is no question about Sliding Billy's speed. He proved that on August 31, 1894, against Washington pitcher Arthur (or William) Wynne, who was making his first (and only) appearance in a big league game. Hamilton ensured that it would be a memorable one by stealing seven bases off the befuddled hurler to tie a nineteenth century record.

When he retired in 1901, Hamilton had 937 total steals (other sources credit him with a bit less), which was the most ever recorded. This mark would last for nearly 75 years, until surpassed by Lou Brock.

Being knocked down to number two (and subsequently, to number three by Rickey Henderson) in lifetime steals probably would not have sat well with Sliding Billy if he had witnessed it. (He died in 1940.) This fiery competitor was immensely proud of his baseball accomplishments, as indicated by a hand-written letter he dashed off to the *Sporting News* in 1937 when he thought the paper had done him an injustice "I was and will be the greatest stealer of all times. I stole over 100 bases on many years and if they ever re-count the record I will get my just reward."

Another superb base stealer of this era was John Montgomery Ward, who is more famous today for leading a player's revolt over the reserve clause in 1890 that nearly sank the National League. Twice Ward led the N.L. in steals, including a personal-best 111 in 1887.

What was remarkable about Ward's base stealing prowess was that he began his baseball career as a pitcher—a position not normally associated with speed on the bases. On the hill, Ward used an excellent curve and pinpoint control to win 165 games (including 47 in 1879) from 1878–1884. When his mound abilities declined, Ward switched to shortstop and began a new career as a hitter and base stealing threat. His advice to base stealers was to get a quick start and slide away from the fielder's tag.

While both Hamilton and Ward were excellent base stealers, neither had the flamboyance and sheer crowd-pleasing presence of King Kelly (although Sliding Billy was a favorite wherever he played because of his intensity). The same cannot be said, however, of another notable base stealer of this era: Arlie "The Freshest Man on Earth" Latham.

Actually a contemporary of Kelly's, Latham played third base on the powerhouse St. Louis Browns of the American Association during the 1880s. But whereas Kelly thrilled the fans with his sliding and derring-do on the bases, Latham took another route to win over the crowd. On a team famous for rowdiness (*Sporting Life* editor Francis C. Richter called the Browns "vile of speech, insolent in bearing, and about the toughest and roughest gang that ever struck this city"), no one could top the Freshest Man on Earth for rabble-rousing, umpire-baiting, and insult-hurling.

It was not uncommon for Latham to roam up and down the third base line when the Browns were up, screaming insults in paint-peeling language at the opposing pitcher, fielders and umpires. Few were safe from Latham's verbal pyrotechnics. (Eventually the league devised the third base coach's box as a way to keep Latham confined to a specific area.)

When he wasn't inciting the rabid Browns' rooters with his fiery words, Latham was regaling them with comical antics, such as planting firecrackers under third base or dressing up like flamboyant Browns owner Chris Von der Ahe, complete with derby hat and bulbous nose, and sauntering up and down the field.

One stunt, however, backfired on him. In 1889, during a game with Brooklyn, he twice lit candles on the field to "casually" point out to the umpire that it was getting dark. The second time he did it the umpire forfeited the game to Brooklyn. Ultimately, the Browns lost the pennant by one game—to Brooklyn.

When Latham wasn't talking, his bat was. Although his lifetime average was just .269, he was on base often enough to average 117 runs scored over an 11 year period (1884–1894). His true hallmark, however, was his exceptional speed: Latham swiped nearly 700 bases over the course of his career, including 129 in 1887 (when he also scored 163 runs) and 109 the following season. In the 15-game World Series between St. Louis and Detroit in 1887, Latham ran wild, stealing 12 bases.

In Latham's file at the Baseball Hall of Fame is a yellowed, undated newspaper story that describes the Freshest Man on Earth in his speedy prime: "He was the fastest thing on bases. Ty Cobb was just an ordinary player compared to Latham. When he reached first base, it was almost certain that he would score. He was a ten second man in the 100-yard dash."

Another premier base stealer of the 1890s was a hard-hitting native of Queenstown, Ireland, named Patrick "Patsy" Donovan. Donovan stole 518 bases during a career that stretched from 1890 to 1907. In 1900 his 45 steals tied him for the National League lead with George Van Haltren. Donovan lives on today in baseball, not as a stolen base artist, but rather as the man who discovered Babe Ruth. After his playing days were over Donovan worked as a scout for the Red Sox, and went to Baltimore to look over pitcher Dave Danforth. The moment he saw the Babe, however, Donovan quickly forget about anyone else. He was so impressed by Ruth that he urged Boston owner Joe Lannin to buy him immediately. Lannin did just that, and the rest is history. Thus did a former base stealing champ inadvertently pave the way for the demise of the stolen base in baseball.

Hugh Duffy, one-half of the "Heavenly Twins" combination (Tommy McCarthy was the other) that roamed the outfield for the Boston Nationals in the 1890s, was yet another outstanding base stealer of this time. Duffy swiped 599 bases during his 17 year career from 1888 through 1906, including a career high of 85 in 1891.

Duffy, who was elected to the Hall of Fame in 1945, was as good a hitter as he was a base stealer. In 1894 he hit .438, which is the highest recorded batting average in major league history. (This is despite the fact that Duffy's first manager was so unimpressed by his play that he advised him to become a wood chopper and forget about baseball.) Duffy also holds the somewhat dubious distinction of being the first man fined in the short-lived Player's Association in 1890. On April 22, he was fined $10 for kicking.

Hamilton, Ward, Donovan, Duffy and Latham, along with others such as George Gore, Bill Lange, Tom T. Brown and William Ellsworth "Dummy" Hoy, helped to maintain the stolen base's popularity among both players and fans during the 1880s and 1890s.

Others helped popularize the steal too—in their own way. Just as King Kelly was immortalized on a painting, so too was a steal by famed catcher Buck Ewing captured on canvas. Ewing was a sensational backstop who could reportedly throw so accurately from a squat that it seemed he was merely handing the ball to the second baseman. He has been credited with inventing the round, thickly-padded catcher's mitt.

Ewing was also a superb hitter and, for a catcher, extremely fleet. He stole 336 bases during his Hall of Fame career, including a personal high of 53 in 1888. He spent a large portion of his career with the New York Giants, and it was the Polo Grounders for whom he was playing when he singled in the top of the tenth inning of a scoreless game. Ewing promptly stole second and third. Then, while standing on third base, he turned to the Giant faithful and announced: "It's getting late. I'm going to steal home and we can then all have dinner."

Which, of course, is exactly what he did. Soon, paintings of "Ewing's Famous Slide" were popping up in saloons all over New York City.

The Giants also figured in another memorable steal of this era. In 1888, New York was playing the St. Louis Browns of the American Association in the championship series. In the bottom of the third inning of the first game, New York right fielder "Silent" Mike Tiernan walked. Trying to get into scoring position, Tiernan promptly took off for second.

He had reckoned, however, without "Honest" Jack Boyle, the Browns' catcher. When he saw Tiernan speeding for the bag, Boyle unleashed a mighty throw to second. Rockets have been launched with less power than Boyle put on his peg. Not only did the ball fly past second, but it also shot past the Browns' center fielder. Tiernan scored all the way from first, and the Giants won the game 2–1.

While there were numerous fine base stealers during this era, they often stole on an individual basis, and not in any coordinated fashion, as part of their team's overall offensive strategy. That, however, was changed by a man named Ned Hanlon.

When Hanlon arrived in Baltimore in 1892 to take over as manager of the Baltimore Orioles, there was little indication that the team was on the brink of greatness. The club had finished last in the first half of the 1892 season, and then stumbled to tenth place in the second part. (The National League experimented with a split season that year to boost attendance.) In 1893 the Orioles continued their losing ways, posting an eighth place finish with a mark of 60–70.

But there was a silent revolution going on in Baltimore baseball during this time. Even while the club was outwardly struggling,

Hanlon was slowly assembling the pieces that would shortly constitute the legendary Baltimore Oriole dynasty.

Hanlon was a keen judge of talent. He brought together players such as pugnacious John "Muggsy" McGraw, "Wee Willie" Keeler, and Hughie "Eeyah" Jennings, all future Hall of Famers. Yet it was as a strategist that "Foxy Ned" made his mark on the Orioles, and on all of baseball as well.

Hanlon's emphasis on speed, teamwork, and timing plays such as the hit-and-run, sacrifice bunt and the stolen base completely changed the game. Although other teams had used these plays before, Hanlon's Orioles were the best at using them in an integrated manner, making them part of their overall offensive scheme and not just isolated occurrences. The result was a gambling, aggressive style of play that caught other teams flat-footed.

Typical of the Orioles' style was the two-base sacrifice. Often executed by McGraw and Keeler, it required a runner on first and a batter who was adept at bunting. The moment the pitch was delivered to the plate the runner took off. The batter then dropped a bunt down the third base line. While the third baseman was throwing out the hitter, the runner roared around second and slid into third uncontested.

These types of tactics were the chief components of what became known as "inside" or "scientific" baseball, with Hanlon widely acknowledged as the father of this type of play. (At Hanlon's death in 1937, the Yankees' Ed Barrow praised Hanlon as a "pioneer tactician," the "first of the smart baseball managers," and one of the "first advocates of surprise tactics.")

Given Hanlon's background as a player, it wasn't too surprising that he favored aggressive, fast-paced baseball. His career began in 1880, and, although stolen base records were not kept until 1887, Hanlon was apparently dedicated to the proposition that speed wins ball games. In a 1912 article about Hanlon as part of a series on the "Fifty Greatest Ball Players in History," the writer said,

> Ned Hanlon as a player was just as successful as he was as a manager. He played on winning teams and was himself a winning factor. I have seen "Eddie" slide into three bases in one inning, tearing along the ground like a battering ram, when his legs were

like raw beef from ankle to hip—yes, and come out the next day and do it again. And Hanlon was as good a base runner and stealer as he was daring. That was one of his strongest points, and many is the tight game he has won by his speed and long slides.

Hanlon's "speed and long slides" accounted for stolen base totals of 69, 38, 53, 65 and 54 in the years between 1887–1891.

The inside game that Hanlon instituted at Baltimore was as revolutionary as it was effective. To the opposition it seemed like there were always Orioles in motion somewhere, whether it was on the bases, or out in the field, where Hanlon perfected the cutoff man and other defensive innovations. Hanlon's tactics were a complete departure from what some called the "roundhouse" form of baseball (or, as another period article put it, a "mere slugging game in which brute strength was paramount to brains") that was popular at the time.

To ensure that the Orioles had the inside game down pat, Hanlon took the team south to Macon, Georgia, before the start of the 1894 season to work on it undisturbed (and thus popularized the notion of spring training). When the Orioles returned, they had perfected a style of play not widely seen before. Like a wolf lurking in the shadows, the Orioles waited to fall upon the other unsuspecting teams.

The New York Giants were the consensus choice to take the National League pennant in 1894. The defending champion Boston Beaneaters were also expected to be in the thick of the fight.

The Orioles, however, had other plans. They served notice of what was to come by sweeping four straight from the favored Giants in the very first series of the season. A major factor in Baltimore's victory was 14 stolen bases. Watching the Orioles scurry around the bases, Giants manager John Montgomery Ward shook his head and said, "That's not baseball they're playing."

But it was baseball—a new, fast-paced brand in which the stolen base played a major part. The Orioles ran from the first game of the season to the last. When they finally stopped, the birds were in first place with a record of 89–39, three games ahead of the favored Giants. For the year, the Orioles stole 324 bases. (The previous year, when the Orioles had finished eighth with a 60–70 mark, they had almost 100 fewer steals.)

Proving that 1894 wasn't a fluke, the Orioles took the N.L. pennant in the following two seasons. Both years featured plenty of baserunning and stolen bases. In 1896 the Orioles capped their first place finish by stealing a whirlwind 441 bases, which was nearly 100 more than any other team in the league.

Despite all of the stolen bases, the Orioles were not a team of speed demons flying about on the wings of Mercury. Certainly, they had players with exceptional speed, such as McGraw, Keeler, Jennings, outfielder Joe Kelley, and utilityman "Dirty Jack" Doyle. Yet they didn't have one outstanding base stealer, in the manner of a Ty Cobb, to lead the running game. Rather, it was more the Orioles' emphasis on the team game and exploiting their opponent's weaknesses that paved the way for their base thievery.

Stealing, for the Orioles, was part of their strategy. Stealing *against* the Orioles, however, was tantamount to waving a red flag in front of a bull. It enraged them, and made them seek revenge on the base thief bold enough to try to use their own tactic against them.

Take, for example, the plight of one base stealer, as related by John McGraw years later: "[he] spiked our first baseman on the foot. Our man retaliated by trying to trip him. He got away, but at second Heine Reitz tried to block him off while Hughie [Jennings] ... covered the bag to take the throw and tag him. The runner evaded Reitz and jumped feet first at Jennings to drive him away from the bag. Jennings dodged the flying spikes and threw himself bodily at the runner, knocking him flat."

(Normally, the umpire might have been expected to put an end to such tactics. But on that play, the Orioles' catcher had spiked him, and put his mitt in front of his face so that the umpire couldn't see the play. The Orioles, as has often been written, were a dirty team.)

Of course, managing this bunch of high-spirited birds was no picnic either, even for a respected man like Hanlon. Long before Babe Ruth drove little Miller Huggins to distraction, McGraw and Keeler did the same thing to Foxy Ned. One of their favorite gimmicks was to invent their own hit-and-run sign and not reveal it to Hanlon. Just when the manager thought he had it figured out, McGraw and Keeler would change it again.

Although the Oriole dynasty ended in 1897, when Boston took

the flag, the lessons that Hanlon and his team had taught were not forgotten. The value of scientific baseball was proven beyond a shadow of a doubt. Suddenly, a single, sacrifice, and stolen base were key offensive weapons. A walk followed by a sacrifice and a stolen base was as good as a triple, for it put a runner on third before the defense could catch its breath.

In 1898 the method for awarding a stolen base was changed to that which has existed (with minor modifications) up to modern times, i.e., giving credit for a steal when the runner reaches the base on his own, without benefit of a hit or error.

This rule change had an immediate effect on stolen base totals. In 1897, the 12 National League teams had combined for 2,696 stolen bases; in 1898, that number dropped by over 600 bases, to 2,069. Individual stolen base totals declined as well. In the five years prior to 1898, the top base stealers in the league had compiled totals of 66, 99, 97, 87, and 73 thefts. In the five years after the rule change, including 1898, league-leading totals were significantly lower: 58, 77, 45, 49, and 42.

As the twentieth century dawned, another significant rule change occurred in baseball. This one, however, was so radical as to completely transform the game: beginning in 1901 in the National League and 1903 in the American League, a foul ball was counted as a strike.

In one giant step, the advantage in baseball swung to the pitcher, and from the offense to the defense. Batters who had been used to fouling pitches off without consequence until they found one they liked suddenly found themselves two quick strikes in the hole. (In fact, the rule was put in because one batter, Phillies outfielder Roy Thomas, was a master at fouling off balls. Once he reportedly fouled off 22 pitches before finally drawing a walk.)

In one fell swoop the entire strategy of the game changed; hitters now came to the plate in a defensive posture, intent on not striking out, rather than in an offensive mode, seeking to put the ball in play.

While batters were cursing, pitchers were smiling. In the era of the spit ball, the shine ball, the emery ball and the mud ball, providing hurlers with another weapon was tantamount to putting a cape with a big red "S" on them; the foul ball strike made pitchers virtually invulnerable. The average runs per game dropped by nearly two, and remained low for years afterward.

Hitters became so desperate because of the foul strike rule that in 1904 the great Pittsburgh Pirate shortstop Honus Wagner made a public plea for help. The Flying Dutchman suggested that pitchers move three feet farther back, that the number of balls needed for a walk be reduced to three, and—above all—that baseball get rid of the dreaded foul ball strike.

He was not alone. Students of the game such as Henry Chadwick and Francis Richter also advocated repeal of the foul-strike rule. Other ideas to help batters included having a special player bat for the pitcher. In jest, a Detroit sportswriter suggested chaining outfielders to posts.

But no help was forthcoming. The offense was on its own. Teams had to cope as best they could, and one way they did was to use the stolen base differently. Suddenly stealing was not just a way to manufacture runs, but a way to save a precious out. If a runner on first could steal second, then an out wouldn't have to be wasted sacrificing him there. Even better, a steal of second voided the double play.

So it was that stolen bases went through yet another metamorphosis. Instead of being used in an aggressive, attacking manner, stealing became almost a defensive tactic of the offensive team. They used it to stay out of trouble, rather than to cause trouble. Stealing was still a necessary and vital skill, but one that was used cautiously. As no less a base stealing authority than Ty Cobb said: "Rarely should a base runner risk a steal when the game is in the balance. It's to be used when you can afford to fail."

A player who rarely failed at the steal—or just about anything else associated with baseball—was the aforementioned John Peter "Honus" Wagner.

Even today, over 80 years since he last trod on a ballfield, Wagner's lifetime stolen base total of 722 ranks ninth all-time. He led the National League in steals five times during his career; his peak came in 1907, when he swiped 61.

From 1901 through 1908 Wagner averaged 51 steals per year. This is despite the fact that his running style was anything but graceful. The *New York American* once said that Wagner's "movements on the diamond have been likened to the gambols of a caracoling elephant. He is so ungainly and so bowlegged that when he runs, his limbs seem to be moving in a circle after the fashion of a propeller."

Caracoling elephant or not, Wagner could, in the words of umpire Hank O'Day, "run bases like a deer." He was a swift and sure runner, who was once timed running to first from a standing start in 3.4 seconds. A 1903 newspaper story aptly titled "Hans Wagner Excels In Every Department" described the "Flying Dutchman" on the bases:

> There are some faster men in both leagues, but when they reach first base it takes a hit to advance them. Wagner is different. Let the pitcher make one false move or the catcher err a trifle in his throw and Hans will land safely at second. Indeed, even though the ball may reach the baseman before his arrival it is not a certainty that he will be put out, for Wagner is adept at sliding away from the outstretched hand. He can slide head first or feet first and never gives the first baseman more than an ankle or a wrist to touch.

Wagner also excelled in the hardest steal of all: home. The Flying Dutchman's 27 thefts of home rank fourth all-time in that department. Anything that Wagner could not do well on a baseball diamond simply didn't need to be done.

The great shortstop (who, incidentally, at first was considered the game's best utility player and was strongly opposed to being positioned full-time at shortstop when it was initially proposed to him) was not above enjoying himself on the bases. In the fifth game of the 1909 World Series against the Detroit Tigers, Wagner reached first after being hit by a pitch. Then, according to contemporary reports, he gyrated like a "circus clown" to unnerve the Tiger pitcher—and promptly stole second. While on second Wagner again went into his act, performing what was described as a "combination hornpipe, reel, and jig between second and third"—then broke for third. When the throw sailed into left field, Wagner scored.

It was in this same World Series that the celebrated clash between Cobb and Wagner was supposed to have occurred on the bases. According to the story, the two great stars, each of whom had led his respective league in batting that season, clashed in the opening game of the Series. In the fifth inning, after Cobb got on first via a force-out, he was reported to have called out to Wagner, "Look out, Kraut-head, I'm coming down," and then proceeded to take off for second. When Cobb slid into the base, with spikes high, Wagner is supposed to have jammed the ball into his mouth, splitting his lip.

Many people claim that this encounter is just pure baseball fiction—among them, Ty Cobb. In his autobiography *My Life in Baseball: The True Record*, Cobb called it "100 per cent concoction" and a bag of "journalistic hot air."

"At the time it was supposed to have happened," Cobb wrote, "I wasn't even the runner at first base."

In the biography *Honus Wagner*, the authors report that it was merely a straight steal with a poor throw from the catcher that Wagner short-hopped and slapped onto Cobb, but the Tiger was called safe. They also indicate that contemporary newspaper reports contain no mention of hurled insults or split lips.

It may well have been Wagner himself who helped to spread the story. In his later years the great shortstop was fond of spinning yarns about "the old days" on the diamond, and would occasionally support the "split lip" version of the story.

Whether or not this famous episode happened, it is now part of baseball lore. What is certain, however, is that Wagner and Pittsburgh ran the Tigers and Cobb ragged, stealing a record-tying 18 total bases to just six for Detroit. In their personal battle, Wagner swiped six bases and hit .333, while Cobb managed just two steals and a puny .231 batting average.

This style of play characterized baseball in the first two decades of the 20th century. The single and stolen base became the dominant offensive threats. Realizing that a single run could win a game, teams began hoarding them like misers.

Home runs virtually disappeared. In 1899, the 12 National League teams had combined for 348 home runs; Washington's Buck Freeman led the league with 25. In 1905, the 16 teams from both the American and National leagues combined to hit just 283 round-trippers. The Boston team led both leagues with 29 home runs, or just four more than Freeman had hit by himself six years earlier. The leading slugger was Cincinnati's Fred Odwell, with nine homers that year.

(Stolen base totals, however, did not soar in relation to the drop in hitting. In 1899 the 12 National League teams stole 2,666 bases. In 1905, the 16 combined American and National league teams stole 2,931 bases—even more evidence of the dominance of the pitchers, since you can't steal first base!)

Base stealing blossomed into a vital team asset. It became a given in baseball during this era that teams leading the league in steals would finish at or near the top of the standings.

Pushed into a corner, is it any wonder that base runners became more aggressive? With a single run looming so large, runners had little regard for base path etiquette. Players sliding with spikes high and fists flying became a common sight. An entire breed of players emerged who were willing to do virtually anything to safely steal a base.

Of all of these, the most memorable was a man from Georgia named Ty Cobb.

3

Cobb:
Demon on the Loose

"To him, a ball game wasn't a mere athletic contest. It was a knock-'em-down, crush-'em, relentless war. He was their enemy, and if they got in his way he ran right over them"—Moe Berg on Ty Cobb.

To say that Tyrus Raymond Cobb wanted to win is like saying that Moby Dick was a big fish. For Cobb, losing was not an option; winning was his white whale, and he pursued it with Ahab-like zeal. Cobb felt that baseball was not just a sport, but a struggle for supremacy in which only the strong survived. "Baseball is a red-blooded sport for red-blooded men," he said. "It's not pink tea, and mollycoddles had better stay out of it."

For almost two decades, Cobb's indomitable will and slashing style of play dominated baseball. It is a measure of his greatness that this era is sometimes called the "Cobbian Era." It took a player of equal greatness—Babe Ruth—to end this era and begin his own.

One of the hallmarks of the Cobbian Era was the stolen base, which Cobb made into an art form. From his palette he dabbed speed, aggression, and daring onto the canvas of the stolen base, until he had created a masterpiece that other teams and players tried to copy. Yet no one could equal Cobb. On the diamond, this Old Master stood alone. He was so adept at his craft that once his type of game was superseded by Ruth and the home run, stealing became a lost art. After Cobb, it would take decades, and the emergence of another supremely talented runner, before the stolen base would once again become an integral part of baseball.

Ty Cobb was born on December 18, 1886, in Narrows, Georgia. His father, the main influence in Ty's life, was a forceful man but not an unreasonable one. Although he wanted his son to pursue a career in medicine or the law, he did not stand in his way early in 1904 when the baseball-smitten 17-year-old told him he wanted to go to Augusta and try out for the Tourists, a team in the Class C league. After a long speech in which the elder Cobb warned his son that he might end up a "mere muscle-worker" if he pursued his baseball dream, the father gave Ty six checks for $15 each, plus some spending cash. "Go get it out of your system, and let us hear from you," he said.

Cobb was a good but not great minor league ballplayer, giving little indication of the legend he would become. He ran the bases with abandon, excelled at bunting, was a solid hitter, and played an erratic outfield. By the end of July, 1905, Cobb was leading the Sally League in hitting, and it was rumored that he might soon be heading for the Detroit club in the major leagues.

Then, on August 9, 1905, Cobb received a telegram informing him his father had been shot to death. When he arrived home, Cobb discovered that his mother had been the shooter. Apparently suspecting that his wife was having an affair, the elder Cobb had pretended to leave town, only to sneak back that evening hoping to catch her in the act. When his wife heard someone jiggling the bedroom window, she grabbed a shotgun and fired twice, killing her husband.

Some biographers, as well as Cobb himself, point to this incident as the trigger for what would become his almost fanatical desire to succeed. While this certainly may have been a contributing factor, the need to win was present in Cobb long before this tragedy. In fifth grade, for example, he beat up a boy whose mistake in a spelling bee gave victory to the girl's team. Quite possibly, Cobb's smoldering urge to be the best was fanned to the incendiary point by his father's death. The result was an explosive combination of a great ballplayer with a violent personality.

Shortly after he returned to baseball Cobb was sold to the Detroit Tigers. Still four months shy of his nineteenth birthday, he arrived in Detroit in late August, 1905, scared and uncertain that he had the ability to stick in the majors. Unfortunately, his combative personality made him ill-suited to endure the severe hazing that rookies received back then. When his teammates sawed his bats in half or ripped the crowns out of his hats, Cobb took it personally.

"He came up with an antagonistic attitude, which in his mind turned any little razzing into a life-or-death struggle," said "Wahoo" Sam Crawford, who patrolled the Detroit outfield with Cobb for many years. "He always figured that everybody was ganging up against him."

Soon Cobb was at war not only with the opposition but his own team as well. Although things gradually improved, the pattern of his big league career—as well as his life—was set: Cobb against the world.

Cobb arrived in the major leagues at the height (or depths, depending on one's viewpoint) of the dead ball era. Quite simply, the game was ruled by pitching. Hitting had declined so severely that in 1908 Francis C. Richter, editor of *Sporting Life*, urged that outfielders be prohibited from using gloves so that more base hits could fall in.

Since one run was often critical to the outcome of a game, stealing was usually employed defensively, as a way to remove the threat of the double play or move a runner up without wasting an out via the sacrifice. This was much different from the aggressive manner in which the Baltimore Orioles and others had used the steal to probe and attack their opponents' weaknesses.

Despite this, stealing was a smart play for several reasons. The first was that pitchers had little experience in holding runners on, and didn't practice the skill much. With long hits so rare, it didn't matter how many runners were on base, as long as they didn't score. The second reason was that catchers had the same trouble accurately throwing the scuffed-up, mushy, discolored balls then in use as batters had in hitting them. A runner with any speed at all had a reasonable expectation of successfully stealing.

Thus stealing was an important skill for players to have at the time Cobb joined the Tigers. But the young Georgian, unsure of himself and rattled by his teammate's antagonism, initially showed little of the fire for which he would become famous. In 41 games in 1905 Cobb hit .240 and stole just two bases.

The following year Cobb revealed a bit more of the player he would ultimately become, hitting .320 with 23 steals. Unfortunately, he missed nearly six weeks of the season with a nervous breakdown caused by the constant hazing he was subjected to.

By 1907, however, things began looking up for Cobb. Tiger manager Bill Armour and his "boys will be boys" attitude was replaced by Hughie Jennings, the former Baltimore Oriole. A scrappy base stealer himself in his playing days, Jennings saw something special in Cobb. He knew that to win, he needed Cobb healthy, and so he tried to smooth things out between the young Georgian and the other players.

(Just when Jennings thought everything was going well, however, Cobb assaulted a black groundskeeper and his wife during spring training. The attack resulted in a fight with Detroit catcher Charley Schmidt and again put him at odds with the other Tigers. Exasperated, Jennings tried to trade Cobb to Cleveland for outfielder Elmer Flick. The deal fell through because of Cobb's difficult reputation.)

The presence of Jennings acted like a tonic for Cobb, because 1907 was his breakthrough year. In 150 games he hit .350, with 212 hits, 116 runs batted in, and 49 steals—all league-leading totals.

Thus began a string of unprecedented excellence by the man from Georgia. Cobb won the American League batting title nine years in a row, and 12 out of the next 13 years. (The only year he missed, 1916, he hit a gaudy .371, but lost to Tris Speaker's .386.)

He also led the league in stolen bases five more times, peaking in 1915 when he swiped 96 to establish a major league record that stood for 47 years. Cobb's other league-leading steal totals were 76 (1909), 83 (1911), 68 (1916), and 55 (1917). In all Cobb stole 892 bases, another mark that lasted for years until shattered by Lou Brock in 1977.

But more than just the amount of bases Cobb stole is *how* he stole them. Certainly, speed helped, and this Cobb had; he once was timed going from home to first base in 3.5 seconds. He needed just 13.5 seconds to circle the bases. If not the fastest man in the game, Cobb was near the top.

However, Cobb used other weapons besides speed to help him steal. One of these was his ferocious slide. Third baseman Ossie Bluege of the Washington Senators described what it was like watching Cobb approach: "He didn't slide. He just took off and came at me in midair, spikes-first, about four or five feet off the ground."

This is what Cobb called "sliding with my steel showing," and it was extremely effective. Even during this time of tough players who ignored injuries that send modern players scurrying to the disabled list, few men were brave enough to stand in the way of Cobb's slashing spikes.

Sliding high not only helped Cobb steal, but it was also an excellent means of self-defense. To try and slow him down, catchers would sometimes throw their heavy masks onto the third base line when Cobb was racing home. Instead of tripping on the mask, or sliding into it and risking injury, Cobb would slide high so he could harmlessly sweep the mask aside with a hip or hand.

"He always reminded me of Man-o'-War coming down the home stretch," said shortstop Everett Scott, who watched Cobb thundering toward him enough times to know.

And, like the famous racehorse, getting hit by Cobb in full throttle was an open invitation to a debilitating injury. Browns catcher Paul Krichell found this out during a game in 1912. According to Cobb, Krichell had a "vicious" habit of hooking Cobb's leg when Cobb slid and then flipping him over, so that the Peach wound up eating a face full of dirt. After several times, Cobb warned the catcher not to do it again. Ignoring this advice, Krichell tried it again; Cobb scissored his legs so that he caught the catcher under one arm and, as Cobb put it, "almost detached it from his body." The injury was so severe that it ended Krichell's major league career.

As if knowing that here was a player who could end your career with one blow wasn't enough to make the opposition dislike him, adding to their dismay was the controversial claim that Cobb sharpened his spikes. To some players, like Tiger second baseman Charlie "The Mechanical Man" Gehringer, there was no doubt about it.

"He was a spiking fool," Gehringer said. "He'd cut you to pieces if you gave him any trouble on the bases."

Cobb denied this allegation—after his playing days were over. He claimed that he pretended to do it once, to psyche out the opposing team (the New York Highlanders). Soon there were stories about how Cobb, "with mouth twisted and eyes ablaze," was constantly sharpening his spikes like a demented surgeon.

Whether or not Cobb honed his spikes to razor-sharpness will forever be debated. Just the thought that he did it was enough to give him a psychological advantage, and that was what he craved above all else. Cobb stole many a base not only because he won the physical battle, but because he won the mental battle as well.

"My stealing," he wrote in his 1961 autobiography *My Life in Baseball— The True Record*, "was 90 percent mental. At all times on the field, I tried to be as sensitive as a burglar alarm to every pulse of the game. The greatest weapon of all ... is an astute understanding of an opponent's thought processes, and application of that knowledge."

Cobb used any trick he could think of to gain an advantage. One of his best was to frequently kick the base bag; although the habit was dismissed as a superstitious ritual, Cobb knew that the bag often was not strapped down tight, and that each kick would push it an inch or two closer to the next base. As Cobb was well aware, a single inch could make the difference when stealing.

Another favorite Cobbian caper was to fake an injury. As he described it: "I'd writhe around on the ground, in agony. Then I'd call time and hobble to my feet and limp around painfully. When the game resumed, I'd go on the first ball pitched and steal second."

Cobb's goal, in his mad charge around the bases, was to instill fear of the unexpected in his opponents—what he called "The Threat." He realized that if the other team never knew what he might do, they'd always be on edge, and more likely to make a mistake. One mistake was all Cobb ever needed.

The Georgia Peach constantly studied the opposition, looking for anything that would give him an edge. When he realized that Boston pitcher Jesse Tannehill squeezed the ball before he threw home, he stole three times on him in nine innings. Another pitcher stiffened his right leg just before he threw to first; the moment Cobb saw the leg relax, he took off. Even the immortal Cy Young fell victim to Cobbian analysis. The Georgian noticed that Young slightly flexed his elbows when he was going to throw to first. Cobb stole on the great pitcher so successfully that one day Young asked him, in frustration, "What am I doing [wrong]?" Cobb said nothing. Once he got an edge he wasn't going to reveal it to anyone.

Perhaps in no other phase of the game was Cobb's awesome combination of physical and mental abilities more on display than in stealing home. A theft of home is the most difficult of all, requiring equal measures of precision, speed, surprise and luck. According to *The Sporting News Complete Baseball Record Book*, Cobb stole home 50 times in his career. No other player has even come close to that number.

The Georgia Peach also holds the record for steals of home in a single season, with eight in 1912. (For years the record was thought to be seven, held first by Pete Reiser and later tied by Rod Carew, but in 1991 the Society for American Baseball Research uncovered Cobb's eight thefts.)

Another of Cobb's records is that he is the only player to steal second, third and home in the same inning three times. He did it on July 22, 1909, against the Red Sox, on July 12, 1911, against Connie Mack's A's, and on July 4, 1912, while playing the Browns. As if stealing three bases in one inning weren't enough, Cobb even managed to top himself in the A's game by stealing the three bases on three consecutive pitches. No wonder he is considered one of the greatest players the game has ever produced.

To steal home, Cobb often used one of his typical hell-bent-for-leather breaks off the bag, and sometimes threw in a ruse to further increase his edge. New York Highlander catcher Fred Mitchell described how Cobb used this technique in a 1906 game:

> Cobb was the runner at third base. Frank LaPorte was our third baseman. Cobb made a sudden move to the plate. I shot the ball to LaPorte, but Cobb got back safely. LaPorte took a few steps toward the pitcher. Cobb slightly sauntered off the bag. LaPorte tossed the ball a foot or two in the air and caught it while talking to the pitcher. Cobb was apparently paying no attention. LaPorte again tossed the ball into the air and did it twice more. With the fourth toss, at that instant, Cobb made a break for the plate. I never in my life saw a man spring into action so fast. There was yelling and confusion. LaPorte didn't see Cobb, didn't

realize what was happening. By the time LaPorte awoke and
threw home, Cobb had slid across the plate.

This was the essence of Cobb's base stealing—using surprise,
skill, speed and aggression to create havoc in the defense, and then
taking advantage of that havoc. No one has ever done it better. He
was a genius—although his genius came with qualifications.

"To taunt him or to try to frighten him was to make him burn
with a cold fire," wrote Robert Smith. "He turned into a frenzied
genius."

Added Branch Rickey, "His genius was a kind of insanity—a
compulsion to beat you at anything in any way he could."

Cobb made no apologies for his behavior on the diamond. It was
beat or be beaten, and he had no intention of being the loser.

"I had to fight all my life to survive," he said. "They were all
against me ... tried every dirty trick to cut me down. But I beat the
bastards and left them in the ditch."

Despite the animosity that Cobb instilled, other American
League teams couldn't help but notice his success. It was impossible
for other players not to be influenced when watching Cobb and the
manner in which he ran the bases. The more successful Cobb was,
the higher stolen base totals rose in the American League.

In 1907, when Cobb led the American League in steals with 49,
the eight A.L. teams stole a combined 1395 bases. The following year,
a dismal season for hitters overall, this total dipped to 1353. But in
1909, when Cobb pilfered 76 sacks, total steals jumped to 1544. This
was followed by increases in the next three years: 1671 in 1910, 1712
in 1911, and a whopping 1809 in 1912.

Naturally, individual player totals also increased during this
time. In 1908, Chicago's Patsy Dougherty led the American League
with 47 steals. Just two years later, Eddie Collins of the Philadelphia
A's paced the circuit with 81 thefts (Cobb was second with 65).
Dougherty's 47 steals of two years earlier would have ranked fifth.
Thanks in large part to Cobb, players were running more, and with
greater success.

Over the next several years, stolen base totals continued to climb,
despite a rule change that reduced the number of steals credited.

Beginning in 1909, a stolen base was no longer given to a runner on an attempted double-steal if either runner was thrown out. Yet, with Cobb leading the way, individual player totals kept rising. In 1911 Cobb paced the American League with 83 steals. The following year Washington's Clyde Milan topped that with 88.

It wasn't only A.L. players who were running more. In the National League, two players who were similar to Cobb on the bases were Bob Bescher and Max "Scoops" Carey.

Nicknamed the "London Flash" because he came from London, Ohio, Bescher was a hook-sliding specialist who led the National League in steals four consecutive seasons from 1909 through 1912, averaging 68 stolen bases per year during that time. His peak came in 1911, when the Cincinnati Reds outfielder swiped 81 sacks, establishing an N.L. record that stood for 51 years until broken by Maury Wills in 1962.

Although a forgotten player today, in his heyday Bescher was as big a star as Cobb, and, at one time, was the highest-salaried player in the National League. In 1910 a newspaper story labeled Bescher a "clever base runner": "One of the paramount issues among fans at present is whether Bob Bescher of the Cincinnati Club is the equal or superior of Ty Cobb of the Tigers in the gentle art of base running."

Bescher ran on his toes, like a track athlete, raising his knees high and pumping his arms like pistons. On the bases Bescher was a Cobbian-style terror, coming in with spikes high and using his muscular body as a battering ram on any poor infielder foolish enough to get in the way.

"The dude was fast," said one observer. "When he went in to slide you better get out of the way because he was coming right at you."

Another person who saw him play said Bescher had "amazing speed" and "paid no attention to anyone when he ran. The coach at third base was lucky if Bescher didn't run over him."

"No one gave him any guff," observed a friend of Bescher's. "It would have been useless to because he would have knocked the hell out of you."

In another similarity to Cobb, the big, 200-pound outfielder had

Bob Bescher set a new N.L. mark with 81 steals in 1911 (courtesy of the Base-ball Hall of Fame Library, Cooperstown, New York).

a hair-trigger temper, and once punched out Cardinals' manager Roger Bresnahan after he cursed Bescher during a game.

Yet, despite his ferocity on the field, Bescher was mild-mannered off of it. His mother had asked him not to go out with girls until he got older, and Bescher stayed true to her wishes. His idea of a good time was playing Parcheesi, checkers and dominoes in the evening with the family at whose house he stayed during the season, and he never drank anything stronger than lemonade or milk.

In 1914 Bescher was dealt to the New York Giants, where his temper quickly led to trouble with fiery manager John McGraw. Traded to St. Louis the following year, Bescher couldn't find the old base stealing magic. He swiped just 66 bases over the next two seasons with the Redbirds, a total that he had accumulated in just one season a few years before. Two years later he left the major leagues and played out the string in the minors. During his 11 years in the majors he stole 428 bases.

Bescher never married, preferring to live at home with his parents. However, he eventually did go out with women, and it was in the company of one that he met his death on November 29, 1942. While driving late at night, he and a female companion were struck by a train at a country road crossing two miles west of London.

Max Carey played his entire career in the National League, most of it with the Pittsburgh Pirates. In many ways he was the N.L.'s equivalent to Cobb, dominating the league in stolen bases year after year. "Scoops" Carey led the league in steals 10 times, with his peak coming in 1916 when he swiped 63 sacks. From 1911 through 1925 Carey averaged an amazing 45 steals per season. His career total of 738 stolen bases ranks eighth all-time. In 1958, Carey received a singular honor when a three-man committee for *The Sporting News* rated Carey as the best base stealer of all time—even better than Ty Cobb.

Carey was a keen student of the game, and was constantly studying other players. He claimed to have learned his base-stealing technique from watching Bob Bescher and Ty Cobb. Of Cobb, Carey said, "He had an easy motion in galloping bases. He had a long stride and an ability to run properly."

He also developed a unique way of knowing when to steal. While others watched the pitcher to get a good jump, Carey kept his eye on the first baseman. The instant that his feet shifted to return to his fielding position, Carey knew that there wasn't going to be a pickoff attempt, and took off for second.

In 1922 Carey had one of the finest seasons ever for a base stealer when he recorded 51 thefts while being thrown out just twice. No one before or since has ever recorded such a high percentage while stealing 50 or more bases in a single season.

According to Carey, the secret to base stealing was getting a good jump. "The great base stealer gets that way by developing the perfect jump," he said. "The secret lies in a long lead, physical balance and mental agility. The runner must establish mobility. He must have the right mental angle. He must watch the pitcher's every move and translate thought into immediate action."

Carey put on his greatest performance in the 1925 World Series against the Washington Senators. With the Pirates down three games to one, Carey sparked his club to victory in the fifth game by stealing second and scoring the first run in an eventual 6–3 Buc triumph. Pittsburgh then won the sixth game to force a seventh, and momentum seemed to be on their side. But in the finale, the Pirates fell behind Walter Johnson by four runs, and things looked bleak. But with Carey slamming three doubles and stealing yet another base, the Pirates rallied for a 9–7 victory, thus becoming the first team to rebound from a 3–1 deficit to take the championship.

Carey was superhuman in the Bucs' triumph. He hit .458, scored six runs, stole three bases, and was a constant worry to the Senators whenever he got on. "It seemed," said Hughie Jennings, the former Tiger skipper who covered the series for the *New York Times*, "as if he [Carey] could steal a base any time he wanted to advance."

Only after the series ended did Carey reveal that he had played the final two and one-half games strapped in a corset to protect two fractured ribs that caused him intense pain with every breath. After the series ended Carey spent the next 11 days in a hospital. "I couldn't have gone any further than I did," Carey said about that memorable series.

In 1926, at the tail end of his career, Carey was sent to the Brooklyn Dodgers. The speedy outfielder's arrival in Brooklyn was greatly anticipated by manager Wilbert Robinson. "This fellow steals as many bases by himself as my whole team steals every year," "Uncle Robbie" said, and he was right. In 1925, the Dodgers had swiped just 37 sacks, while Carey stole 46. "Scoops" proceeded to delight Uncle Robbie by swiping 32 bases in 1927, which helped the Dodgers finish second in the National League in steals (but sixth in the standings).

Max Carey was one of the N.L.'s most prolific base stealers in the 1910s and 1920s (courtesy of the Baseball Hall of Fame Library, Cooperstown, New York).

But while both Bescher and Carey were similar to Cobb in many ways, perhaps no one matched him better steal for steal than "Cocky" Eddie Collins.

Plucked out of Columbia University by Connie Mack in 1906 before he had finished school, Eddie Collins soon became part of the fabled "$100,000 infield," of the Philadelphia A's which included Stuffy McInnis, Collins, Jack Barry, and Frank "Home Run" Baker. Collins was a slick fielder and superb hitter, once called "the greatest player on the field" by no less a judge of talent than John McGraw. Over the course of his 25 year career he banged out 3,313 hits and compiled a lifetime .333 batting average.

Collins emerged as a base stealing threat in 1909, when he swiped 67 to finish second behind Cobb's 76 thefts. The next year Collins stole 81, which not only beat Cobb for the league lead but was also the highest total ever in the American League. (Two years later, Clyde Milan topped the mark with 88.)

For the next dozen years Collins consistently ranked among the top base stealers in the American League. Between 1909 and 1917, Collins averaged 55 steals per season. He paced the league in steals three more times: in 1919 with 33, in 1923 with 47, and in 1924 with 42 steals. (He was 37 when he led the league in 1924, thus becoming the oldest player to lead the American League in steals.)

Like Cobb, Collins' base stealing garnered him numerous accolades. A 1911 newspaper article called "Cocky" the "best base runner the game has known since the days of Bill Lange and Billy Hamilton."

"Base stealing seems to come natural to Collins," said the story. "He does not appear to be as speedy as some runners, but always has such a big lead, even with southpaws pitching, that it is almost impossible to catch him."

As his nickname suggests, "Cocky" was not shy about voicing his opinion on the diamond. An undated clipping in his file at the National Baseball Hall of Fame Reference Library describes him as "one of [the] noisiest of ballplayers."

"The impression seems to prevail that Collins is a brilliant ball player, but a silent one," said the story. "Far be it from such. Eddie is one of the noisiest ball players that there is." Among the chatter that Collins supposedly engaged in on the diamond was "Call that base running? You look like a goat tied to a post!" and "If I had a 4-year-old baby and he couldn't stop that one, I'd disown him." (Obviously, the definition of cutting sarcasm has changed since then.)

Collins' speed caused some of baseball's most memorable moments. In 1912, the A's second baseman stole six bases in a single game twice within two weeks. The first time was against the Tigers on September 11; on September 22 the Browns were the victims.

Even more unforgettable was an incident that occurred in the 1917 World Series. By then Collins was on the Chicago White Sox, having been sold for $50,000 by Connie Mack in 1914 when he decided to gut his talent-laden A's ball club. In the sixth game of the series, with the Sox leading the New York Giants three games to two, Collins was trapped in a rundown between third and home. With Giants third baseman Heinie Zimmerman holding the ball, Collins saw that New York had left the plate uncovered. He streaked for home, leaving the hapless Zimmerman little choice but to chase after him, holding the ball in his outstretched hand.

Watching Zimmerman hopelessly chasing one of the fastest players in the game across home plate immediately became part of baseball lore. It left an indelible image that was burned into every fan's mind as "Zim's boner." The day after the game (which, incidentally, the White Sox won to clinch the series), sportswriter Hugh Fullerton immortalized the scene in a ditty paraphrasing *Gunga Din*:

> Heinie Zim, Heinie Zim,
> Chasing Collins home.
> I'm a faster man than you are,
> Heinie Zim!

After playing big league ball for 25 years, Collins retired in 1930. (Before that, in 1929 he had been seriously considered as a replacement for Yankee manager Miller Huggins.) Today, more than 75 years after he last set foot on a diamond, Collins' lifetime stolen base total of 743 ranks seventh on the all-time list.

Collins, Bescher, Carey, and other base stealing contemporaries of Cobb owed the Georgia Peach a debt of gratitude. Cobb took base stealing and raised it to the next level. His determination to get to the next base, no matter what it took—a hard slide, a trick play, or even slashing a fielder—put a new face on stealing. In a scenario that would be repeated several decades later, managers and players watched Cobb run the bases and realized just how important stealing could be to an offense. The result was a generation of talented runners like Collins, Carey, Bescher and others taking their cue from Cobb and running the bases with abandon.

There was even an entire team that parlayed stealing into a pennant. The 1911 New York Giants, managed by John McGraw, the old Oriole who was as keen a practitioner of the inside game as there ever was, were running fools. The team stole 347 bases that year, which remains the single-season record for most steals by a team. Five of the top six stolen base leaders in the National League that year were Giants (Josh Devore, Fred Snodgrass, Fred Merkle, Red Murray and Buck Herzog). Only Cincinnati's Bob Bescher, with his league-leading 81 thefts, prevented a Giants' sweep of the category.

The Giants stole and slid so much that they literally ripped their uniforms to shreds. As McGraw recalled: "On one trip west we arrived in Chicago with a club in rags and tatters. Every player on the club had slid out of the seat of his pants." No sooner had McGraw sent an urgent telegram to New York requesting more uniforms than Devore slid into second base and couldn't get up because his pants had come apart. To avoid public embarrassment, players had to surround Devore and walk him off the field. Was it any wonder that McGraw referred to the 1911 club as the team that "stole the pennant"?

Unfortunately, the Giants' running failed them in the 1911 World Series against the Philadelphia A's. New York stole just four bases in falling to the A's in six games. The World Series was also where Ty Cobb met his Waterloo. The Tigers played in three consecutive World Series (1907-1909) during Cobb's tenure with the club, and lost each one. In two of the series Cobb performed poorly: he hit just .200 in the 1907 World Series with no steals, and a paltry .231 in the 1909 games, with two stolen bases. Only in the 1908 Fall Classic did he shine, batting .368 and swiping two bases.

Because of the pounding that his legs took from sliding, Cobb's stolen base totals declined long before his hitting skills. He usually stole without the use of sliding pads, and his legs were a mass of cuts, bruises, and welts. Manager Jennings once said that Cobb lost "a cup of blood" in each ball game because of his sliding and base running. Since these were the days of rock-hard, stone-pitted infields that had just a nodding familiarity with a rake, Jennings may not have been exaggerating too much.

In 1917, Cobb led the league in stolen bases for the sixth and final time with 55. After that, injuries and age increasingly took their toll, and he could no longer run with the recklessness of youth. A severe knee injury (torn ligaments) in 1920 further hampered his running ability.

After leaving the Tigers in 1926, Cobb played two years with Connie Mack in Philadelphia. Proving that the old fire was still there, he hit .357 and .323, respectively, in the 1927 and 1928 campaigns, while stealing 22 and 5 bases. Unfortunately, the A's finished second to the powerful Yankees both years, and Cobb missed out on a shot at one last pennant and World Series.

By 1929, Connie Mack's team was ready to embark on three straight pennant-winning seasons, but without the help of Ty Cobb. He had finally retired from the game he had played so well, and so hard. For 24 seasons the man from Georgia had slashed and burned his way through the American League, taking no quarter and asking for none in return. No matter how anyone felt about him on the diamond, his mastery of the game of baseball was unquestioned. "It will be a long time before the game develops a second Cobb," wrote one observer, "and then it will be just that—a second Cobb. You've seen the first and only."

This was Ty Cobb the baseball player. Ty Cobb the human being was, unfortunately, another story. Even someone sympathetic to Cobb has to conclude that he was unpleasant, at best. The intense anger and determination that made him great between the lines made him miserable outside of them. "Tyrus was always angry," said boyhood friend Joe Cunningham. A famous quote about Cobb was that he would "climb a mountain to punch an echo."

This anger, never far from the surface, frequently boiled over. He had dozens of fights both on and off the field. The most infamous was when he leaped into the stands and pummeled a fan who had lost nearly all of his fingers. The fact that he was a racist led to even more unpleasant altercations. Alienated from everyone, including his teammates, he might well have been the loneliest man in base-ball.

When Cobb was around, no one was safe, not even those who thought they were his friends. As Ring Lardner wrote, "If you called him some name on the field, he'd of walloped you with a bat, even if you was his best pal."

Even after Cobb left baseball, the warlike fury that fueled his play on the diamond did not die out but continued to glow white hot, as if stoked by some inner flame that could not be turned down. Although he received more votes than any other player (including Babe Ruth) among those to be initially inducted into the Baseball Hall of Fame at Cooperstown in 1939, Cobb deliberately missed the opening ceremonies so that he would not have to be polite to base-ball Commissioner Kenesaw Mountain Landis, with whom he had been feuding for years.

Proving that he could give no quarter, even when it had long since ceased to matter, when he was 60 years old Cobb asked 57-year-old catcher Wally Schang to back up during an Old-Timers Game at Yankee Stadium, because he was afraid that the bat might slip out of his hands due to his advanced age. No sooner had Schang stepped back than Cobb dropped a perfect bunt in front of the plate.

In his later years Cobb was an embittered man. He continued carping at modern baseball and its players, still consumed with his lonely crusade to bring back his cherished scientific game. In 1952 he wrote in *Life* magazine that most present day ballplayers "limped along on one cylinder," and were obsessed with hitting home runs. Only Phil Rizzuto and Stan Musial gained the Cobbian seal of approval for playing the game the right way.

Having failed at two marriages, estranged from his children and isolated from the close-knit fraternity of former ballplayers thanks to the animosity he had caused while playing, Cobb in his later years was almost totally alone. He roamed the country aimlessly, the glory that had once been his on the diamond now just a mocking mem-ory. According to one writer, he carried a gun and a paper bag filled with a million dollars in securities everywhere he went, and drank a quart of bourbon mixed with milk each day to dull the pain of the cancer that was killing him.

"Where's anybody who cares about me?" he cried out one day, toward the end. "Where are they? The world's lousy—no good."

Alone, ill, and ignored, he worked with writer Al Stump on an autobiography whose title—*My Life in Baseball: The True Record*—explained the book's purpose. In it Cobb set right all the "stories" about him—the spikings, the "dirty" plays, even the altercations with fans and players. Cobb claimed that his bad reputation was a bum rap, that he was really just playing the game hard and wasn't out to hurt anyone.

On July 17, 1961, at age 73, Ty Cobb died. Just three ex-ballplayers (Mickey Cochrane, Ray Schalk and Nap Rucker) and one Hall of Fame representative came to the funeral of the man whom many consider the greatest player in baseball history.

But although Ty Cobb lived for many years after he left baseball in 1928, his era did not fare as well. The "scientific game" of bunting, hit-and-run, and base stealing that symbolized the Cobbian Era was supplanted by the home run frenzy of the Ruthian Era.

In 1919 Babe Ruth hit the then-unbelievable total of 29 home runs. Almost overnight, baseball was transformed. Suddenly everyone was swinging for the fences. For Cobb and other players, who thrived via their wits and finely-honed running and batting skills, the new, swing-from-the-heels type of baseball involved no more thought than it took for a gorilla to peel a banana. Surely, they thought, the game's fascination with the home run wouldn't last.

But they were wrong. It would indeed last, and for far longer than anyone could imagine. And, although no one knew it at the time, the birth of the home run meant the near-death of the stolen base.

4

The Babe Blasts the Steal

Everything about George Herman "Babe" Ruth was larger than life: his appetites (for food, sex, and whatever else he desired), his personality, his profligate ways, and his habit of hitting home runs.

The Babe's arrival onto the baseball scene was providential; not only did he restore public faith in the game after the Black Sox scandal, but he also injected a much-needed boost of excitement that helped bring people back through the turnstiles. Attendance soared as fans flocked to ballparks to watch Ruth hammer the ball into the seats.

The offensive revolution wrought by Ruth and his cadre of sluggers in the 1920s was one of the most dramatic changes in the history of baseball. Almost overnight, the game changed from a low-scoring chess match to a run-filled slugfest.

However, for every action there is a reaction. The rise of the home run meant the decline of the "inside game" so beloved by Cobb and others. Slowly but surely, the steal, bunt, hit-and-run, and other strategic elements of the "scientific" game were relegated to the baseball doghouse in favor of the game's new pet, the home run. It would be a long time before they were let out to play again.

In 1919, while with the Boston Red Sox, Ruth hit what was considered the unbelievable total of 29 home runs. Not only did this lead both leagues, but it was almost as much as the combined total of the next three top A.L. home run hitters, each of whom hit 10.

Baseball experts agreed that Ruth's home run record would stand for some time. The 1920 *Spalding Guide* suggested, "Perhaps, and most likely, Ruth will not be so successful in 1920." According to the *Guide*, it would be years before someone else hit more than 29 home runs.

With his usual disdain for authority, Ruth thumbed his nose at the *Guide's* prediction the best way he knew how—by belting the astronomical total of 54 home runs during the 1920 season. This time, there were fewer voices crying about the chances of breaking *that* record. It was a good thing, too, because the following year Ruth did it again, sending 59 baseballs into the seats. Fans, who just a few years earlier had celebrated as superhuman the ability of anyone who hit a dozen home runs, could barely believe their eyes. Best of all for them, it was only the beginning.

Starting in 1920, Ruth ignited an offensive explosion through-out baseball. That year, American League batters hit a combined .283 and clubbed 369 homers, both records. Not to be left out, National League batters hit .270 and blasted 261 round-trippers.

These were extraordinary totals, representing a complete rever-sal of the game's priorities. Just two years earlier, the combined Amer-ican League batting average was .254 with 98 home runs, while the National League tallied .254 with 139 homers. To put it another way, in 1919 the Yankees hit 45 home runs; Ruth beat that all by himself in 1920. In fact, his 54 home runs in 1920 were more than the com-bined total of any other team in baseball in 1920 except the Philadel-phia Phillies, who hit 64 homers (and still finished last).

Of course, all of this offense came at the expense of someone, and that was the hapless pitcher. Formerly the lords of the game in the dead-ball era, hurlers had the unpleasant duty of watching as their former serfs rose up in angry revolt. As the collective earned-run average kept rising—from 2.68 in 1917 to a whopping 4.33 in 1925—pitchers must have wondered what they had done to deserve being condemned to such purgatory.

There are numerous theories as to why offense suddenly became dominant in the 1920s. These run the gamut from the banning of trick pitches such as the spitball, to the persistent use of clean base-balls following the death of Ray Chapman in August 1920 from being hit in the head by a dark, discolored baseball, to a so-called "lively ball" that was made differently than in the past so that it traveled farther when hit.

In the book *Big Sticks: The Batting Revolution of the Twenties*, William Curran systematically demolishes any possibility that a "lively ball" caused the offensive explosion. Instead, he effectively argues that it was a combination of the banning of spitballs and their no-account cousins (such as the shine ball and the emery ball), the use of clean balls, and more batters learning how to uppercut the ball just like the Babe, that led to ball parks suddenly resembling launching pads in the 1920s.

(For those who scoff at the "clean baseballs" part of this argument, there is a famous story about how, in a game in the early years of the American League, a single ball was kept in play for so long that the pitcher could actually squeeze it like a sponge. All the batters could do with it was hit weak grounders. Finally, after repeatedly begging for a new ball and being turned down by the umpire, Nap Lajoie snatched the dilapidated ball out of the catcher's mitt and threw it out of the ball park.)

Of all those factors, the one that should not be underestimated is the influence of Ruth. Curran points out that not only did Ruth bash home runs, he also hit for a high average. Ruth's success seemed to disprove the popular theory that trying for the long ball was detrimental to the batting average and made the Babe an even better model, since there didn't seem to be a downside to imitating him. As Curran wrote,

> Throughout the country there had to be college, high school, and even sandlot ballplayers pondering the Babe's performance. What their coaches had been telling them was obviously not true. Choking up on the bat and trying to poke the ball past an infielder was clearly not the only way to a high average, success, and fame on the diamond, especially if you had broad shoulders. We can guess that many strong young hands began to slide down to the knob of the bat as cheap spikes or sneakers dug in at the plate.

Besides the fact that it looked and felt good to knock balls out of the park, major league ballplayers had another, more practical reason for imitating Ruth: money. Long before Ralph Kiner announced that "home run hitters drive Cadillacs," Ruth was living proof of that statement. His salary soared from $10,000 in 1919 to $52,000 by 1922. The Babe was well aware of what was putting all that filthy green into his pocket—and it wasn't his mastery of the scientific game. "There's more jack in it for me in this home run racket," said Ruth once to a reporter who asked him if he wouldn't rather hit for a higher average than go for home runs.

Measured against the possibility of fame and fortune by hitting home runs, the inside game never had a chance. As F.C. Lane wrote in *Baseball Magazine*, "He [Ruth] has not only slugged his way to fame, but he has got everybody else doing it. The home run fever is in the air. It is infectious."

If the home run was an infection, the part of the baseball body that it killed was the stolen base. In normal times, stealing could have relied upon the owners to devise an antibody to rid the game of the long ball plague. The men who ran baseball had proven themselves quite willing to tinker with the rules throughout the years to strike a balance between offense and defense. Since the home run explosion had definitely turned the tide in favor of the offense, the owners would have likely tried to quell the home run outbreak.

But these were not normal times in baseball. In September, 1920, after months of rumors, word of the Black Sox scandal broke publicly. The worst fears of the owners were realized; the integrity of the game had been severely compromised. Not only attendance, but the future of baseball itself, was in peril.

News of the Black Sox did not just suddenly descend on baseball like a thunderbolt. Allegations of players throwing games, or teams throwing games, had dogged the sport for years. In fact, the Black Sox scandal became public because a grand jury was investigating allegations of a rigged game between the Phillies and the Cubs and was also taking a look at baseball's gambling problems in general.

Thus in the fall of 1920 baseball owners were faced with a curious dilemma. On the one hand, Ruth and his home runs had fueled enormous interest in the game; on the other, scandal and resultant fan disillusionment were threatening to crush this blooming interest like a bulldozer rumbling over a flower. Faced with this situation, the owners reacted in two ways: one, by making Kenesaw Mountain Landis the game's first commissioner, with broad powers to clean up baseball; and two, by giving the public what it wanted in not meddling with Ruth and the offensive barrage he had begun.

In retrospect it wasn't a very hard decision to let the homers fly. All the owners had to do was look at the Yankees' attendance figures. In 1917, before Ruth, the team drew 330,294; in 1920, with the Babe belting balls into the seats, New York set a major league home attendance record with 1,298,422. Any owner who called for a return to the scientific game would have undoubtedly been sent away for a nice long rest.

So was the course of baseball set for generations to come. "Hitting them where they ain't" became "hitting them into the seats." The home run became baseball's crowd-magnet.

And what of the stolen base? Like its other strategic cousins from the inside game the stolen base quickly fell out of favor. After all, there was little strategy involved in hitting home runs; all a manager had to do was wait for somebody to connect. With at least one run, and possibly more, always just one swing away, managers had little incentive to try to fashion a run from bunting, stealing, and the like. Stealing simply became unnecessary.

The decline of the stolen base was quick. In 1918, the average team was stealing 9.8 bases every ten games. One year later it had dropped slightly, to 9.3 bases per ten games. In 1920, when Ruth hit 54 homers, this figure nose-dived to 6.9. By 1926, the average steals per ten games had dropped still further, to 5.2. By 1929 it had settled below 5.0. Here it would remain for generations.

Even pugnacious John McGraw, who symbolized the inside game both as a player and a manager, admitted in 1923 that baseball had changed. "[With the] ball being hit all about the lot the necessity of taking chances on the bases has decreased," the Little Napoleon said. "A manager would look foolish not to play the game as it is… There is no use in sending men down on a long chance of stealing a bag when there is a better chance of the batter hitting one for two bases, or, maybe, out of the lot."

McGraw's actions proved his point. In 1911, his pennant-winning Giants' team had stolen 347 bases, setting an all-time record. In 1924, just 13 short years later, his pennant-winning Giants stole a mere 82 bases. That's how quickly the steal disappeared from baseball.

The fact that even people like McGraw were turning their backs on the inside game must have been a bitter pill for Cobb and other scientific game stalwarts to swallow. Cobb, as was his nature, would not abandon the inside game without an argument. "Given the proper physical equipment—which consists solely in the strength to knock a ball 40 feet farther than the average man can do it—anybody can play big league ball today," Cobb carped. "In other words, science is out the window." (One day in 1925, just to prove how simple it was to smack round-trippers, Cobb announced that he would deliberately hit home runs. He hit three homers in six at bats that day and two more the next before he felt he had made his point.)

The Peach's complaints were echoed by numerous contemporary magazines that considered the skyrocketing rise in home runs to be just slightly less serious than a foreign invasion of the United States. Articles with titles like "Baseball Shudders at the Home Run Menace" and "The Growing Problem of the Home Run" must have warmed the hearts of those who longed for those not-so-distant days when a single, a sacrifice, and a stolen base constituted an offensive explosion.

But if advocates of the inside game hoped that a few magazine articles would turn the tide in their favor, they were sorely mistaken. Even Cobb could see the handwriting on the wall for his type of baseball, particularly when it was announced in *The New York Times.* "Cobb [is] in eclipse for the first time since he began to show his remarkable ability," said the newspaper. "Ruth has stolen all of Cobb's thunder."

Besides, club owners had no intention of stifling something that was proving so profitable. Historically, an increase in offense has been followed by an increase in attendance, and the 1920s were no exception. As more runners crossed the plate, more fans clicked through the turnstiles. During the 1920s, average club attendance increased 50 percent over what it had been during the previous low-scoring decade. In 1920, when runs per game jumped from 3.8 in 1919 to 4.4, major league attendance leaped to a record 9.1 million. Thereafter, new attendance records were set from 1924 through 1927; yearly attendance averaged approximately 9 million throughout the decade.

Instead of bringing back scientific baseball, club owners seemed content to stimulate the offense some more. In 1926, a new cushioned cork center ball was introduced. Curiously enough, it resulted in an offensive decline. Batting averages that year dropped .012 percentage points in the National League and .011 in the American League, while home runs plunged 31 percent and 20 percent, respectively, in the two leagues.

By 1927, however, when Ruth belted his record-breaking total of 60 home runs, hitters had regained their momentum. Home runs and batting averages rose that year in both leagues.

In 1930, the National League added fuel to the offensive fires by introducing a new ball for the upcoming season. Wrapped more tightly, and with less prominent stitching rendering it more difficult to grip, this ball heralded an offensive barrage that dwarfed all that had come before it and undoubtedly sent the boosters of scientific baseball running for cover.

In 1930, nine out of the sixteen major league teams hit .300 or better. Pitching was so atrocious that in both leagues, only the Washington Senators' mound staff had an earned run average of less than 4.00 (and with an e.r.a. of 3.96, they just made it under the wire). Individual hitting statistics were equally prodigious; the Phillies' Chuck Klein hit .386, with 40 home runs, 250 hits, and 170 runs batted in, and led the league in *none* of those categories.

Hitters were so dominating in 1930 that John McGraw, who had seen the game change considerably since his playing days in the dead ball era, argued unsuccessfully for an immediate reduction of the pitching distance to 58 feet to give the poor pitchers a fighting chance.

True to form, fans responded to this latest outburst of offense by hurrying to the ballparks like never before. Major league baseball's attendance for 1930 was 10,132,272, a new record. Any owner contemplating a return to the inside game was quickly dissuaded by a look at the bottom line.

Thus, with the home run the unquestioned king of baseball, stealing slowly atrophied as an offensive weapon. Throughout the

1920s, stolen base totals steadily declined. In 1917, N.L. teams stole a combined 1,145 bases, while A.L. teams swiped 1,268. By 1920 those numbers had dropped to 969 and 751, respectively. Ten years later, they had fallen even further, to 481 and 598.

Individual stolen base totals plummeted as well. In 1914, no less than 34 players stole at least 20 bases. By 1923, however, that number of players had shrunk to 11. Soon it would shrink even further, to the point that 20 steals would be considered an exceptional total. These were dark days indeed for the stolen base.

It's incorrect, however, to assume that stolen base totals dropped each time home runs increased. For example, in 1924, National League teams hit 40 fewer home runs than the previous year, yet stole 70 fewer bases. Moreover, in 1927 in both leagues the total number of home runs and steals increased from the previous year. This was especially noticeable in the American League, which saw just 15 more home runs but 124 more stolen bases.

So while baseball lore usually holds that Ruth and his booming bat sounded the death knell for stealing, a closer look at the numbers tells a different story. In reality, stealing reached a pinnacle in the 1910s, and was dropping even before the Babe swaggered onto the scene. The years from 1910 through 1912 were the peak seasons for stealing. In the National League, base stealers swiped 1,594, 1,692, and 1,576 bags during those years, respectively, for an average of 1,620 bases per season. American League totals were even higher at 1,671, 1,712, and 1,809 steals for those three years, averaging out to a gaudy 1,730 steals per season.

After 1912, base stealing numbers flattened out. In the National League, the number of stolen bases (1,576) stayed the same in 1913 as in the previous year, then began falling. The American League had a drop of 134 stolen bases in 1913 as compared to 1912. By 1915, A.L. base stealing had declined by 366 from the high water mark set in 1912, while in the N.L. there were 528 fewer sacks swiped in 1915 than there had been in the peak season of 1911.

Clearly, then, stolen base totals were already slipping before Ruth's home runs changed the offensive outlook of the game. There doesn't seem to be any obvious reason for the stealing slowdown; no rule changes occurred that had a major impact on stealing. It's almost as if base stealing had reached its limits in the early years of the 1910s, and then slowly began to constrict, for no other reason than it couldn't extend any further.

Although Cobb and others blamed Ruth for killing the steal, it's perhaps more accurate to say that the Babe didn't put the knife into the back of the stolen base—he just knocked it in firmly with his big bat.

It's not likely that the Sultan of Swat cared much about the demise of the scientific game anyway. "If I'd just tried for them dinky singles I could've batted around six hundred," he once snorted, perfectly summing up his feelings about pre–Ruthian baseball.

But others did mourn for the days of inside baseball. One of these was legendary baseball writer Ring Lardner. Early in his career, Lardner's baseball-related writing was realistic and good-natured. However, as the home run took over, his tone turned bitter and sarcastic:

> It ain't the old game which I have lost interest in it, but it is a game which the magnates has fixed up to please the public with their usual good judgment ... the master minds that controls baseball says to themselves that if it is home runs that the public wants to see, why leave us give them home runs, so they fixed up a ball that if you don't miss it entirely it will clear the fence, and the result is that ball players which used to specialize in hump back liners to the pitcher is now amongst our leading sluggers.

Ultimately, Lardner became so disillusioned with the game that he gave up writing about baseball.

Another who mourned the decline of stealing was sportswriter Hugh Fullerton. As early as 1911 he was already publicly commenting on the "death" of the stolen base.

Others believed the steal's demise was long since past. For them, the "good old days" of base stealing featured men like Sliding Billy Hamilton and Harry Stovey, who swiped box cars full of bases under the old rules, before the modern interpretation of the steal came into effect in 1898. To them, if you weren't stealing at least 100 bases in a season, you just weren't trying, and so they probably didn't know what all this talk was about the "death" of the stolen base. They figured it had died a long time ago.

The offensive production of 1930, while good for attendance and personal statistics, was bad for stolen base totals. National League runners swiped just 481 bases that year, down 211 from the previous season. American Leaguers stole 598 bases, which was a drop of 33 from 1929.

In 1931 baseball owners finally took steps to curtail the offense. The National League introduced a ball with a slightly thicker cover and raised stitches instead of countersunk ones. The American League kept the existing cover, but raised the stitches on their ball as well. This tinkering with the ball's aerodynamics enabled pitchers to put more movement on their pitches. The strategy worked; the National League's collective batting average dropped from .303 to .277, and home runs declined by 400. In the American League, batters hit nearly 100 fewer homers and suffered a batting average drop of ten points.

But even though the hitters had been cooled off slightly, stealing—much to the chagrin of Cobb and others, no doubt—did not make a comeback. Just like the U.S. economy, stealing was in its own Great Depression, but this one would take many more years to dissipate. Nobody was running anymore, and stolen base totals that would have looked pathetic 20 years before were now leading the league. Bugs Baer wrote: "Today thirty [stolen bases] will get you in the Hall of Fame and a player is considered a terrific runner if he doesn't get thrown out at first on a base on balls."

Throughout the 1930s and 1940s, stolen base totals in both leagues were like bad club fighters—they couldn't get off the canvas. In 1938, the eight National League teams stole a combined 354 bases, or an average of 44 bases per team. Those running fools, the Cincinnati Reds, stole a grand total of 19 bases for the *entire season*—or just about one month's worth for Cobb during his peak years.

Obviously, individual league-leading stolen base totals during these years were deplorably low. In 1938, Chicago Cubs' third baseman Stan Hack led the National League with 16 steals. The top five base stealers in the National League combined for just 74 steals, a total that Cobb beat by himself three times.

Although he never stole many bases, Stan Hack was one of the leading N.L. base thieves in the nonrunning 1930s (courtesy of the Baseball Hall of Fame Library, Cooperstown, New York).

Stolen base totals in the American League were generally higher during the 1930s and 1940s. The difference was often not very significant, however; in that stealing-challenged year of 1938, for example, Yankee shortstop Frank Crosetti led the league with 27 steals.

Stealing was a lost art during this era, and it didn't matter how much Cobb and other old-timers bemoaned the sad state of the game, the steal wasn't coming back anytime soon. Inevitably, the mechanics of stealing—like reading the pitcher and jockeying for a good lead—were ignored by those who taught the game. This meant that kids coming up didn't know how to steal and helped to ensure the continuing neglect of the stolen base.

An example of how much the perception of stealing, as well as the circumstances under which it was taught, had changed was illustrated in a 1939 instructional book by former player Ethan Allen called *Major League Baseball*. In the book, Allen described "when to steal": "All single steals are gamble plays and should only be attempted by fast runners and under certain conditions. For instance, a steal of second base is usually advisable with two outs, your team in the lead, the score tied, or the opposing team ahead no more than one run and preferably a left hand batter other than the pitcher at the plate."

Gamble plays? Only steal with a left-handed hitter at the plate? Only for fast runners? There were so many warnings attached to stealing, it's a wonder that runners weren't told to bring galoshes with them in case the base paths were muddy. One can only imagine what rugged base stealers like Cobb and Bob Bescher would have thought of such trepidation.

Even though stealing was in critical condition during these years, a few skilled practitioners kept it on life support. The Cardinals' Pepper Martin, "the Wild Hoss of the Osage" (described in more detail in Chapter 12), led the National League in steals three times in four years.

Another outstanding base stealer of this era was Frankie Frisch. Nicknamed "The Fordham Flash" because of his speed, Frisch's peak years were in the 1920s, before stealing totally dropped off the baseball radar screen. Frisch stole 419 bases over the course of his career, and led the league three times: 1921 (49 steals), 1927 (48 steals), and 1931 (28 steals).

After breaking into the big leagues with John McGraw's Giants, Frisch was traded to St. Louis in 1927 for Rogers Hornsby. After the season began, the irascible Hornsby was bombarded with newspaper clippings sent by gleeful St. Louis fans, pointing out how wonderfully The Fordham Flash was doing and how much faster Frisch was than Hornsby on the bases.

Hornsby, who had an extremely low boiling point, could take only so much of this. In May 1927, he issued a $1,000 challenge to Frisch to race around the bases and find out who was faster.

"Frisch is a good friend of mine," said Hornsby, who never stole more than 17 bases in a season in his life. "I have nothing against him. But I'd like to prove I can beat him in a race around the bases just for the fun of the thing—and to silence a lot of my old boosters."

To his credit the Flash, who probably could have beaten Hornsby while running backwards and eating a turkey sandwich, ignored the challenge.

"This is all a laugh to me," he said.

In the American League, the Yankees' Ben Chapman was the league's top base-stealer in the early 1930s. He swiped 61 in 1931 to account for almost half of New York's total of 138 steals. The premier base-stealer of the late 1930s and 1940s was George Case. Playing virtually his entire career for mediocre Washington Senator teams, Case almost single-handedly kept the stolen base alive, both as an offensive weapon and in the memories of baseball players, managers and fans. Both of these men are covered in more detail in Chapter 12.

A disturbing characteristic of the stolen base during this time was that it was no longer a hallmark of winning teams. During the first two decades of the twentieth century, it was almost a given that winning teams stole bases. During 1900–1909, the National League team that stole the most bases finished first six times, and second twice. This trend wasn't as pronounced in the American League, but the leader in steals still finished first twice, and third once. From 1910 to 1919 it was more of the same: the team that led the National League in steals finished first four times and second once, while in the Junior Circuit it was two first-place finishes and six second-place results.

Things changed in 1920, when offenses began to be structured around the home run. From 1920 through 1929, the team that led the National League in steals finished first just twice, second once, and third three times. In the American League it was even worse: the league-leader in steals landed in the top spot just once (the 1925 Washington Senators), and in second only one time. Hitting homers had replaced stealing as the key ingredient for winning baseball.

Soon after he became manager of the Brooklyn Dodgers in the early 1930s, Max Carey, one of the best base stealers in National League history, noted that stealing didn't mean what it used to: "The boys seem to think that because I used to do some running the Dodgers are going to dash wild on the bases. Well, you can't win a pennant these days by stealing bases."

Carey's statement was very true, and the deterioration in the value of stealing as a component of winning baseball continued throughout the 1940s. In the American League, every club that led in steals finished fourth or lower during the decade except for the 1945 Senators, who came in second, and the 1941 White Sox, who finished third.

The National League fared better, primarily because of Jackie Robinson. Teams that led the league in steals recorded two first-place finishes during the 1940s, both by the Robinson-led Brooklyn Dodgers (1947 and 1949). Robinson was a large part of this success, as he led the National League in stolen bases both those years with 29 and 37 steals, respectively.

Besides Brooklyn's two pennant winners, N.L. teams that led the league in steals also came in second three times, and third three times. Only in 1945 did the team with the most steals (the Boston Braves) finish below third. (This was a harbinger of things to come in the 1950s, when N.L. teams that led the league in steals were far more successful than their A.L. counterparts.)

Stolen base patterns during the 1940s were also affected by the talent drain precipitated by World War II. With so many skilled players in the military by the mid–1940s, managers were forced to use strategy to score runs. Thus stealing made a brief comeback, although by necessity rather than choice.

After dropping in the first two years of the decade, stolen base totals in the American League bounced up in 1942 and 1943. In fact, the A.L. total of 626 stolen bases in 1943 was the highest in the league in 12 years. At the same time, home run totals plummeted, going from 883 in 1940 to 473 in 1943. The next year, however, both home runs and steals dropped, possibly because 1944 is often cited as the nadir for talent in the majors due to the war.

In the National League it was a somewhat different story. Steals continued to drop, even throughout the middle 1940s, when they were rising in the American League. Suddenly, in 1945 N.L. stolen base totals jumped up to 525, a gain of 147 from the previous season. Since home run totals stayed nearly identical in both seasons (575 in 1944, 577 in 1945), the rise in stolen bases for that one year is difficult to understand.

By 1946, with many players returning from the war, home runs shot back up, and stolen bases resumed their familiar decline. By the end of the decade, yearly steal totals in both the National and American leagues were averaging about 45 per team.

As major league baseball entered the 1950s, the stolen base had reached an historic low point. The American League's 366 total steals in 1949 was the lowest total ever recorded, while the National League's 364 thefts were just ten greater than in 1938, when the all-time low mark of 354 had been posted. It would get even worse in the 1950s.

Sadly, the stolen base had become an afterthought in baseball— a "trick" or "gimmick" play. The days when a Cobb or Collins would plan exactly when to steal, hoping to maximize disruption in the defense, was a thing of the past. Now, once a player got on base he knew that nothing was expected of him except to stay out of trouble and run when the ball was hit. It was brainless baseball at its best.

Stealing was considered a risky play that should only be tried in certain situations. The unpredictable element that the stolen base represented in Cobb's day, when at any moment a runner might bolt for the next base, was replaced by a school of thought that developed strict rules as to when stealing should be attempted. These conditions were spelled out by Joe DiMaggio, in his 1948 instructional book *Baseball for Everyone*: "There is no sense in trying to steal second if the runner's team is more than one run behind. A steal should be attempted only when the potential tally, which the base runner represents, is an important one. It is rarely good judgment to steal with none out."

Not only was stealing considered risky, it was also thought to be dangerous. During spring training in 1948, Yankee manager Bucky Harris looked with dismay at a sliding pit that the team's grounds-keeper had built. "We cannot afford to risk broken legs," Harris sniffed, and that was the end of the sliding pit. True to Harris' feelings, the Yanks finished next-to-last in stealing in the American League that year with 24, or approximately one successful steal every six games.

This attitude carried over to the Yankees' training camp the next year, even though Casey Stengel had replaced Harris as manager. In camp, coach Johnny Neun tried explaining to a group of Yankees how to run the bases. One player was horrified. "You mean I've got to steal bases?" he gasped, clearly alarmed at the prospect. "No," Neun replied. "You don't have to know how to steal bases, but you do have to know how to run bases."

As predictable as stealing had become for the players, it was even more so for the fans. Generations of spectators were being denied one of the most quintessential experiences in baseball: a runner unexpectedly streaking toward a base, his legs pitted against the catcher's arm and the pitcher's guile, the outcome tantalizingly suspended until the umpire's call.

Once, baseball had presented an interesting challenge to its fans: watch the batter, and miss the possibility of a daring base runner like Cobb, Carey, or Collins suddenly doing something unexpected. Or, watch the runner, and miss what the hitter might do. But with the virtual extinction of stealing, once a man reached base the fans could ignore him, knowing that he almost certainly wasn't going anywhere until the batter made contact.

Indeed, it was not inconceivable that a spectator during this period could go an entire year without seeing the home team ever steal a base. For instance, the 1949 St. Louis Cardinals stole just 17 bases the entire season. Over the course of 154 games, this averages out to one steal every nine games. Thus it is likely that a Cardinals' fan who attended a dozen or so games during the year might never see a Redbird steal successfully.

Ironically, the stolen base was scraping the bottom of the baseball barrel at precisely the moment when one of the most exciting runners the game had ever seen arrived. When he joined the Brooklyn Dodgers in 1947, Jackie Robinson brought the gambling, scrambling, running style of play that personified Negro League baseball back into the major leagues. As Buck O'Neil, star first baseman of the Kansas City Monarchs of the Negro National League noted: "At the time [major league] baseball was a base-to-base thing. You hit the ball, you wait on first base until somebody hit again. See? But in our baseball you got on base if you walked, you stole second, you'd try to steal, they'd bunt you over to third and you actually scored runs without a hit. This was our baseball."

This, indeed, was "their" baseball. It was Negro League baseball, and it was where the stolen base had gone after being banished from the white major leagues. Like the players, the stolen base found a home there, and thrived.

5

Thriving in the Shadows

"That was our game—run, steal, make them make mistakes."

That quote, by William Julius "Judy" Johnson, one of the slickest fielders ever to man the hot corner, accurately describes a type of baseball played in the United States for over three decades. But Johnson was not talking about the game featured in the American and National leagues. Instead, it was the style of baseball played in the Negro Leagues—where the bunt, the hit-and-run, and the stolen base could be found once the white major leagues largely abandoned these tactics in favor of the home run.

During most of its existence, black baseball was the game that big league baseball had once been: exciting, sudden, innovative, and unpredictable. Yet few fans of the white major leagues knew of this thrilling alternative to the plodding, one-base-at-a-time game that increasingly dominated both the National and American leagues after 1920. While these fans were watching games that were becoming as routine as punching a time clock, Negro League players were using the tools that the majors had discarded to fashion their own distinctive brand of baseball.

"Black baseball was fast and aggressive, with lots of stealing, bunting, hit-and-run play," said Buck O'Neil, in his book *I Was Right on Time*.

Even though stealing was a major part of the Negro League game, modern baseball fans are sometimes puzzled that stolen base totals of Negro League players aren't greater than statistics indicate. For example, the highest single season steal total that the ninth edition of *The Baseball Encyclopedia* credits Hall of Famer Oscar Charleston (sometimes called "the Black Ty Cobb" or "The Hoosier Comet") with is 34, in 1921—a good number, certainly, but not even close to Cobbian.

However, this illustrates the risk of judging a Negro League player (or any athlete, for that matter) strictly by the numbers. Charleston was an explosive, terrifying force on the base paths, one whose worth as a game-breaking stolen base threat went far beyond mere numbers.

(What makes it even more difficult to evaluate Negro League players by "official" statistics is that not only did many games go unreported, but the reports that were made were often erroneous. In addition, the Negro League season was much shorter than that of the white major leagues.)

Charleston's 34 steals are much more impressive when coupled with the fact that they were obtained in just 60 games, during 212 at bats. That same year, Frankie Frisch needed 153 games and 618 at bats to lead the National League in steals with 49. Given the same 618 at bats, Charleston, if he would have maintained his 1921 pace throughout an entire season, would have stolen approximately 99 bases.

Perhaps, in the case of Negro League players, it's best to let the deeds of the men speak louder than the numbers attached to their names. In Oscar Charleston's file at the National Baseball Hall of Fame reference library in Cooperstown is a newspaper story about a series in 1922 between Charleston's team and the major league St. Louis Cardinals. Three times during that series, after reaching first base Charleston boldly informed the Cardinals' pitcher that he was going to steal second on the next pitch. All three times he did precisely that. You can't measure that type of ability with just numbers.

The tone of black baseball, with its emphasis on stealing, the hit-and-run, and other aggressive tactics, was set early by another Hall of Famer: Andrew "Rube" Foster. The man often called the

"Father of Black Baseball" fervently believed that a winning ball club is built on speed.

Foster was a sensational pitcher in the early years of the twentieth century. He won his nickname "Rube" when he beat the legendary Rube Waddell in a 1904 game. At one time Foster was such a dominating force that a newspaper headline simply read, "Foster Pitched, That's All."

Yet it was as a manager, not a pitcher, that Foster made an indelible impression on black baseball. Becoming skipper of the Chicago American Giants early in the 1910s, Foster installed an offense that featured more running than a mass jailbreak. Speed was his elixir for winning baseball, and he made sure that everyone on his team drank from the same cup.

Foster devised numerous plays to maximize the use of speed, such as the hit-and-run bunt (which was the same as the hit-and-run, only the batter bunted instead of swinging away) and the triple steal.

Another favorite Foster tactic was the steal-and-bunt. As Cool Papa Bell once explained: "The runner on first would take off and the batter would bunt the ball so the third baseman had to field it. If he threw to first, the lead runner just kept going to third. If he held the ball, it was runners on first and second. It was a beautiful play, and Foster's team made it work over and over again."

Dave Malarcher, third baseman on the Chicago American Giants, once observed that "Rube knew the value of speed." Indeed he did; Foster's ball club bristled with lightning-quick players. In the book *Blackball Stars*, Malarcher described the Giants' speed-laden lineup: "We had Jimmy Lyons, [Cristobal] Torriente, and Jelly Gardner in the outfield. They're all fast. I was on third, I'm fast. Bobby Williams shortstop, real fast. Bingo DeMoss second, he's fast. We had George Dixon and Jim Brown catching. Brown was fast ... when James Brown was catching, we had seven men in the lineup could run a hundred yards in around ten seconds. All speed..."

Through incessant practice, Foster made sure that the Giants were able to use their speed to maximum advantage. One of his favorite drills was to have the players bunt into a circle drawn in front of home plate; they'd keep at it until they were so proficient that they could successfully bunt on a third strike. During a game, Foster used these plays and his team's well-honed ability to execute them to manufacture runs out of situations that other teams ignored. "If you walked a man against Rube, that was a run," said pitcher Webster McDonald.

What Foster was doing was the same as Ty Cobb was doing in the white game: using speed as a weapon to shake up the defense. As Malarcher said: "He taught this: that in order for a man to put you out going from base to base, the other team must make a perfect play. If you can run, if you're fast, he's got to make a perfect play, and if you surprise him, he can't make a perfect play, he can't make it."

Foster's constant use of speed drove opposing defenses wacky. The other team knew that the moment a Giant got on first, he was going to be running, be it a hit-and-run, bunt-and-run, straight steal, or via some other devilish play concocted by Foster's fertile brain. The opposition played cautiously, realizing that the Giants' speed meant that no lead against them was ever truly safe. In 1921 the Indianapolis ABCs found this out the hard way; after surging to an 18–0 advantage over the Giants, they watched helplessly as Foster's team used 11 bunts and 6 squeeze plays to forge an 18–18 tie.

Not only was Foster a great pitcher and a superb manager/tactical, he was also a visionary. In 1920, he formed the Negro National League (NNL) to provide an organized structure for both black players and their fans. It was, Foster said, an attempt to "do something concrete for the loyalty of the race."

Until destroyed by the Great Depression in 1931, the NNL was very successful. Foster's Giants dominated the league in its early years, winning championships in 1920, 1921 and 1922.

Just how much Foster used the stolen base is evident in the statistics of five key players from the 1921 team who combined for 82 steals in just 58 games: Lyons (28), Torriente (18), DeMoss (14), and Gardner & Malarcher (11 each). (If accurate statistics for jackrabbit shortstop Jimmy Williams are ever found, this total will almost certainly reach 100.)

In the major leagues during that same year, Washington led the American League with 111 stolen bases. The top five Senators in steals were Bucky Harris (29), Sam Rice (25), Joe Judge (21), Howard

Shanks (11), and Frank O'Rourke (6). Their combined total of 92 is just ten more than the five Giants compiled in 96 fewer games. The mind reels at what Foster could have accomplished if given a major league season of 154 games with which to work his magic.

But whereas the success of Foster's teams alone might have been enough to convince teams to run, there were also other reasons why Negro League teams resorted to a game of speed and skill rather than home run hitting.

One factor that limited the amount of homers in the Negro Leagues was that the baseballs were usually in such terrible shape that hitters couldn't possibly belt them out of the park consistently. Unlike the major leagues, where a conscious effort was made beginning in 1920 to use only clean balls, Negro League balls would rarely be removed from a game. Thus the ball would get progressively darker, mushier and more lopsided as the game went on.

Negro League pitchers did their best to add to a ball's distress. While doctoring the ball was banned in the early 1920s in the white league, there was no corresponding action taken in black baseball. Emery balls, spit balls, shine balls, and a variety of other "balls" were permissible weapons in a black pitcher's arsenal, and most did not hesitate to use them. "We had to hit balls doctored up so bad you'd think carpenters worked on them," said second baseman Mahlon Duckett.

Naturally, the more unpredictable a ball's movement, the less likely it would be that a batter could time a pitch and hit it out of the park. As Bobby Robinson of the Detroit Stars noted: "You couldn't hit those spitters. That ball would come in about halfway and then start dancing. It would be all over the place. You'd just close your eyes and swing."

"Spit balls, shine balls, emery balls," Roy Campanella once said about catching in the Negro League. "I never knew what the ball would do once it left the pitcher's hand."

Black pitchers also made liberal use of the knockdown pitch to move batters off the plate and keep them from digging in. "People say my best pitch was my fast ball," said Leon Day. "Wrong. My best pitch was my knockdown pitch."

Trying to connect with a dark, soft, lopsided ball that was dipping and darting across the plate, while keeping one eye open for a knock-down pitch, was not exactly a recipe for home run hitting. Sometimes, even making contact seemed impossible. Never was this more obvious than in a 1930 game between the Homestead Grays and the Kansas City Monarchs dubbed the "Battle of the Butchered Balls." Chet Brewer and Smokey Joe Williams used emery balls, sandpaper balls, and "goo balls" (the "goo" was a black, tar-like substance that Williams put on the ball) in pitching 12 devastating innings each. Williams struck out 27 batters and Brewer 19. Not surprisingly, the final score was 1–0 (in favor of the Grays).

As if hitting a ball that looked like it had been repeatedly run over by a train and had the resiliency of an old beanbag wasn't hard enough, Negro League players also had to endure a traveling schedule that would sap the stamina of Superman. In *Invisible Men*, Willie Wells bemoaned the endless traveling, relating how the Homestead Grays once played games in Pittsburgh, Toronto, and Detroit all on successive days. "We'd just eat and ride and play," pitcher Chet Brewer said. "That was the size of it. It wasn't easy street."

Playing two and three games a day, then riding all night to get to the next game, did little to improve the eye and hand coordination necessary to hit a ball over the fence.

This is not to say that home runs were a lost art in Negro League baseball. The league had its share of sluggers, like George "Mule" Suttles, Willard Jessie "Home Run" Brown, and the legendary Josh Gibson. But just as the long ball became the prevailing theme in the white game, so did aggressive plays like the hit-and-run, bunt, and stolen base become dominant in the black leagues. The beloved "scientific game" of Ty Cobb and others hadn't been completely wiped out by the homer-happy 1920s—it had just found a new home.

Not only did Negro League players know how to steal, they also knew how to defend against the steal. This was never better illustrated than in a classic confrontation between legendary shortstop John Henry "Pop" Lloyd and Ty Cobb in 1910.

The Detroit Tigers were playing an exhibition series in Cuba against the Havana Reds, a team that included Lloyd and other Negro League stars such as Bruce Petway and Grant "Home Run" Johnson. In the fourth inning of a game Cobb walked, and everyone knew what was coming next: the man who had run roughshod over American League infielders while swiping 65 bases that year was preparing to go into second with spikes high.

What Cobb didn't realize, however, was that Lloyd was ready and waiting. Knowing that the Tiger outfielder liked to come into bases with his "steel showing," Lloyd was wearing his custom, cast-iron shin guards underneath his stockings. When runners came in high on Lloyd, he would merely plant a "stilt" (as he called them) in front of the bag and swing the runner off to one side, out of harm's way.

Sure enough, Cobb came hurtling toward second with fire in his eyes. Lloyd calmly took the throw, hooked a stilt between Cobb's leg and the bag, and flipped him away as easily as he would a pebble on the infield.

Cobb didn't steal second base that game. Nor did he steal it during the next five games, although he tried twice more. Lloyd kept him off the base handily. (One can only imagine the racist Cobb's reaction to being dealt with so easily by black ballplayers.)

As the 1920s gave way to the '30s and the '40s, the Negro Leagues underwent many changes; teams came and went, whole leagues dissolved only to reform, and players shuttled back and forth between teams, leagues, and even countries. Yet the game remained essentially the same—fast, aggressive, and intelligent, as full of strategic moves and counter-moves as a chess match. In this type of game, the stolen base continued to thrive.

This was in direct contrast to the white leagues, where the home run grew strong at the expense of the steal. As the 1930s dissolved into the 1940s, the disparity between home runs and stealing in the major leagues grew even greater. In 1931, the eight American League teams hit 576 home runs, and stole 627 bases; N.L. teams hit 492 homers and swiped 462 bases. Ten years later, home runs in the American League had jumped to 734, while steals had shrunk to 471. In the National League the totals were 597 home runs versus 411 steals. By the time Jackie Robinson broke the major league color line in 1947, the distance between home runs and stolen bases had widened to Grand Canyon–like proportions: 886 home runs in the National League as compared to 361 stolen bases, while in the American League the totals were 679 and 399, respectively.

Although not a base stealer, Josh Gibson was one of the Negro Leagues' most feared hitters (courtesy of Noirtech Sports).

This growing gulf between homers and steals is one reason why black ballplayers did so well in their exhibitions against teams of white all-stars. As Cool Papa Bell once explained, while the whites would play for one big inning and the home run, the blacks would play "tricky baseball": bunting for base hits, hitting away when the situation called for a bunt, and throwing curves on 3–2 counts when the major league "book" dictated fastballs.

Stealing—especially in unexpected situations—was part of "tricky baseball." The more the white leagues gravitated toward the home run, the less able the players were to defend against stealing and consequently to prevent blacks from using stolen bases to disrupt defenses, manufacture runs and win games. In 1929, future Hall of Famer Willie Wells stole home twice in successive days to win games against a team of white all-stars.

Naturally, in a league where stealing was king, great theft artists emerged. One was the aforementioned Oscar Charleston.

Some rate Charleston on a par with Joe DiMaggio, Willie Mays, and other legendary outfielders; others say he was even better. He had speed, power, quickness, and panther-like reflexes. His burning desire to win and hell-bent-for-leather style of play elicited comparisons to Ty Cobb. Nowhere was he more like the Georgia Peach than on the bases.

Some sources credit Charleston with leading the league in stolen bases three times during his career: 1921 (34), 1923 (31), and 1927 (11). During his career, which spanned from 1915 through the early 1940s, Charleston has been credited with stealing 144 bases. Considering the haphazard manner in which Negro League statistics were recorded, the actual total may be much higher.

Charleston was also a powerful hitter, whose awesome strength both on and off the diamond was the stuff of legend. One often-told story is that he was driving a car filled with players when it spun out of control and rolled over. Scrambling from the car, the other players saw Charleston sitting in a ditch, still holding the steering wheel, which he had ripped off the car as it was bouncing around.

But it was on the ball field that Charleston's physical gifts were most evident. He consistently batted in the high .300s–low .400s, and hit with power as well. In the outfield, he used his great speed to reach balls that others couldn't, sometimes catching easy flies behind his back or on his hip.

On the base paths, particularly when he was young and his body nothing but chiseled muscle, Charleston was like a runaway locomotive. Cool Papa Bell, who knew a little something about running, once said, "He could really run, and he was the smartest and most aggressive baserunner I ever saw. You talk about comin' in with spikes high or runnin' over a catcher. You shoulda' seen Charleston. He was as tough as they come."

Another great Negro League base bandit was Jimmy Lyons, who swiped 82 bases over ten years. Frank Warfield, who spent much of his career with the Philadelphia Hilldales in the 1920s, also was a superb base thief. Hard-hitting Cristobal Torriente is credited with stealing 166 bases during his long career.

And then there was Cool Papa.

The man whose name is still synonymous with speed, even though he last played over a half-century ago, was not just the premier base stealer in the Negro Leagues, but in all of baseball. There may never have been anyone faster. "All these years I've been looking for a player who could steal first base," the sports editor of the *Denver Post* once wrote. "I've found my man; his name is Cool Papa Bell."

James Thomas Bell got his nickname of "Cool" as a young man, when he was unafraid of playing ball before large crowds. When "Cool Bell" seemed somehow lacking, "Papa" was added and a legend was born.

So many stories exist about Bell's great speed that it would take an entire book to relate them all. Satchel Paige told how Bell once hit a ground ball past him on the pitcher's mound, and then got struck in the back by the ball as he slid into second. Others describe Cool Papa stealing two bases on one pitch, or scoring from first on a single. "Cool Papa ran like he stole something," said Quincy Trouppe, manager of the Cleveland Buckeyes.

The quintessential Bell story, again related by Paige, is that Cool Papa was so fast he could flip off the light switch and jump into bed before the light went out. While this story is often considered typical of the exaggeration that has grown up around Bell (as well as an

Possibly the fastest man ever to play the game—Cool Papa Bell (courtesy of Noirtech Sports).

example of Paige's colorful story-telling ability), it turns out that the tale was indeed true.

At the 1981 Negro Baseball Reunion in Ashland, Kentucky, Bell explained how he and Paige were rooming together in California when he noticed there was a short in the light switch. After the switch was turned off, it would take several seconds before the light actually went out. Bell decided to have some fun with Paige; when the pitcher returned to the room, Bell began talking about how fast he was.

"Why, I'm so fast, I can turn out the light and be in bed before the room gets dark," said Bell. Paige answered with a bemused "Sure, Cool. Sure you can."

Satchel Paige was one of the best pitchers in the Negro Leagues (courtesy of Noirtech Sports).

Bell then turned off the switch, jumped into bed, and pulled the covers up to his chin—all before the light went out. For once, the loquacious Satchel was speechless.

Usually, however, it was Bell's on-the-field exploits that left people speechless. He was once timed circling the bases on a wet field in

Cool Papa Bell in the outfield (courtesy of Noirtech Sports).

13.1 seconds. Cool Papa, however, might have considered this an off day. In 1924 he reportedly circled the bases on a dry field in 12 seconds, including a blinding 3.1 seconds from home to first.

When he ran, Bell was a thing of beauty to watch, his long legs pumping like two pistons as he gracefully glided around the bases. "When he came around second with a full head of steam, it looked like his feet weren't even touching the ground," said Hall of Fame third baseman Judy Johnson. "He was so fast that if he hit a ground ball to the left side of the infield that took more than one hop, you just couldn't throw him out. Might just as well hold the ball."

Just like Babe Ruth, Cool Papa began his baseball career as a pitcher, signing a contract in 1922 with the St. Louis Stars of the Negro National League. But the pitcher's mound was no place for all that speed; once Bell raced and beat Jimmy Lyons, the Chicago American Giants' speedster considered one of the fastest men in black baseball, he was moved to the wide open spaces of the outfield. And the Stars' wide open spaces were wider than most. The left field line at Stars Park was extremely short (250 feet) in order to accommodate a trolley car garage. From here the outfield fell back drastically, with dead center field an eye-straining 500 feet from home plate. Because of this unusual configuration, Stars Park had extremely deep power alleys. Not only did Bell use his great speed to chase down fly balls in those alleys, but after he hit a ball in the gap he could run all day.

Bell played with the Stars for ten seasons, and then moved to other teams, like most Negro League players did. For more than two decades, Bell patrolled the outfield for over a half-dozen clubs. Among these were some of the all-time great Negro League squads, including the Kansas City Monarchs, Pittsburgh Crawfords and Homestead Grays.

In 1933 Bell had perhaps his greatest season, hitting .379 with 63 doubles, 17 triples, and 11 home runs. This is also the year he reportedly stole 175 bases—a total never even approached by a major leaguer. What is truly incomprehensible is that Cool Papa always felt this total should have been higher. "I stole a whole lot more than that [in 1933]," he commented on more than one occasion.

While some may disparage statistics like these because they

Satchel Paige with other Negro League ball players (courtesy of Noirtech Sports).

aren't "official," no one can deny that Bell was the premier base-stealer of his time and, perhaps, of all time. Not only did he steal virtually at will in the Negro Leagues, but he proved just as formidable against opponents from the white major leagues.

In 1931, an all-star team featuring Max Carey and the Waner brothers—all future Hall of Famers—played Bell and the Stars in St. Louis. In the first inning, Cool Papa bunted for a base hit, then stole second, third, and home. This ignited the Stars, who routed their opponents 18–3. Watching Bell race around the bases, one of the white players turned to Lloyd Waner and said that Cool Papa was like "a black Ty Cobb." "You're wrong," replied Waner. "Cobb is like a white Bell."

The eternal question that hangs over Bell, as it does over all of the Negro League stars, is how he and they would have fared in the white major leagues. It's a question that can never be answered, just endlessly debated; however, given the predominance of the home run and the low stolen base totals in the majors during the time that Bell was at his peak, it's likely that the lanky outfielder would have been a dominating player unlike any other in the game at the time.

What makes this plausible is the display that Bell put on in 1948, at the end of his career, in an all-star game against a team of major leaguers. With Cool Papa on first, Satchel Paige bunted; the 45-year-old Bell streaked around second, continued to third when he saw the bag unoccupied, and then, with the infield in a tizzy, turned on the after-burners and raced home. Any player who can incite pandemonium in a major league infield and score from first base on a bunt, at age 45, would surely have been a force to be reckoned with in his prime.

Bell's long career spanned nearly the entire life of Negro League baseball in the 20th century. By the time Bell hung up his spikes, the Negro Leagues were on their way to oblivion.

Ironically, Jackie Robinson's signing prompted the destruction of the Negro Leagues. Once Robinson broke the color barrier and other black players followed him into the majors, fans stopped going to Negro League games. Instead, they traveled to American and National League ballparks to see their heroes play. The Newark Eagles' attendance plummeted from 120,000 in 1946 to just 57,000 the following year, as fans deserted the team in droves to go see Jackie Robinson play for the Dodgers. Within a few short years, Negro League teams like the Homestead Grays and Newark Eagles had vanished. Before long, so too had Negro League baseball.

But although the Negro Leagues disappeared, their style of play remained very much alive. Robinson brought the league's gambling style, including the inclination to steal bases at any time, back to the major leagues. Robinson's aggressive baserunning blew a blast of fresh air across the landscape of major league baseball, which had grown stale after years of base path inactivity. "[Black baseball] was the game Jackie Robinson ... brought to the majors ... speed, intelligence, unbridled aggressiveness on the basepaths," wrote Buck O'Neil.

Setting a Negro League player like Robinson loose in the big leagues in the late 1940s was like setting a lone cheetah down on a planet of chickens. Robinson was a predator on the bases; many pitchers and catchers had simply not seen his like before, and it showed. It is no coincidence that in his first major league season (1947), in which he hit .297, was named Rookie of the Year by the *Sporting News*, and helped spark the Dodgers to the pennant, Robinson led the National League in stolen bases with 29. On his own, Robinson stole more bases than both the Cardinals (28) and Cubs (a pitiful 22), and just as many as the Giants. His 29 steals more than doubled that of the N.L. runner-up in steals, teammate "Pistol" Pete Reiser (14).

On base Robinson was a bundle of quicksilver energy, arrogant, explosive and unpredictable. The game hadn't seen a runner of his swashbuckling caliber since stealing had been bludgeoned out of fashion by the big bats of the home run–happy 1920s. By himself, Robinson could command the entire focus of the game, as Roger Kahn once described: "Balancing evenly on the balls of both feet, he took an enormous lead. The pitcher glared. Robinson stared back. There was no action, only two men throwing hard looks. But time suspended. The cry in the grandstands rose."

What Robinson brought with him to the majors was nothing more than Cool Papa Bell's "tricky baseball." But to teams whose style of play had become calcified by the home run, "tricky baseball" seemed revolutionary. In the Negro Leagues, scoring runs was often achieved without making a hit at all.

Against home run-driven offenses of the major leagues, Robinson's style of play, particularly on the bases, was guaranteed to stand out. In a *Sporting News* article of September 17, 1947, in which the paper announced Robinson's Rookie of the Year Award, J.G. Taylor Spink wrote about Robinson on the bases: "Robinson is not spectacular in a lone-wolf manner. His hotfooting has typed the Dodger play. When Robinson galloped over home plate on a clean steal during Fitz Ostermueller's windup one night in Pittsburgh, there was no showboat aspect to the feat, there was nothing superfluous about the run; it broke a 2 to 2 tie; he scored the big run."

Spink—whose paper had opposed the integration of baseball several months earlier—called Robinson a "demon on the bases" and "an ebony Ty Cobb."

Josh Gibson's accurate arm proved a powerful deterrent to Negro League base thievery (courtesy of Noirtech Sports).

Thanks to this "ebony Ty Cobb," the stolen base was being taken out of storage, dusted off, and looked at anew. In 1947, the Brooklyn Dodgers, led by Robinson, paced the National League in steals with 88. This was the first time that an N.L. pennant-winner had topped the circuit in stolen bases since 1934, and it started something. People like to emulate winners, and Jackie Robinson and the Dodgers were winners—not only in 1947, but in subsequent years as well. In 1949, 1952, 1953, and 1955, the Dodgers led the league in steals and won the pennant.

The only year during this period that Brooklyn took the flag but didn't lead in steals was 1956, when their total of 65 was just two behind the league-leading Giants. Even in 1950 and 1951, when the Dodgers finished a close second both years, they still led the league in stolen bases.

By reintroducing the stolen base into baseball, Robinson had wrought a change in the game as fundamental and important as the Babe Ruth–inspired emphasis on the home run several decades earlier. Nestled within the "ebony Ty Cobb's" success on the base paths were the seeds that would blossom into a profound shift in the balance of power between the two leagues.

Until the emergence of Robinson, it can be argued that the American League was superior to the National. Nowhere was this superiority more obvious than in the All-Star game; by 1950 the American League held a whopping 12–4 advantage over the National League in All-Star victories. In the World Series it was the same story; during the 1930s and 1940s, the American League team won 13 contests, the National League just seven.

But in the 1950s, things began to change. During that decade, the National League surged to seven victories in All-Star competition, versus just four for the American League (two games were played in 1959). The N.L. edge would become even more pronounced in subsequent decades.

In the World Series, while the early part of the 1950s was marked by Yankee dominance (the Bronx Bombers won it all in 1950, 1951, 1952, 1953, and 1956), by the end of the decade the Bombers had shot their bolt. Throughout the remainder of the 1950s and into the early 1960s, the Yankees lost more World Series than they won, until the "great collapse" of 1965, when their dynasty finally crumbled. Even before this, however, the National League was extending its dominance into World Series play as well: after 1962, N.L. teams won 12 of the next 20 Fall Classics.

Was the re-emergence of the stolen base in the National League one of the reasons for the National League's surge to superiority in head-to-head competition with the American League in All-Star games and the World Series? Conventional baseball wisdom usually holds that it was the Senior Circuit's greater willingness to sign black ballplayers as compared to the American League that helped them gain the upper hand. While teams like the Yankees and Red Sox moved glacially toward integration, National League clubs were signing Willie Mays, Ernie Banks, Hank Aaron, Roy Campenella, and other talented African-American players. In 1957, 18 blacks held roster spots on various N.L. clubs, compared to just eight black players on A.L. teams.

It seems likely that the return of stealing as an offensive weapon in the National League also contributed to its superior play. Beginning with Robinson's first season in 1947, up through 1960, the team that led the National League in steals won the pennant six times, and came in second twice. This indicates that stealing was becoming part of a winning formula for N.L. teams in a way that it hadn't since the dead ball era.

In the American League, however, things were exactly the opposite. From 1947 through 1960, the A.L. team that led the league in steals came in first just once—the 1959 "Go-Go White Sox." In fact, the White Sox led the American League in steals every year from 1951 through 1960, but could claim just one pennant and two second-place finishes for all their running.

National League clubs also stole more total bases during the 1950s (3,870) and averaged more steals per year (387) than the American Leaguers (3,551 and 355, respectively).

It seems like more than just coincidence that the National League began to assert dominance over the American League in the 1950s at the same time the stolen base was coming back into vogue in the Senior Circuit. While there were other factors at work, one of the reasons why the National League became stronger was that they began playing the fast, aggressive game prominent in the Negro Leagues, and which the influx of black players into the league brought with them. The American League, hypnotized by the Yankees' success—a success that did not include base path aggression and stolen bases—continued to wait around for the home run and the big inning. The only team running aggressively was the White Sox, and they weren't able to move past the Bronx Bombers.

The stolen base had continued to thrive in the Negro League—existing in the shadows, along with dozens of superb ballplayers who never got the chance to show their skills in the white major leagues. In breaking the color barrier, Jackie Robinson had also liberated the game itself from the predictable rhythms into which it had fallen. The next step in the reclamation of the stolen base—as well as of baseball itself—was destined to be taken by a man from Venezuela named Luis Aparicio.

6

Luis and the Go-Go Sox

Like any sport, baseball is a game full of ironies. Tracy Stallard was the epitome of the journeyman pitcher, compiling a record of 30–57 during seven relatively undistinguished seasons in the majors. But Stallard will forever be remembered for giving up Roger Maris' record-breaking sixty-first home run in 1961. Thus the irony is that the name of an otherwise nondescript pitcher will live forever in baseball lore, not for winning an important game but for giving up a landmark home run.

The great irony for the stolen base is that it began its renaissance in the 1950s, the decade that is most identified with plodding, slugging, station-to-station baseball. However, stealing didn't exactly spring back overnight like a parched flower after a summer rain; the return of stealing was a long, slow process that, like almost everything else in baseball in the 1950s, seemed to move in slow motion.

In the American League during the 1950s, the New York Yankees were lambasting opposing pitchers with mechanical regularity. From 1950–1958, as the club won eight pennants and six world championships, the Bronx Bombers lived up to their nickname by leading the American League in homers and slugging average five times, and batting average four times.

In the National League, Brooklyn was the dominant team

throughout most of the decade. The Dodgers led the Senior Circuit in home runs from 1950 through 1955 and in batting average in four of those years, while winning three pennants and one World Series.

The 1950s saw the stagnation and calcification of baseball that had begun in the 1920s reach full maturity. Hitting and slugging were in, and everything else—especially stealing—was out. In 1950 the Red Sox's Dom DiMaggio introduced the era of plodding baseball in fine style by leading the American League in stolen bases with a miserable 15, the lowest league-leading total ever recorded.

But Joltin' Joe's little brother was only mirroring the rest of his lead-footed league. In 1950 the eight A.L. teams stole just 278 bases, which is also the lowest total ever recorded for an eight-club league. (The National League would make its contribution to this period of molasses baseball in 1954 by recording *its* lowest steal total ever for an eight-club league: 337.) The era of slow-motion baseball was off and (barely) running.

But the seeds of a new type of baseball had been planted. After taking a few years to germinate, these seeds would burst into full flower in the subsequent decade at the expense of the old homer-happy game.

As previously noted, the first green shoots of this new game began sprouting in Brooklyn in the mid–1940s. In 1946, the Dodgers' "Pistol" Pete Reiser led the National League with 34 steals. This was the highest league-leading total in the National League in 16 years, since Hazen "KiKi" Cuyler's 37 steals in 1930. The following year, another Brooklyn player, Jackie Robinson, paced the circuit with 29 steals. In both years, the Dodgers finished in first place. (In 1946 they tied for first with St. Louis and lost in the playoffs to the Cardinals.)

Before 1946, Reiser had also led the league in steals in 1942 with 20. If his brilliance hadn't repeatedly been dimmed by injuries, Pistol Pete might have brought back the stolen base all by himself, even before Jackie Robinson's arrival.

When he was healthy—which wasn't often—Reiser ran the bases as if he had been reincarnated from the dead ball era. Running and stealing in a manner not seen in baseball for decades, Reiser was the scourge of pitchers and catchers. A 1946 *Sporting News* cartoon shows N.L. catchers cowering in their bed from the nightmare of Reiser stealing on them. That was the year he stole home seven times to set a new record (later tied by Rod Carew and subsequently surpassed when new research revealed that Ty Cobb had stolen home eight times in 1912). Reiser often claimed that he actually stole home eight times that year, but that umpire George Magerkurth erroneously called him out on one steal in which he was clearly safe. "I'll be a son of a gun. I missed that one," Reiser swore Magerkurth said, moments after punching him out.

With his speed, and the fact that he played in the media center of the baseball universe, a healthy Reiser might have reignited interest in stealing a full ten years before Luis Aparicio arrived on the scene. Unfortunately, it was not to be. Fate had other plans for the man that announcer Red Barber once called "as quick as a startled monkey."

During his too-short career, Pistol Pete was carried off the field 11 times due to injury. Once, he smashed into the outfield wall at Ebbetts Field so severely that he was given the Last Rites. The injuries destroyed not just his amazing speed, but his career. When he retired in 1953, Reiser had just 87 total steals—with 54 of them coming in two of the seasons that he was relatively healthy. If the phrase "unfulfilled potential" is ever defined in the dictionary, surely it will include a picture of Harold Patrick Reiser.

When he wasn't injured, Reiser, along with Jackie Robinson and shortstop Pee Wee Reese, was the prime architect of a running, base-stealing philosophy employed by the Dodgers that resulted in winning baseball.

The Dodgers' aggressiveness on the bases—so rare in the sedate 1950s in baseball—meant that anyone on the team might run at any time. In a game against the St. Louis Cardinals in 1954, Brooklyn catcher Roy Campanella—who was many wonderful things on the diamond, but "base stealer" was not one of them—stole home in the twelfth inning, to help ensure the Dodgers' 7–5 victory. It was the only base Campanella stole all year. This steal by Campanella, who began his career in the Negro Leagues, also illustrates how the National League's greater willingness to sign black players caused its teams to surge ahead of the A.L. as far as implementing a running, base-stealing philosophy. Since one of the facets of the Negro League game was stealing bases, it was only natural that as black players started filtering into the National League, they brought their style of play with them.

In the 1950s, this aggressiveness led to N.L. teams consistently stealing more than their American League counterparts. From 1950 through 1959, the N.L. stole more bases than the A.L. every year except one (1954). Overall, the senior circuit stole 319 more bases during the decade. Not only was the emphasis on speed and stealing helping N.L. teams win, but it was also elevating the entire league to a level of play well above that of the American League—a point that would be emphatically proven in the 1960s.

But while in the National League stealing helped a team win, in the American League it was a different story. The Chicago White Sox led the Junior Circuit in steals for 11 straight seasons, from 1951 to 1961. In the midst of this streak the Sox were joined by one of the best base stealers in history, future Hall of Fame shortstop Luis Aparicio. No team was more speed-and-steal oriented than Chicago.

Yet all that the Sox could show for their running and stealing was one lone pennant (1959). Despite all their speed, Chicago was simply unable to run past the Yankees, who remained rooted in first place like a giant sequoia thanks in no small measure to their slugging offense.

At least, however, speed and base stealing had enabled the White Sox to once again attain respectability in the American League. Ever since the Black Sox scandal had decimated a team loaded with potential Hall of Famers, fortune had not smiled on the White Sox. The team consistently finished in the second division during the 1920s and 1930s, and this trend continued throughout much of the 1940s. From 1944 through 1949, the best the Pale Hose could muster was a fifth place showing in 1946, a whopping 30 games behind the first-place Red Sox.

In 1949 the Chisox stumbled to a sixth-place finish with a record of 63–91, 34 games behind the pennant-winning Yankees. As poor as this was, however, it was actually an improvement over the previous year's abysmal last-place record of 51–101. The White Sox had finished so far behind the first-place Boston Red Sox (44 games) in 1948 that just looking up in the standings gave them a nosebleed.

What was even worse about the 1949 season, however, was the

White Sox's power shortage. While four A.L. teams that year hit over 100 home runs, the best the White Sox sluggers—if that word could be used—could muster was 43. This puny total was almost doubled by Washington, which had the next-lowest number of homers (81) in the league. The leading Sox home run hitter was Steve Souchock, who clouted all of seven.

Amazingly, those 43 homers were tallied, for at least part of the year, in a park in which the fences had been moved in specifically for the purpose of generating more home runs. This had been the brainchild of peripatetic White Sox general manager Frank Lane, who was trying to improve upon the sickly total of 55 home runs that Chicago had hit in 1948. Seeking ways to juice up his team's attack, Lane moved the left and right fences at Comiskey Park in 22 feet from the previous year. Then he sat back and waited for the fireworks to erupt.

Unfortunately, the only fireworks that erupted were generated by Lane himself. After watching his hitters continue to struggle early in the 1949 season, Lane reached the end of his rope in June, when the Senator's Floyd Baker—a born banjo hitter if there ever was one—belted the first (and last) home run of his career out of the diminished Comiskey Park. The moment Baker's ball left the yard the White Sox's experiment with shortened fences was over.

Clearly, trying to out-bludgeon the other clubs was not going to solve the White Sox's problems. If homers wouldn't do it, then it was time to go to the other extreme. And so the Age of Speed began in Chicago.

In choosing to run, it's not as if the Chisox were totally unfamiliar with the concept of stealing bases. The team had led the American League in steals in 1949 with 62. The base stealing, however, was prompted as much by their weak hitting as by anything else; with a league-low slugging average of .347, the team had to do *something* with the runners who occasionally found their way onto the bases. Since big hits were few and far between, stealing was the only other way to move runners along.

(Proof that the team was not deliberately featuring the steal came the following season, when Chicago stole just 19 bases—last in the league.)

But beginning in 1951, the White Sox made an effort to fashion a team built around speed, and, by extension, the stolen base. The result was nothing short of miraculous. Using strong pitching, timely hitting, good defense, and the stolen base, the White Sox actually led the American League for a time during that season before faltering and ultimately finishing fourth with a mark of 81–73.

The White Sox featured speed to such a degree in 1951 that they placed three players on the list of the top half-dozen base stealers in the American League. Overall, the team's 99 stolen bases led the league.

One member of the suddenly fleet Sox was outfielder Jim Busby, whose 26 steals ranked second in the league. Another was shortstop Chico Carrasquel, who tied for fourth with 14 stolen bases. But the real key to the White Sox's running game was a smiling Cuban named Saturnino Orestes Armas "Minnie" Minoso.

Plucked by Frank Lane from Cleveland early in 1951, Minoso battered American League pitching throughout the year. He finished second in batting average and runs scored, fourth in hits, fifth in slugging, and first in triples. Minoso also led the league in stolen bases with 31, which began a three-year streak for him as the top A.L. base thief.

The following year, sparked by Minoso again as well as outfielder "Jungle Jim" Rivera, the White Sox showed that 1951 was no fluke by posting another 81–73 mark in 1952, which this time was good enough for a third-place finish. Rivera proved an excellent comple-ment to Minoso on the bases. He averaged 20 steals during his first seven seasons with Chicago (1952–1958), and led the league in stolen bases in 1955 with 25.

Rivera broke into the majors with the St. Louis Browns in 1952. Not having much else to promote, the talent-poor Brownies played up Rivera's speed. The team claimed that he was even faster than Mickey Mantle, and had beaten Minnie Minoso in a foot race.

St. Louis skipper Rogers Hornsby—who should have known bet-ter—also joined the chorus deifying Rivera by claiming that Jungle Jim was the only player in the game today that he would pay to see. Unfortunately, Hornsby soon had to do exactly that, because he was fired after 51 games of the 1952 season, with the Browns stumbling along at a 22–29 clip. Forty-six games later Rivera also left St. Louis when he was traded to the White Sox. There he joined the man he had supposedly once beaten in a race, and the two formed a formidable base-stealing duo.

During the next several seasons the White Sox kept running. They continued to lead the league in stolen bases, and their record kept improving. In 1954 they cracked the 90-win barrier for the first time since 1920, a feat they repeated in 1955. Unfortunately, the standings didn't reflect their success; the team was seemingly locked into third place, finishing there every year from 1952 through 1956.

But 1956, while not notable for Chicago as far as their pennant hopes went, did produce a milestone of a different sort for the White Sox when Luis Aparicio made his debut with the team.

Over the years, White Sox executives probably got heart palpitations every time they thought about how close they came to losing the great shortstop. In the early 1950s, Red Kress, a coach for the Cleveland Indians who also managed in Venezuela, told Tribe general manager Hank Greenberg about a sensational young Venezuelan shortstop named Luis Aparicio. Greenberg was interested, but wanted Aparicio to come to the U.S. for a closer look before offering him a contract. This enabled Frank Lane to swoop in and sign Aparicio right from under Greenberg's nose. Little did anyone know that, in Aparicio, the White Sox had secured the player who was going to help end their pennant drought, revive the stolen base, and enjoy a Hall of Fame career.

In Aparicio, the stolen base had found its greatest champion since Ty Cobb. Until the advent of Maury Wills, the slick-fielding shortstop was the game's premier base thief. If Jackie Robinson scraped the rust off the stolen base, Aparicio was the one who jump-started it and got it moving again before passing it on to Maury Wills, who shined it to a gleaming finish.

Early on, however, the talk in Aparicio's first spring training camp was not of future greatness but of whether or not the youngster could play at the major league level. "White Sox Hope Aparicio Can Fill Shortstop Hole" headlined a typical newspaper story early in 1956. Indeed, the Pale Hose had reason to worry. At the end of 1955 they had dealt Chico Carrasquel to Cleveland for Larry Doby to add more pop to their line-up. If Aparicio couldn't make the grade, the glaring hole at shortstop would negate whatever power Doby generated.

Chisox skipper Marty Marion, a fine shortstop himself, admitted during spring training in 1956 that he had been initially concerned about the Carrasquel deal. "The Kid [Aparicio] at short had to make it," Marion said one March day, as he watched his team stretch and sweat in the Florida sun. "That was the long gamble we took. At first, I wasn't so sure. Now I am. He's definitely big league. Some players have baseball sense. The Kid has it. [He] does everything naturally, effortlessly."

Once the season started, Aparicio left any lingering doubts about his ability in his dust on the base paths. Not since the heyday of George Case had anyone run with such abandon in the American League. "The kid runs like a scalded dog," exclaimed Marion approvingly.

Aparicio's first season was a rousing success. He hit .266, stole 21 bases to lead the American League, and was named the league's Rookie of the Year. But "Little Looie" was just getting warmed up. Like a stream after a steady rain, Aparicio's stolen base totals kept rising, year after year, until reaching 56 in 1959—the highest total in baseball in 16 years. "He makes the Go-Sox Go," exclaimed one article about the swift Venezuelan.

Even more importantly, these steals were laying the foundation for the White Sox's long climb to first place. Finally, in 1959, the years of running paid off; Chicago streaked past the Yankees and everyone else in the American League to post the first pennant at Comiskey Park in 40 years.

There is little doubt that stealing played a major role in the White Sox's drive to the flag. The team was nicknamed the "Hitless Wonders," and with good reason; Chicago hit just 97 home runs in 1959, the fewest of any team in either league, and their batting and slugging averages also languished near the bottom of the collective pack.

Pitching, defense and speed were the Sox's main weapons, and they made them count. (In one game they scored 11 runs in one inning on just one single.) The team's reliance on the running game resulted in a second, more complimentary nickname: the "Go-Go" Sox. Chicago did indeed "go-go" on the base paths, stealing 113 bases to lead the American League in steals by a wide margin. Aparicio and teammate Jim Landis, with 20 thefts, paced the base-stealing attack.

Unfortunately, in the World Series against the Los Angeles Dodgers, the Go-Go Sox faltered. Their vaunted running game didn't impress L.A.'s rifle-armed catcher John Roseboro, who was used to that sort of thing in the more run-oriented National League. Roseboro shut down the speedy Sox, giving up just two steals (to Aparicio and Landis) as the Dodgers took the series in six games. As one of Chicago's high profile players, Aparicio got his share of blame for the loss. One newspaper story labeled him the "Bust of the Series" (even though he hit .308).

True champions, however, always bounce back. The following season, Aparicio shrugged off whatever disappointment he felt over the series by having another superlative year, hitting .277 and stealing 51 bases to lead the American League in stolen bases for the fifth straight year. "If he could hit .300 he'd steal 100 bases," said White Sox manager Al Lopez in 1960.

As Lopez had suggested, Aparicio was not a strong hitter. Most seasons found him in the .250–.260 range. (His lifetime batting average was .262.) But despite this, every time the opposition looked up, "Little Looie" seemed to be on second base. How he got there—a walk, followed by a steal—became known as an "Aparicio double."

Like many base stealers before and after, it was not Aparicio's blazing speed that made him successful, but rather, keen observation of opposing pitchers. "[With] almost every right-handed pitcher," he said, "I always watch the left shoulder. I steal on the pitchers. Even a good throw by a catcher won't stop me once I get a good jump. When I decide to go, I just go. I never say to myself, 'I'm going to steal this time.' But [when] the pitcher gives me my chance, I go."

Although in 1961 Aparicio again led the American League with 53 steals, the big news in stolen bases that year were the performances of rookies Dick Howser of Kansas City and Jake Wood of Detroit, who stole 37 and 30 bases, respectively. When the two sophomores bolted quickly out of the starting gate in 1962, with Howser actually leading Aparicio in steals for a time, there were predictions that the end of Aparicio's consecutive, six-year reign as A.L. stolen base champ was imminent.

"Two Greyhounds Threaten Theft-King Looie," proclaimed *The Sporting News* in June, 1962. In the article, which focused on the threat of Howser and Wood to Aparicio's reign as King of Thieves, the usually mild-mannered shortstop revealed his fierce pride over his stolen base crown. "How many bases will I steal this year? I don't know. But I would like to steal enough to win," he said. Then, in a muted challenge to Howser and Wood, he said, "I'm going to keep running. I know they'll be doing the same."

And run he did. When the season ended, Aparicio again led the American League, this time with 31 steals. Wood was third with 24 while Howser, hobbled by injuries, managed just 19.

Aparicio went on to lead the American League in steals for two more seasons, for a total of nine in a row. Then young legs, in the person of Bert Campaneris, finally caught up to him and the crown passed from his head for good.

Aparicio remained a legitimate stolen base threat until the end of his career. In 1973, when he stole his five hundredth base while with the Red Sox (who let the event pass unnoticed, much to Aparicio's dismay), he was the first American Leaguer to reach that milestone since Eddie Collins over a half-century before. After that season Aparicio retired, with a lifetime total of 506 steals.

Aparicio's career-high in steals was 1964, when he swiped 57 sacks. By then, however, the little shortstop was wearing the uniform of the Baltimore Orioles, to whom he had been traded in January, 1963. After expending so much effort to finally reach first place, the White Sox had found it difficult to remain there for long, tumbling to third in 1960 and fourth the following season.

Eventually the club that had won the 1959 pennant had to be dismantled. With the end of the "Go-Go" Sox era, the team skidded out of the top spot in base stealing. In 1962, for the first time in 12 years, Chicago did not lead the American League in stolen bases. Since then, the White Sox have led the league in steals just once, and have not made it back to the World Series.

The remarkable thing about Aparicio and the White Sox is how long one man, and one team, were able to dominate the league in stealing. For years, the words "Luis Aparicio" and "Chicago White Sox" were synonymous whenever stealing in the American League was mentioned. No other team in the league embraced the stolen base with the fervor of Chicago. Perhaps this was because, for all their running, the White Sox had little to show for it besides one pennant and a slew of also-ran finishes. Or maybe the stolen base was eschewed by other A.L. clubs because the Yankees were handily winning pennants without stealing. Even though some of the Yankees during this era could run, such as Bobby Richardson, Tony Kubek, and Mickey Mantle, the team didn't need the stolen base to win. "That [running and stealing] just wasn't how we played the game then," Kubek later recalled.

It wasn't as if the Yankees were unaware of the value of speed and base stealing. Players such as Aparicio, Busby, and Minoso persistently bedeviled the Bronx Bombers with their base path antics. "Since I've been managing the Yankees," Ralph Houk said, "little Luis Aparicio has beaten me more times than any other player in the American League." But as long as they were winning, the Yankees could safely ignore these gnats buzzing around them.

Possibly because the Yankees were so successful for so long without emphasizing a running attack, by the time stealing emerged from its "dark period" in the American League, just the White Sox had embraced the stolen base. The other clubs continued to try and beat the Yankees at their own game.

The same was not true in the National League. Even though the Dodgers led in stolen bases in 7 out of 10 seasons from 1950 to 1959, they did not dominate the league to the extent that Chicago did. Other teams, such as the Braves, Cardinals and Giants, also emphasized the running game during the decade.

By the same token, there was no counterpart to Aparicio in the National League. Even though the Dodgers as a team usually led the National League in steals, only once during the 1950s did a Dodger actually top the circuit in stolen bases (Pee Wee Reese in 1952, with 30).

Numerous players excelled in stealing in the National League during the 1950s. Sam Jethroe of the Braves swiped 98 bases from 1950–1953 and led the league in steals in 1950 and 1951. In the latter part of the decade, the Giants' Mr. Everything, Willie Mays, proved just how multi-dimensional he truly was by leading the National

League in steals for four straight years (1956–1959). Of course, the Dodgers also had some of the league's premier base bandits. Jackie Robinson stole 197 bases during his ten-year career, while Pee Wee Reese swiped 232 over 16 years. In 1953 these two were joined by Jim "Junior" Gilliam, who piled up 203 lifetime steals over 14 seasons.

Two more of the most prominent base-stealers in the National League during the 1950s were outfielders Richie "Whitey" Ashburn and Bill Bruton.

Ashburn made the Phillies during spring training in 1948, even though he was initially slated to go to Toronto in the International League. The incumbent Philadelphia center fielder was Harry "The Hat" Walker, who had led the National League in batting in 1947 and didn't figure on giving up his position to a rookie any time soon. But Phillies' manager Ben Chapman, a former league-leading base stealer in the 1930s, was impressed enough by Ashburn's raw speed to tear up his ticket to Toronto and give him one to Philadelphia instead.

Once in the City of Brotherly Love Ashburn quickly justified Chapman's faith in him. Whitey hit .333, led the league in steals with 32, and won both the Rookie of the Year Award and the hearts of Phillies fans.

(What the fans didn't know is how close they came to never having Ashburn to adore. In 1944 the New York Giants offered him a contract, but because of a snub by the Giants' Mel Ott during a newspaper-sponsored all-star game at the Polo Grounds for youngsters, Ashburn turned them down.)

Once in the majors, Ashburn's speed on the bases precipitated a media frenzy. Newspapers tripped all over themselves to anoint him "the fastest man in baseball," and it seemed that not a day went by when someone wasn't proclaiming the rookie outfielder as the best ever.

In one story, headlined "Rookie Ashburn Fastest Player in Major Loops," the Nebraska native's speed is reported to have "the fans blinded, the opposing pitchers and fielders jittery, and his manager singing his praises." The story also quoted former player and veteran umpire Babe Pinelli, who said, "I can't think of a player who runs from first to third as fast as Ashburn. And I can't recall any either."

In another article, no less an authority than the legendary Grantland Rice said that "Ashburn is the fastest man in baseball—as fast as Ty Cobb."

But of all the "speed" stories that came out during Ashburn's rookie year, the best may be a short wire service piece in which he complained to Phillies skipper Eddie Sawyer (who took over from the fired Ben Chapman after 79 games) that his uniform was "too heavy" and was holding him back from going even faster on the bases. "Son, we don't want anything holding you back," replied Sawyer. Concluded the story: "Ashburn now has four light-weight suits."

Although exceptionally fast, Ashburn never considered himself a true base stealer. "I'm not a good base stealer," he once said. "I can't seem to get that jump on the pitcher." Maybe there was some truth to this, because despite his superior speed, Ashburn never again led the National League in steals after his rookie season.

He did, however, go on to have a Hall of Fame career, sparking the Phils to the pennant in 1950, leading the league in hitting twice, and playing a peerless center field. In 1957, when it seemed like he might be slowing down, a trade of speedsters was rumored to be in the works that would have sent Ashburn to the Milwaukee Braves for Billy Bruton and Felix Mantilla. This would have made Bruton the Phillies' first black ballplayer, but the deal never happened.

Ashburn ended his career by playing two years with the Cubs and one with the expansion New York Mets in 1962. One year of Mets baseball was enough to convince him to hang up his spikes for good. Over the course of his 15 year career Ashburn swiped 234 bases.

Billy Bruton was another 1950s base stealer who was such a speed demon on the bases that fans debated whether he or Mickey Mantle was the fastest man in baseball.

Bruton's lifetime stolen base total isn't impressive—just 207 over the course of his 12 year career (1953–1964), which averages out to only 17 per season. Yet he led the National League in steals during his first three years in the league (1953–1955), peaking with a high of 34 in 1954. These are excellent totals for the early 1950s, when the stolen base was still covered with cobwebs from years of neglect.

Bruton was spotted playing sandlot ball around Wilmington, Delaware, by the immortal Negro League star Judy Johnson (who later became his father-in-law), who brought him to the attention of the then Boston Braves. In 1950, Bruton scorched the base paths of the Northern League for 66 stolen bases. His speed soon blazed him a path to the majors, where he made the Braves in time for the team's maiden season in Milwaukee in 1953.

Although just a rookie, Bruton was given the green light to run by Braves manager Charlie Grimm, who, with disarmingly simple logic, said, "You're in the majors, you should know when to try to steal and when not to."

Bruton did indeed know when to steal, and during his first three years in the majors he averaged 28 steals per season. But early in 1956 Fred Haney replaced Grimm, and Bruton's green light turned red. That year, his stolen bases dropped from 25 to 8.

In 1957 a serious knee injury robbed Bruton of some of his speed, and even though he continued to steal afterwards, he was never the same "Bullet" Billy Bruton again. He retired after the 1964 season, and shocked the gathering at his retirement celebration by revealing that he was actually 39, and not 35 as believed. (It seems that the scout who signed him had trimmed two years off his age before putting him under contract, and then the Braves organization cut another two years off.)

A few years before he died in 1995, Bruton explained the philosophy of base stealing in the 1950s. "We didn't run for personal records," he said in *Baseball Digest*. "When you steal a hundred or more bases, that's a guy running just because he's on base. We didn't do that. We ran because we represented the tying or go-ahead run. I always had a lot of respect for those bases."

Throughout the 1950s, players like Bruton, Ashburn, Reese, Jethroe and others helped to bring stealing back into vogue in the National League. More and more players and teams began using the stolen base.

In the American League, however, few players besides Aparicio concentrated on stealing bases. While the same faces appeared year after year in the list of top A.L. base stealers, the N.L. leaders were always changing. This reflected a continuing influx of new blood that spread the word of stealing throughout the league.

However, in the American League during the 1950s, there was just a handful of players consistently stealing bases. In 1951, Minnie

Minoso's name first appeared on the list of the top five A.L. base bandits. He continued to appear on that list every year until 1959. The same holds true for Jim Busby, Jim Rivera, Luis Aparicio, and Jackie Jensen; some combination of these same players appeared on *every* list of the top five A.L. base stealers from 1951 through 1959. (It almost goes without saying that, except for Jensen, everyone played for the White Sox at one point.) Minoso appeared eight times, Rivera seven times, Jensen six times, Busby four times, and Aparicio four times. Rather than a breeding ground for new base stealers, the American League was little more than a stagnant pool.

Things were far different in the National League, however, where the waters of aggressive baserunning were flowing swiftly, continually providing a steady stream of fresh talent. Only Reese and Ashburn repeatedly appeared on the list of the top five base stealers, each doing it five times. Both of them, however, did it early in the decade.

By 1955, the list of leading National League base stealers was completely refreshed from what it had been at the beginning of the decade. None of those who were among the top five in steals in 1951 were still listed in 1955; names like Reese, Torgeson, Ashburn and Robinson had been replaced by Bruton, Mays, Ken Boyer and Gilliam. In the American League, on the other hand, both Minoso and Busby were on the list in 1951 and 1955.

Even by decade's end, both Aparicio and Jensen were still on the A.L.'s list of leading base stealers. Aparicio was at the beginning of his distinguished career, but Jensen was fading. He played just one more season (1961) before calling it quits. As for the others on the list, only Mickey Mantle would be a force in the game in the 1960s. In the National League, the 1959 list of leading base stealers had some new names on it, such as Vada Pinson and Orlando Cepeda, players who were destined to make a major impact in the coming decade.

By the end of the 1950s, the two leagues stood at an historic crossroads. The National League, for years the inferior circuit, was on the threshold of a long period of dominance over the American League, thanks in no small part to the faster, more aggressive game that its teams played. It is no accident that the National League, which would win 11 out of the 13 All-Star games played from 1960–1969 and six out of ten World Series, was also the league that boasted most of the best base stealers in the game, such as Maury Wills, Lou Brock, Willie Davis, and Joe Morgan.

The American League, however, would stay with the old, familiar ways. No team demonstrated the continued neglect of base stealing better than the 1957 Washington Senators, who stole a grand total of 13 bases for the entire season, setting an all-time record for fewest thefts that still stands. Their leading runner ("base stealer" would be a misnomer) was Julio Becquer, with three steals.

What the American League didn't know, and would only come to understand much later, was that a new game was beckoning in the 1960s, a game nurtured by artificial turf and new, all-purpose stadiums with standard dimensions. In this game, stealing and power complimented, rather than excluded, each other. The day of the one-dimensional, slow-footed slugger was rapidly drawing to a close. Slow to sign black ballplayers and slower still to develop any base stealing threats beyond Aparicio, the American League was also slow where it counted in the 1960s—on the base paths.

This new era was heralded in 1960 by the emergence of one of baseball's all-time greatest base stealers: Maury Wills.

7

Wills Puts Thievery
Back in Style

Although his deeds have been overshadowed in recent years, Maury Wills remains one of the most important baseball players of the second half of the twentieth century. Although not a large man physically, Wills strode like a colossus through the game during most of the 1960s, casting as long a shadow as such giants of this decade as Harmon Killebrew, Mickey Mantle and Willie Mays. Wills' influence on the game, however, did not stem from his bat, or even his glove—but from his feet.

What Babe Ruth did for the home run Maury Wills did for the stolen base: he brought it into the limelight and made it a highly anticipated, crowd-pleasing part of baseball. It had been decades since people came to the ball park specifically to see a base stealer; Wills not only drew fans to games, but had people all across America rooting for him.

Perhaps most importantly, the skinny shortstop made it once again respectable for players to build a successful career upon a foundation of base stealing. Home run hitters still may have driven the Cadillacs during this era, but Wills got the base stealers out of the economy cars and pointed them in the direction of the luxury vehicles.

When Bill Mazeroski's home run sailed over the left field fence at Forbes Field to give the Pittsburgh Pirates an improbable victory over the New York Yankees in the 1960 World Series, it marked the end of an era. For over half a century, major league baseball had consisted of two eight-team leagues. Even the franchise movements of the 1950s did not alter the size of the leagues, just their configuration.

All that changed in 1961, when two brand new teams began play in the American League: The Los Angeles Angels and the Washington Senators. (The "new" Senators took the place of the old Senators, who had fled to the greener pastures of Minnesota. Fortunately for traditionalists, the new team was as bad as the old.) The following year the National League followed suit, swelling to ten teams by adding the Houston Colt .45s (who later became the Astros) and the New York Mets. Both leagues liked expansion so much they did it again seven years later, each adding two more new clubs in 1969 and, for good measure, splitting into two divisions.

More than just the appearance of the two leagues changed in baseball during the 1960s. By the end of the decade, the homer-happy, station-to-station game of the 1950s would be a rapidly fading memory. Speed, rather than power, would be the hallmark of late '60s baseball. One of the things that aided this metamorphosis was expansion.

Expansion team managers, looking over their squads on the first day of spring training, must have wondered how they were going to compete with the Yankees and Dodgers of the world. After all, they were fielding teams of unproved rookies, cast-offs and also-rans from other clubs against powerful teams with lineups packed with All-Stars and future Hall of Famers.

After checking over the roster, just to verify that Mickey Mantle or Willie Mays wasn't hiding somewhere on the team, an expansion manager probably decided that, as far as offense went, it was best to employ a running game to try and make up for what was lacking in hitting. After all, while stealing couldn't take the place of a home run, it could turn a single or a walk into a double.

(Almost 40 years later, expansion club managers still employ this strategy. In March 1998, manager Larry Rothschild of the first-year Tampa Bay Devil Rays said that "For our situation right now, I'm not looking at power at every spot in the order. So you have to make up for that in certain ways. Speed is the quickest and best way to do that." Using this philosophy, the Devil Rays opened the season by compiling the best record ever for an expansion team after 16 games.)

This is precisely what the "new" Washington Senators did. In their inaugural 1961 season, the Nats swiped 81 bases to finish third in the league. The following year, the Senators stole 99 bases to lead the American League. Not coincidentally, their slugging percentage both seasons was among the A.L.'s lowest.

Unfortunately, while noteworthy in that the Senators' 99 steals broke the Chicago White Sox's streak of 11 straight years of leading the American League in thefts, the stolen bases did little for the team's fortunes. Washington finished in the A.L. basement both seasons. Yet the Senators were on to something. Speed was indeed going to play a more prominent role in baseball in the 1960s, although for reasons that Washington could never have imagined.

To catch a glimpse of baseball's future, one needed to look not to the east and Washington, but to the south, and Houston, Texas. Here, in 1965, two important events that would shape baseball in the coming years occurred: one was the opening of the sport's first domed stadium, the Astrodome; the second, and more significant, was the death of the Astrodome's grass due to a lack of sunlight.

Brown grass, of course, does not a ball field make. Casting about for a substitute, Astros management located a synthetic playing surface that became popularly known as Astroturf. Initially, Astroturf was a layer of macadam covered by a plastic green carpet that was held together by zippers.

But while it might have looked like grass (at least, from a distance), Astroturf acted like concrete. Batted balls picked up speed and topspin as they scooted across it, turning even ordinary infield grounders into potential hits. In the outfield it was a real adventure: a routine line drive single could instantly become a triple or inside-the-park home run if it bounced over a charging outfielder's head. A ball hit into the gap was like a berserk pinball, ricocheting around crazily while fielders gave chase and runners flew around the bases.

Initially, the players didn't care for Astroturf. "If the horses won't eat it, I won't play on it," said Dick Allen, succinctly summing up overall reaction to baseball's new plastic carpet. But its desirability to a horse's diet notwithstanding, Astroturf caused a major change in baseball. Having the opportunity to run all day on a ball hit into the gap didn't matter much to teams populated by players who ran as if they were carrying pianos on their backs. Suddenly clubs began looking at speed and, by extension, base stealing in an entirely new light.

Even before the advent of artificial surface, however, National League teams had been continuing to develop a multi-dimensional attack that included speed as one of its components. Certainly the league had its share of sluggers, such as Willie McCovey, Joe Adcock, and Orlando Cepeda. But they also had pennant-winning teams built on speed and quickness, to whom the home run was a happy accident. In 1965, the Los Angeles Dodgers won the pennant (and subsequently, the World Series) with a club that hit just 78 home runs all season—far and away the fewest in the National League. However, they did lead the league in stolen bases with 172.

Many National League teams incorporated a balanced blend of speed and power. The pennant-winning 1961 Cincinnati Reds hit 158 homers, good for fourth in the league, but also stole 70 bases to finish tied for third in steals. When the St. Louis Cardinals won the pennant and World Series in 1964, they did it with an offense that hit 109 home runs and stole 73 bases.

Baseball was also changing in the American League in the 1960s, although not in the same way. No one saw it coming, but the early years of the decade were the last gasp of the mighty Yankee dynasty. After winning another five pennants in a row (1960–1964) and two more world championships, the bottom finally fell out for the Bronx Bombers. A sixth-place finish in 1965 was followed by a plunge to the cellar the following year. It would be another decade before New York regained the top spot in the standings.

With the Yankee roadblock to first place finally removed, Minnesota, Baltimore, Boston, and Detroit all took turns winning A.L. pennants. These teams, however, did not rely on running attacks to help them win. The Boston Red Sox, who finished third in steals in their "miracle" pennant year of 1967, posted the best showing among

A.L. clubs that won the flag from 1965 to 1969. The following year, the lead-footed Tigers won both the pennant and World Series, despite stealing a dismal 26 bases.

Just as when the Yankees ruled the roost, leading the American League in steals was not the recipe for a pennant-winning season. From 1960 through 1969, the best showing that an A.L. club leading the league in steals could manage was third by the 1960 Chicago White Sox. Six out of ten years, the league's steals leader failed to contend.

As might be expected, things were much different in the more steal-oriented National League. Thanks to the Dodgers, who led the league in stolen bases six straight years (1960–1965), the N.L. steals leader finished either first or second four out of those same six years. In 1967 the St. Louis Cardinals joined the club by winning the pennant and World Series while leading the league in stolen bases.

Throughout the 1960s, the National League stole more bases every year than the American League except for the final two years of the decade. (Although the American League actually had more steals in 1961, they also had two more teams. After subtracting the bases stolen by the two American League expansion clubs, the National League beats the American League by eight.)

The 1960s were also a time when new base stealing champions emerged to challenge the old. In the American League, Luis Aparicio's consecutive nine-year reign as King of Thieves was finally ended in 1965 by Kansas City's Bert Campaneris. The National League also had a new stolen base leader in the 1960s: Maury Wills.

Just the fact that Maurice Morning Wills stayed in baseball long enough to make the big leagues, never mind his becoming one of the greatest base stealers of all time, is a tribute to the glory that baseball, more than any other sport, will sometimes bestow on those with the patience and perseverance to wait for it. Signed by the Dodgers in 1950 as a 17-year-old pitcher, Wills bumped around the minor leagues for nearly ten years, giving absolutely no indication that he was the man who would someday break Ty Cobb's record for most stolen bases in a season.

In the spring of 1959 the Dodgers sold Wills on an option basis to Detroit; the Tigers, faced with a choice of keeping either him or

Rocky Bridges, kept the latter and sent Wills back to L.A. It would turn out to be one of the best deals the Dodgers never made.

Early in 1959, with Wills resigned to yet another year in the minors, Don Zimmer, the Dodgers' starting shortstop, broke his toe. Wills was called up and surprised everyone by doing a respectable job for the team that ultimately became world champions. In 83 games the switch-hitter batted .260 and stole seven bases. In the World Series against the White Sox he stole one more, which was just as many as base-stealing king Luis Aparicio. Little did anyone suspect that in Wills they were watching the man who was about to supplant Aparicio as the most well-known base thief in the game.

In 1960, Wills became the Dodgers' starting shortstop. He hit .295, and set a team record with 50 steals, a total that also led the league. In 1961, Wills again led the league in thefts with 35, while hitting .282. In honor of the offensive power generated by this spindly 170-pounder, his teammates began calling Wills "Mighty Mouse."

But although he had led the league in steals two years in a row, Wills was still not assured of being the Dodgers' number one shortstop. Each spring, the team brought in several contenders for the position whom he had to beat out before he was guaranteed of a job. As Wills wrote in his book *On the Run*, "Not until I stole 104 bases did I go to spring training knowing that I had the job and could take my time getting in shape."

This illustrates how lightly regarded speed and stealing bases were in the early 1960s, even by the Dodgers, a team that had been successfully using speed as a weapon for over a decade. Despite leading the league in steals twice, and clearly having the ability to do it again, Wills still had to overcome the doubters who maintained that what he brought to the Dodgers wasn't as important as the home runs. As Wills wrote: "That's the reason I spent so many years in the minor leagues. I didn't fit into the long-ball style of play. They weren't even scouting speed at that time. They were looking for big guys who hit the long ball. I do believe that after I stole 104 bases, they started scouting for speed."

Wills' pursuit of Cobb's single-season record of 96 steals in 1962 came as something of a surprise. The year before, all the talk and attention in baseball had been on the home run. The assault by the

Yankees' "M&M" boys (Roger Maris and Mickey Mantle) on Babe Ruth's single-season home run record dominated the sports headlines. But in 1962, for the first time in anyone's memory, the stolen base took center stage, thanks to Maury Wills.

Throughout the season, Wills stole bases at a phenomenal pace, until it began to dawn on everyone that he was making a serious run at Cobb's mark of 96, set in 1915. Long thought to be "unbreakable," Cobb's record had certainly seemed safe during the decades that the stolen base had been abandoned by baseball, and entire teams were stealing far fewer than 96 bases per year. Arthur Daley of the *New York Times* wrote in 1954, "Cobb's record of ninety-six stolen bases in a season probably never will be broken, because modern ball has virtually eliminated the steal as a method of progression."

What gave Wills' efforts added emphasis was that the Dodgers were involved in a bitter pennant race with the San Francisco Giants throughout the 1962 season. Each time Wills stole, he was not only drawing nearer to Cobb, he was also helping his team in their dogfight with their ancient and recently-transplanted enemy.

Ironically, Wills didn't specifically focus on breaking Cobb's mark until late in the season. As he wrote in *On the Run*: "I was just interested in trying to win the pennant because it was a tight race between us and the Giants. I didn't put any special emphasis on stealing bases. I had to do it to win games."

In late summer, Wills stole his seventieth base. Now, suddenly, alarm bells started going off around the sports world that something extraordinary was occurring. Since 1920, just three players had stolen 60 or more bases: Sam Rice, with 63 in 1920; Ben Chapman, with 61 in 1931; and, George Case, also with 61, in 1943. No one had stolen 70 sacks since Cobb's 96-steal season in 1915. Wills had run himself into elite company. Public attention shifted to the skinny shortstop who had always had to fight to make the team. At every city in the National League, large crowds began showing up whenever the Dodgers came to town, crying "Go-Go-Go" as soon as Wills got on base. At Dodger Stadium, attendance soared (it would ultimately be nearly one million more than the previous year) as fans flocked to the ball park to urge Wills on.

With about one month to go in the season, Wills stole his eighty-second base, eclipsing the National League mark set by Cincinnati Reds outfielder Bob Bescher in 1911. By the time he reached 90 steals, Wills was national news; a horde of writers followed him and the Dodgers around the country. Base stealing was back in the spotlight, and in a big way.

But as the stolen bases mounted up, the physical pounding that Wills' body endured began to take its toll. He developed a hemorrhage in his leg from sliding. The leg turned a nasty shade of purple, and it hurt him to run. But with the Dodgers locked in combat with the Giants, he had little choice but to continue running, sliding and stealing.

It's never easy to break a sports record. Usually just having the physical ability isn't enough; it's the mental toughness that's critical when the pressure mounts, the media contingent grows to mammoth proportions, and the same questions are asked day after mind-numbing day. For Roger Maris, the pressure caused his nerves to fray and his hair to fall out. While Wills appeared unshaken by the media scrutiny, other distractions plagued him both on and off the field.

Opposing teams were ready and waiting for Wills when the Dodgers arrived. The field would be doctored in an attempt to slow the speedy shortstop down, and Wills never knew what he might find when he stepped onto the diamond. The base paths at Candlestick Park would have been right at home in the Okefenokee Swamp, because the Giants saturated them with water to prevent Wills from getting good traction. In Pittsburgh it was the other extreme; the Pirates loaded the area around first base with so much sand that it wouldn't have been surprising to see a camel stroll by.

Off the field things were heating up as well. As Wills zeroed in on the record, Baseball Commissioner Ford Frick, that lover of asterisks, decreed that the Dodger would have to break Cobb's record in 156 games, the same number that the Georgia Peach played in 1915. Any steals Wills accumulated after that, and for the remainder of the 162 game schedule, wouldn't count toward the record.

The pressure, the media, the asterisks, the pennant race, and everything else that Wills carried with him in his pursuit of Cobb converged on September 23 in St. Louis, where the Dodgers were playing their 156th game of the season. By then, the "young man who looks like a church deacon and runs as if the hounds of Hades were eternally snapping at his heels" was just two bases away from breaking one of baseball's most hallowed marks.

On the mound for the Cardinals was right-hander Larry Jackson, whom Wills called the toughest pitcher to steal against that he ever faced. Nevertheless, in the third inning, with the Dodgers trailing 3–2 and a crowd of 20,743 watching, Wills singled and stole second to tie Cobb's record, as catcher Carl Sawatski's hurried throw bounced past second baseman Dal Maxvill.

Unfortunately, the errant throw was the last good thing that happened for the Dodgers that night. By the seventh inning the Cardinals were routing them 11–2, and about all that was left for the team and the crowd was to root for Wills to break the record. As he came to bat in the seventh inning, he knew that it was probably his last chance to pass the Georgia Peach.

Wills kept hope alive by singling to right field off Jackson. With the game comfortably out of reach the Cardinal pitcher could afford to give Wills his full attention. After several throws to the bag, Wills shortened his lead, and Jackson figured it was safe to pitch to the batter. But Wills, whose chase of Cobb had been improbable from the beginning, had decided to pin all his hopes on one of the most improbable stealing tactics of all: the delayed steal. It was the ultimate gamble by a man who all season long had faced down every opponent through a combination of guts, guile and skill.

Jackson went into his stretch, peered over his shoulder at Wills, and began his delivery to the plate. Wills hesitated for a moment— just enough to lull the defense to sleep. Then he exploded toward second. Sawatski was so anxious to get Wills that he double-clutched, then threw the ball into center field.

It was fortunate that the throw was high, for Wills was so pumped up that he dove headfirst for the bag, instead of sliding feetfirst as usual, and wound up five feet short of second. Then, as he wrote in *On the Run*: "I crawled the rest of the way and when I got there I just hugged second base as if it were a pillow with my head on it. As I hugged the bag, it was like, 'Thank God it's over.'"

Maury Wills, hardly a household name when the season started, had broken a record that had stood for nearly 50 years. He would go on to steal an incredible 104 bases that year, hit .299, and be named the National League's Most Valuable Player—not too shabby for a guy who hadn't even been guaranteed a job when the season began.

Unfortunately the Dodgers would not fare as well. They ended the season in a tailspin, losing 10 out of their final 13 games and allowing the hard-charging Giants to tie them for first on the final day of the season. In the three-game playoff series that followed, the Dodgers led the final contest 4–2 in the eighth inning, and visions of a pennant danced in the heads of the L.A. faithful. But the Giants pushed across four runs in the ninth to win the game, take the pennant, and reawaken the ghosts of 1951. The Dodgers may have escaped Brooklyn, but they could not escape their destiny.

(They also could not escape the Candlestick Park infield, which was saturated almost to the point of flooding by groundskeeper Marty Schwab, ostensibly to keep the dust from flying around in the swirling breezes. The Dodgers screamed that it was done to slow down Wills, but to no avail. Schwab was voted a full World Series share by the Giants.)

There is little doubt that Wills' 1962 season was one of the great individual accomplishments in baseball up until that time. His achievement becomes even greater in light of the fact that in the first seven years of the 1950s no team in either league stole 100 bases during a season. Just the year before, only one team in the major leagues had stolen 100 bases in a season, and that was the White Sox, who swiped exactly 100. Wills topped that all by himself in 1962.

Yet Wills also accomplished something far more permanent. All of the publicity that he received for breaking Cobb's record had reawakened interest in stealing. "The new Nijinsky of the base paths also has stolen the headlines from the home run hitters," said the New York Times. This was particularly true among youngsters who did not have the size or strength to clout balls into the seats, but did have the speed to make it to the big leagues as base stealers. If we can imagine the many budding ballplayers who slid their hands down on the bat thanks to the influence of Babe Ruth, so can we visualize the countless players who stared at their spiked shoes, gauged their reflexes, flexed their legs, and realized that here were attributes that could compensate for their lack of home run-hitting power.

"The effect of Wills will be on a long-term basis," said Cleveland Indian Manager Birdie Tebbets. "The kids in schools and the lower minors will polish their techniques as base stealers. It'll be another five or ten years, though, before they reach the major leagues."

Tebbetts was exactly right. Within a decade, an explosion of speed and base stealing unprecedented in baseball history would occur. While it might be too perfect to attribute all of this to Wills' influence, it also seems like more than mere coincidence that a new generation of base stealers came along less than ten years after the Dodger shortstop reignited interest in the stolen base as an offensive weapon.

What had to be encouraging to youngsters without all the physical tools who dared to dream of a big league career was that in Wills they saw themselves. He was the classic overachiever, making the most of his natural abilities and using his wits to compensate for what he lacked in strength and size. Wills often admitted he wasn't the fastest or the quickest runner; his bases were often stolen less on speed than on intelligence.

For example, by studying the rule book he learned that the bases are 15 inches on each side, so if he ran from the back inside edge of the first base bag to the back inside edge of the second base bag, it's 22½ inches shorter than the 90-foot distance from the first base line to the middle of second base. And in stealing, where every inch counts, who knows how many successful thefts those extra 22½ inches accounted for?

Wills also used this analytical approach to dictate when he should run. He wasn't a cheetah, like teammate Willie Davis, relying on sheer speed and luck to make it safely. Instead, he was more like an accountant; he calculated the odds, and if they were in his favor, he went. "A man should never try to steal," Wills told the *Los Angeles Herald-Examiner* in 1969, "unless the odds are 80 percent in his favor. My steals are calculated. I've never tried to be a gambler on the bases."

Wills said that, when he first broke into the big leagues, the player that he often watched on the bases was Willie Mays. "I picked up a few valuable hints, his little mannerisms, feinting with his head, a certain way he runs, the way he goes for the extra base, the way he runs full stride on the outfielders."

Those "few hints," along with his own natural ability, helped Wills lead the National League in steals for six straight years (1960–1965). In 1965 he was on his way to another great season; the stolen bases were piling up, and, as he said in *On the Run*, he felt sure that he was going to break his own single-season record. But once again a hemorrhage in his leg slowed him down. Wills finished the year with a league-leading 94 steals.

It was his last hurrah. Although Wills averaged 33 steals over the next six seasons, never again did he pace the circuit in thefts.

In 1967 Wills was traded to Pittsburgh. There he helped the Pirates rekindle their moribund running game. In 1968 the Bucs led the National League in steals with 130. (Wills chipped in with 52.) But the team finished in the middle of the pack both years that Wills was with them, and by 1969 he was on the move again, this time going to the expansion Montreal Expos.

Wills retired after the 1972 season. Over his 14 year career he swiped 586 bases, a total that even in 1998 placed him seventh on the all-time career stolen base list. Sadly, his star dimmed rapidly after he left the game, and a brief, ill-fated stint as manager of the Seattle Mariners in the early 1980s further tarnished his image, as did a widely-publicized battle with drug addiction.

Yet despite his later misfortunes, there is no denying the fact that, like Babe Ruth, Wills profoundly changed the game of baseball. In October, 1977, Bob Broeg, writing about Lou Brock breaking Ty Cobb's record for lifetime steals that year, said, "If, however, there was an unsung hero in the saga of King Louis of St. Louis, it would have to be Maury Wills, the former Los Angeles flash who, after lingering nine years in the minors, became a switch-hitter, reached the majors and suddenly turned the game around." Wills, Broeg wrote, had triggered a new era of stealing by awakening baseball to the possibilities of the stolen base.

While Wills was stealing bases and focusing attention on the National League, in the American League it was the same old story: Luis Aparicio was setting the pace. The slick-fielding shortstop rolled right along in the early 1960s just as he had in the previous decade. Aparicio led the league in steals each year from 1960 to 1964, which made it nine straight years that he had been the A.L.'s top base thief.

Occasionally some new challenger to Aparicio's streak would emerge, and the newspapers would be full of "this is the guy that's going to break Looie's streak" type of stories, but at season's end Aparicio would be atop the list of stolen base leaders once again.

Then, just when it seemed as if no one was *ever* going to beat Aparicio, along came Bert Campaneris.

When Campaneris was called up to the Kansas City A's from the minors in the midst of the 1964 season, he was so small and looked so little like a ballplayer that the team's equipment man refused to give him a uniform when he initially reported to the locker room. Soon, however, no one would doubt his right to be in the major leagues.

In 1965 the versatile "Campy" (he once played all nine positions during a game) swiped 51 bags to dethrone Aparicio and lead the American League. It had taken from Ike to LBJ, but at long last the American League had a new stolen base king. Aparicio, with 26 steals, finished in a fourth-place tie.

As might be expected, once it was clear during the 1965 season that Campaneris represented the most serious threat to break Aparicio's streak in years, he became big news. Twice in one month *The Sporting News* ran extensive features on the youngster. "Campy Kicks Up Cloud of Dust in A.L. Theft Race," proclaimed one *TSN* headline. In the article, the A's speedster received high praise from Elston Howard, Yankee manager Johnny Keane, and others. A few weeks later brought another story and more accolades, including one from A's coach Gabby Hartnett. "He's got the best pair of wheels I've ever seen. I saw a lot of great base stealers, including Max Carey, but I wouldn't rate any of them ahead of this kid." Two other A's coaches, Luke Appling and Whitey Herzog, also chipped in with praise for the Cuban-born Campaneris. (With such top-notch coaches, how could the A's always have been so bad?)

The article revealed that Campaneris was a self-taught base stealer. Because of his limited English, he had trouble communicating with the A's manager and coaches. Thus Campy learned everything through observation, and trial and error. Since he was new to the league, most of the bases he stole in 1965 were swiped on sheer speed alone.

After breaking Aparicio's stranglehold on the stolen base crown in 1965, Campaneris went on an Aparicio-like streak of his own, leading the American League in steals for the next three years in a row. In 1969, his four year streak was snapped when Tommy Harper stole 73 sacks for the Seattle Pilots, even though Campaneris tied his personal best that year by swiping 62 bases. Later, when he spoke about losing the title to Harper, the normally easy-going Campaneris displayed the pride and arrogance common to all champion base stealers. "Last year [1969] I was stealing bases only to make runs," he said. "But Harper was stealing when they were 10 runs ahead or behind or whatever. When I see this, I started to run all the time like he did. I don't like to steal bases just to steal bases."

Then, just as Aparicio had done eight years earlier when challenged by Howser and Wood, Campaneris threw down the gauntlet to all rivals, present and future. "No one is going to stop me from stealing," he said defiantly.

In 1970, Campy was as good as his word. His 42 steals paced the American League once again. Harper, plagued by injuries, finished second with 38. Although both players had off years, there was conjecture that either one was likely to break Maury Wills' eight-year-old mark of 104 steals.

But it was not to be. Neither man ever mounted a serious challenge to Wills' record after 1970.

Campaneris probably would have benefited by taking a stab at the mark, because when great base stealers are mentioned today Campy is usually not included. Despite finishing with more lifetime steals than Wills and Aparicio, Campaneris lacked that one sensational, eye-popping season that would have defined him as a thief of the same caliber as Wills, Brock and Aparicio.

Another problem for Campy was that during his best base stealing years, the A's were usually buried in the second division, and publicity was hard to come by. Wills, Brock and Aparicio played for winning teams during much of their careers. By the early 1970s, as the pieces that would form Oakland's world championship teams were coming together, Campy's best base stealing years were behind him. In 1972, when the A's finally broke through and took first place in the A.L. West, Campaneris led the league in stolen bases for the last time with 52. After that, although he consistently registered theft totals in the 20s and 30s (excluding 1976, when in a final blaze of glory he stole 54) throughout the 1970s, the base stealing limelight shifted to players like Lou Brock, Joe Morgan and Davey Lopes.

When he retired after the 1983 season Campaneris had 649 lifetime stolen bases, which in 1998 ranked him tenth on the all-time list.

Campaneris' league-leading 62 thefts in 1968 helped propel the American League to a victory over the National League in total steals; A.L. runners swiped 811 bases, while the National League tallied 704. Not only was this the first time in the 1960s that the American League had bested its rival in steals, it was only the third time in almost two decades; from 1949 to 1967, the American League stole more bases than the National League just twice (1949 and 1954).

That's why someone in the A.L. front office should have broken out the balloons and party hats in 1969, when the junior circuit topped the National League in steals for the second year in a row. Not only did the American League steal 216 more bases than the National League, but the 73 steals rung up by Tommy Harper were the most in the league since Cobb's 96 thefts in 1915.

The obvious conclusion is that all those years of watching the N.L. jackrabbits racing around the diamond and making a mockery of interleague competition (particularly in the All-Star Game) had finally made an impression on the American League, which decided to fight speed with speed.

Baseball was on the verge of enormous changes as the 1970s loomed—changes both in how the game was played as well as where it was played. Thus the American League's adoption of the running game was not just a recognition of what had happened in the past, it was also a bow toward the future.

Indeed, the 1970s would see the stolen base become an integral and necessary part of many teams. No one epitomized the importance of the steal more during those years than a lanky deer of a man from St. Louis named Lou Brock.

8

Brock's Ballet on
the Base Paths

Lou Brock came along at precisely the right time for the stolen base. Just as Maury Wills was slowing down, Brock burst into prominence as the game's premier base thief. Not only did Brock keep public attention focused on the stolen base, but he also took the art of stealing to the next level by breaking both Wills' single-season mark as well as a record long thought to be untouchable: Ty Cobb's 892 lifetime stolen bases. Pleasant, articulate and intellectual, the St. Louis Cardinal outfielder was the perfect ambassador for the running 1970s in baseball, and for stealing in particular.

Yet if Brock's timing was right for the continuing evolution of the stolen base, the time was also right for Brock in baseball. Some might argue that only in an era where speed was highly valued could Brock have excelled. Certainly, as a lead-off hitter he was far from ideal: he struck out far too often (over 100 times in nine seasons) and walked far too little (just 761 times over 19 seasons). In the outfield, the seven times he led the National League in errors did not evoke images of Joe DiMaggio, either.

But what Brock did well on the diamond, he did better than anyone had ever done before: steal bases. That was more than enough to earn him superstar status during his playing days, and a ticket to the Hall of Fame after he retired.

The story of how Lou Brock wound up with the St. Louis Cardinals and became baseball's premier base stealer has to start with one irrefutable statement: It was the worst trade the Chicago Cubs ever made. In fact, to take it one step further, the Lou Brock for Ernie Broglio deal between Chicago and St. Louis in June, 1964, ranks high in the Terrible Trade Hall of Fame, alongside such infamous deals as Jim Fregosi for Nolan Ryan. Still, when the Cubs and Cardinals pulled off the swap, neither had reason to suspect what the final outcome would be.

For the Cubs, the object was pitching. The team had made great strides in 1963, posting a record of 82–80 to finish above .500 for the first time since 1952, when they broke even at 77–77. Although they still ended up 17 games out of first, the Chicago pitching staff had posted the second-best ERA in the league. Another top-flight pitcher would add to an already formidable mound corps, and quite possibly help the club rise even higher in the standings.

In the Cardinals' Ernie Broglio, the Cubs thought they had found that pitcher. The big right-hander, a former 21 game winner, had been a solid performer for St. Louis for five straight seasons, racking up 67 victories against just 50 losses. In 1963 he had posted a mark of 18–8. At age 28, he seemed to be in his prime.

The Cardinals, meanwhile, were also on the rise. The club had rebounded from a dismal sixth-place finish in 1962 to end up second the following year, just six games behind the pennant-winning Dodgers. Anticipation ran high in St. Louis for the 1964 season. But the Redbirds began the year slowly, and couldn't get untracked. By June the team was mired in the bottom half of the league, watching the surprising Phillies pace the circuit. Clearly, the team needed a jump-start before it was too late.

So on June 15, the Cardinals and Cubs pulled the trigger on a deal that would be talked about throughout baseball for years to come. St. Louis sent Broglio, pitcher Bobby Shantz (the American League's Most Valuable Player in 1952 with the Philadelphia A's) and outfielder Doug Clemens to Chicago in exchange for journeymen pitchers Paul Toth and Jack Spring, and a young outfielder with enormous potential named Lou Brock.

Ironically, the trade was condemned by both sides. Bob Kennedy, who was the Cubs' "head coach" at the time (owner P.K. Wrigley having temporarily done away with managers for a revolving system of head coaches), remembered that the Cubs' on-the-field brain trust was against the swap. "The other coaches and I opposed the deal," he said. "We all told John Holland [Cub general manager] how we felt, but he said we needed a pitcher." To try and scotch the deal Kennedy and the other coaches scattered on the June 15 trading deadline so that Holland couldn't find them. But when Kennedy—who was playing golf in the rain—got a phone call from his wife saying Holland wanted to see him and Brock, he knew what it was about.

Yet despite their disappointment over losing Brock, the Cubs were excited about the pitching they obtained in return. Although in sixth place at the time, with a record of 27–27, the team was just 5½ games behind the first-place Phillies and Giants. They felt that obtaining two veteran pitchers would enable them to make some noise in what was turning out to be a wide-open pennant race. In fact, Kennedy was particularly thrilled about the acquisition of Bobby Shantz. "We haven't had a left-handed reliever for some time," Kennedy exulted. "We'll give Shantz about 15 minutes [to get acclimated to his new surroundings] and then use him."

Over in the Cardinal clubhouse, however, the mood was anything but optimistic. Clemens had shown so much potential in the Redbird farm system that he had been dubbed "the next Stan Musial," while Broglio was a dependable veteran pitcher. To many St. Louis players, the trade seemed like a promising prospect and a workhorse pitcher for a mediocre outfielder.

Indeed, while Brock had shown flashes of promise, there was little reason to rate him on a par with a proven commodity like Broglio. In two seasons with the Cubs, Brock had hit .263 and .258, with 16 and 24 stolen bases, respectively. There was absolutely no indication that this was the man who would one day wipe both Maury Wills' and Ty Cobb's names out of the record books and make his own name synonymous with the stolen base.

In fact, Brock had little interest in stealing bases at this stage in his career. To him, base stealers were puny leadoff hitters who survived on scrub singles and Texas Leaguers. He fancied himself a no. 6 hitter—a good RBI man with some power who could hit late in the order. (He did indeed have power. In a 1962 game against the Mets, Brock smashed one of the longest home runs ever hit at the Polo Grounds.)

"The ultimate insult to me was saying I had to start stealing bases," Brock remembered. The man who delivered that "ultimate insult" was Cards skipper Johnny Keane, who had been pushing St. Louis to get Brock in the first place. Keane, having watched the havoc wreaked by Wills throughout the National League, saw the same potential in Brock, and urged Cardinals general manager Bing Devine to obtain the young outfielder from the Cubs. "When I told him [Keane] we had a chance to get Brock, he said, 'What are we waiting for?'" Devine said.

So the deal was made just before the June 15 trading deadline expired. Baseball lore is full of stories about "can't miss" prospects that *do* miss—sometimes badly. The Cubs can be forgiven for thinking that Brock's saga might have ultimately wound up among those stories as well.

Unfortunately for Chicago, they had written the wrong end to the story. Injuries hampered Broglio's effectiveness for the remainder of his career; he won just 7 games total for the Cubs over the next 2½ years before retiring at the end of the 1966 season. The trade that was supposed to lift the Cubs instead turned out to be a millstone around their necks; the team sank to eighth place in 1964, ten games below .500.

For Brock, however, the trade was a classic case of a player who just needs a change of scenery to blossom. Keane helped take some of the heat off his new outfielder by asking the St. Louis press to back off a bit and let Brock get oriented to his new surroundings.

It didn't take the former Cub long to get his St. Louis sea legs. Hitting just .251 at the time of the deal, the young outfielder from El Dorado, Arkansas (the same home town as pitcher Lynwood "Schoolboy" Rowe), proceeded to spank the ball for a .348 average the rest of the season, winding up at .315 for the year.

Another area in which Brock improved once in St. Louis was base stealing. Keane had told him that to be a regular player he'd have to start stealing bases. If Brock didn't like the idea at first, his performance certainly didn't show it. He ended up with 43 steals, second in the National League behind Maury Wills' 53.

The all-around excellence of Brock's play ignited the Cardinals, who got hot and plunged into the thick of the pennant race that was being waged by the Phillies, Reds, and Giants. When the dust settled from the wild, four-way fight, St. Louis found themselves on top by one game over the Phillies and Reds, with the Giants three back.

Flushed with confidence, the Cardinals roared into the World Series, where they beat the Yankees in an exciting seven game contest. Brock, shrugging off any post-season jitters, contributed a .300 average and one home run (but no stolen bases) to the Cardinal cause.

Because Brock was given the lion's share of credit for righting the Cardinals' listing ship and sending it sailing toward the pennant and, ultimately, the World Series, Devine (who, ironically, was fired in August before the Cards caught fire) wound up looking like a genius. A headline from the October 17, 1964, *Sporting News* summed up the general feeling about the trade: "Brock Turns Bing's Folly Into A Steal." Keane also credited the addition of Brock as the turning point of the Cardinals' season, and predicted that he could steal as many as 50 bases per year.

Unfortunately for Keane, he was never able to enjoy the fruits of what he had set in motion by bringing Brock to St. Louis and telling him to steal. Miffed at Cardinal management, Keane left the team after their World Series triumph and signed to manage the Yankees. Thus Keane presided over the dissolution of the once-mighty New York dynasty. Keane has always taken more than his share of heat for his role in the Great Yankee Collapse that began in 1965; maybe the knowledge that he saw something in Brock that no one else did will restore some of the luster to his reputation.

Yet even Keane's perceptiveness did not go far enough. In 1965, Brock raced past his former skipper's prediction by swiping 63 bases. This set a Cardinals' team record, shattering the old mark of 48 set by Red Murray in 1908 and tied by Frankie "Fordham Flash" Frisch in 1927. Contacted at home, the Old Flash managed to sound both congratulatory and critical toward Brock in one sentence. "Good boy and good legs, but the way pitchers have forgotten how to throw to first base, he ought to steal 490," Frisch grumped.

Despite his sensational 1965 season, however, Brock once again finished second to Wills in steals. The Los Angeles shortstop pilfered 94 sacks that year to lead the National League for the sixth straight time.

But even as the Dodger base stealer was enjoying a banner year, there were indications that his reign as King of Thieves might be coming to an end. In September 1965, the *Christian Science Monitor* seemed to look past Wills, toward the up-and-coming base stealers: "But even those who laud the Los Angeles player's remarkable achievements admit that they wonder what another swifty will do when he acquires Maury's experience and finesse."

That "swifty" was Brock, who was also quoted in the article. From his remarks, it is apparent that he had done a complete about-face from a year ago. Instead of belittling base stealing he was now embracing it, and had already begun the thoughtful analysis of stealing that was to mark his entire career. The man who had only recently considered base stealers as inferior now obviously felt a kinship with his fellow thieves. "Being fast is only the beginning," Brock told the *Monitor.* "You have to learn the habit of every pitcher you'll face, just as the hitters do. You have to watch when a pitcher changes his habits…. Basically, good base runners all have to have the same things. You have to have speed and quick reflexes. After that you succeed or fail on what you learn by observation."

Ironically, the man who would one day wipe Maury Wills' name out of the record book denied that he was a threat to do just that. "He's [Wills] the greatest," Brock said. "He has it down to a science. Nobody knows as much as he does. Maybe nobody ever will." By the following year, however, Brock demonstrated that he was learning fast. He swiped 74 bases to easily outdistance Wills and the rest of the league and pace the National League in steals for the first time.

Beginning in 1966, there was a new base stealing king in the National League, and he hailed from St. Louis. Brock proceeded to dominate the National League in steals like no one had dominated it before. He led the league in stolen bases eight out of the next nine seasons, falling short only in 1970 when his 51 steals ranked him second to the 57 swiped by Cincinnati Reds outfielder Bobby Tolan. Ultimately Brock set a record by stealing 50 or more bases for 12 straight years. Not since the great Cobb had anyone left the rest of the league so far in the base path dust.

As Brock warmed to base stealing, he became more sophisticated in learning his craft. He moved beyond merely observing pitchers to using more advanced techniques, such as timing the throw home. He filmed pitchers, then spent hours studying the movies looking for that one almost imperceptible clue that would give him the edge on the bases. Once, Don Drysdale saw Brock filming him in spring training and, realizing what the base thief was doing, chased him away. "But it was too late," Brock chuckled. "I could spend every night with him and his motion stuck in a frame so I could study it. And there was nothing he could do about it."

As any eager pupil would do, Brock sought out the best in the business, Professor Maury Wills, for some further pointers. There was a rumor in the National League that Wills kept a little black book containing the most detailed and fundamental knowledge of pitchers ever recorded. This was a book that Brock yearned to read.

"Whenever I'd see him, I'd put my hand in his pocket looking for the book," Brock said. "But of course none existed. If there was such a book with that kind of information, it would have to be as big as an encyclopedia."

Failing to find such a treasure trove of information, Brock came up with his own method of analyzing pitchers. "All you need to know about pitchers is that they are in one of two categories, the two-motion throw to first or the three-motion throw," he said. "Soon as you can read the pitcher well enough, you can eliminate the catcher. He won't have a chance of nailing you."

Clearly, in Brock the stolen base had found one of its most articulate and thoughtful practitioners. As age and injury took their toll on Wills, all of this meticulous attention to detail made Brock the premier theft artist in the league, despite the fact that he admittedly wasn't the fastest man in the National League.

"Speed helps, of course," he said. "But you have to blend, to coordinate a combination of things into a technique. Once you acquire a technique, all you have to know is when, for sure, the pitcher is going to throw to the plate. Obviously you acquire that knowledge through your own observation and experience. The pitcher knows I'm going.

The catcher knows I'm going. I know I'm going. Everybody in the park does. But I'm the only guy who knows *when* I'm going."

In both the 1967 and 1968 World Series, Brock demonstrated to a national audience just how far his observation and experience had taken him. In the 1967 classic he not only battered Red Sox pitching for a .414 average but also stole a record seven bases (which accounted for all of the Cards' steals in the Series) to spark the Redbirds' triumph over Boston. The following year, against Detroit, he was even better, hitting .464 while again stealing seven sacks.

By stealing 14 bases, Brock tied Eddie Collins' World Series record. The difference was that Collins had set his mark over the course of 34 games in six World Series, while Brock had done it in just 14 games and two Fall Classics.

Yet much of the luster was taken off Brock's performance in the 1968 series by a controversial play that some said led to the Cardinals' losing the Series to the Tigers in seven games. In Game Five, with St. Louis up 3–2 and ahead in games 3–1, Brock was on second with a double when second baseman Julian Javier singled. Racing for home, Brock inexplicably did not slide. Just as his left foot was poised to come down on the plate Detroit catcher Bill Freehan pushed it away and tagged him out. When the Tigers rallied to win that game 5–3, and ultimately the series, that play was singled out as the turning point.

Nothing, however, could temper his soaring popularity in St. Louis among both fans and Cardinals management alike. Cards President August A. Busch, Jr., was so enamored of his star outfielder's base stealing abilities that he urged him to try for 90 steals in a season. Brock, while obviously intrigued by the possibility, nevertheless poured cold water on it. "I believe honestly I might do it," Brock said, "but I won't because it would mean unnecessary wear and tear on myself and useless risk." He pointed out that, because of Wills, pitchers and catchers were much more aware of the steal than ever before, which made it difficult to swipe many bases.

As the years went by, it seemed that Brock had made a self-fulfilling prophecy. From 1966 through 1973, he averaged 61 stolen bases, with his high being 74 in 1966. Ninety steals seemed like an impossible dream.

In 1973, Brock stole 70 bases, and baseball fans might have been forgiven for thinking that they had seen his last hurrah. After all, at season's end he was 34 years old, an age at which many players' skills begin to deteriorate. Along with the advancing years there was the physical abuse that Brock's body endured from the constant sliding. Few people would have been surprised to see his base stealing total drop drastically in 1974 as an acknowledgment of the effects of Father Time. Brock instead put together the greatest single season in the history of base stealing.

Brock put everyone on notice early in 1974 that there was still life left in his muscular legs by stealing 28 bases in a row after being thrown out on opening day. As the months rolled on, his stolen base total soared, and by the end of July the speedster had swiped 65 bases.

Then came August. During a month in which heat and humidity can sap the strength of even the strongest player, Brock became a base stealing machine, pilfering an incredible 29 bases in 41 attempts.

By September 1, Brock had 94 steals, and it was obvious that he had Wills' single season record of 104 in his sights. But unlike the Dodger shortstop, who carried his quest to break Cobb's record down to the wire, Brock eschewed any suspense. He stole 11 bases over the next ten days to collect the magic one hundred fifth in the Cardinals' one hundred forty-second game of the year.

The record-shattering stolen base came on September 10, in a game against the Philadelphia Phillies in St. Louis. With Dick Ruthven pitching and Bob Boone behind the plate, Brock took off for second in the seventh inning after singling. He made it easily, as the crowd of 30,000 roared its approval. At that point the game was stopped. Cool Papa Bell, a St. Louis native who was in attendance that night, came onto the field and presented the milestone base to Brock. "We decided to give him his 105th base because if we didn't, he was going to steal it anyway," Bell joked.

When reached for comment, Wills was philosophical about the loss of his record, which had stood for just 12 years. (In contrast, Cobb's single season mark had survived for 47 years.) "My hat's off to him [Brock]," said the graceful Wills. "I never thought anyone would approach the record this soon, probably not in my lifetime. I was hoping he wouldn't break the record, but when Lou got around 80, it became pretty obvious."

Brock ended 1974 with 118 steals, a mind-boggling mark that everyone assumed would last for many years. Unfortunately, his base stealing heroics were not enough to help the Cardinals overtake the Pittsburgh Pirates, who finished 1½ games ahead of St. Louis in the N.L. East race. One thing that did benefit, however, was the Cardinals' attendance, which surged to 1,850,000 from 1,535,000 the previous season. Base stealing had finally caught up to the home run as a fan magnet in baseball.

With his record-breaking season behind him, most baseball fans again probably figured that Lou Brock had sipped the sweet nectar of glory for the last time. Becoming the greatest single season base stealer in baseball's long history was quite a feather in the cap of a 35-year-old outfielder. What else could be left to accomplish? Besides, the physical wear and tear, not to mention the emotional tumult, of the 1974 season had been enormous. Surely, most thought, Brock would now sit back, rest on his laurels, and give way to some of the new base bandits in the game, such as Davey Lopes and Joe Morgan. But Lou Brock wasn't finished yet.

While 1974 would be the last year that he led the league in steals, the man with the long, lean sprinter's legs was not quite done thrilling the baseball world. There was one more mountain for him to climb, and climb it he would; just like Wills had taken Cobb, and he had taken Wills, Brock now set his sights on Cobb, and another of the Georgia Peach's seemingly "untouchable records": his lifetime stolen base total of 892. This, however, was no easy task; formidable obstacles blocked the path to the Georgia Peach. At the beginning of the 1975 season, Brock had 753 stolen bases. Not only was he 139 steals short of Cobb, but he would be 36 in June—not exactly the age at which a man begins the quest for a base stealing record. Davey Lopes once noted that a base-stealer can't rely on his speed anymore once he hits his thirties. Brock had not only reached his thirties, but was now able to see forty closing in on him in the rear view mirror. How could he hope to catch Cobb with his speed ebbing and his body battered from over a decade of sliding? He seemed more like a candidate for a featherbed than a stolen base record.

But now, when he needed it most, Brock's long hours of learning the intricate art of base stealing paid off. Although superbly conditioned, he certainly wasn't as fast as he once was. Yet, that was the beauty of it; he didn't have to be. His brain, packed with years of information gleaned from observation and study, could pick up the slack from his aging legs.

Thus Brock began his assault on Cobb. He stole 56 bases in both 1975 and 1976 to draw within 27 of the record, once again defying the maxim that the older a base stealer becomes, the less he steals. He wasn't getting on base through charity, either; in those years he hit .309 and .301, respectively.

By the time the 1977 season began, it was obvious that, barring catastrophic injury or the end of civilization, Cobb's record would fall that year. Since the Cardinals were never a factor in the pennant race, Brock's relentless pursuit of the Tiger outfielder took center stage in St. Louis. Before long, it had captivated the entire nation as well. As summer waned and turned the corner into late August, the "Brock watch" was in full swing. People who didn't know a stolen base from a stolen car began following the Cardinal outfielder's remarkable run at a baseball icon and his record.

Finally, on the night of August 29 in San Diego, in the seventh inning of a game against the Padres, Brock reached first via a fielder's choice. He had already tied Cobb in the first inning by stealing number 892. With the crowd roaring with anticipation, Brock mysteriously called time and walked off first base.

He later said he had heard "something"—no one was sure quite what—but when he asked the first base umpire, the San Diego first baseman, and his own coach if they had said anything, they all shook their heads.

"Maybe," said Cardinal publicist Marty Hendin, "it was the ghost of Ty Cobb."

Maybe it was indeed the spirit of the irascible Tyrus Raymond Cobb, crying out from beyond the grave in a final act of protest against the loss of one of his most cherished records. If it was, the objections fell on deaf ears. A few moments later the game resumed, and Brock took off for second, sliding in safely ahead of catcher Dave Roberts' wide throw. Lou Brock had become the most prolific base stealer of all time—and presumably shut the ghost of Ty Cobb up for good.

Just as when he had broken Wills' single season mark in 1974, the game was stopped and the bag uprooted to give to Brock. Called upon to make an impromptu speech, he was, as always, gracious. "I think it should not be remembered as an evening when Lou Brock stole a base to set a record," he said, "but as an evening in which the record of a tremendous ballplayer was surpassed."

In California Shirley Cobb, daughter of the great Georgia Peach, gave her family's approval to the event. "I don't think even the old man would object," she said, obviously not having heard the same plaintive cries as had Brock.

Brock finished the 1977 season with 35 steals, but did not finish among the top five base thieves in the National League. By now the generation that had grown up watching his accomplishments had come into the game and outstripped their idol, just as Brock had once surpassed Maury Wills.

After the adulation and accolades of 1977, the following year was a tremendous disappointment for Brock. Hampered by injuries, he had his poorest season ever, hitting just .221 with 17 steals as the Cardinals tumbled to fifth place in the N.L. East with a 69–93 mark. His pride stung, Brock came back for one final campaign in 1979. In 120 games he hit .304 and stole 21 bases, helping the Cardinals surge to third.

And then he was gone. The player who had initially thought of himself as an RBI-producing outfielder retired with 938 lifetime stolen bases, the most anyone had ever accumulated up to that time. On his way to that mark he had brought acclaim, recognition and respect to base stealing and base stealers.

He had also used the steal like no one else. As he explained in later years, Brock viewed stealing as a match to light a fire under his ball club. Eschewing the traditional view that a player should only steal if it would influence the game and that he should not risk getting thrown out if the team was several runs down, Brock stole whenever he thought it would inspire his teammates. "My biggest asset was being able to light the fuse to a ball club," Brock said. "Someone on every team has to do that to create enthusiasm. Being able to do it with the St. Louis Cardinals gave me a great deal of satisfaction."

All too soon, his base stealing records were under attack by Rickey Henderson. The first to fall was his single season mark of 118, which Henderson shattered in 1982 by swiping 130. Like the classy individual that he is, Brock followed Henderson around from town to town, wanting to be on hand to present the historic base to Rickey when the A's outfielder set the new standard. When it finally happened in Milwaukee, after several days' delay, Brock joked, "It's like waiting for your wife to have a baby. Now I feel my wife had the baby."

As always, he was very complimentary toward Henderson, a man to whom he had offered advice and hospitality when Rickey had visited Brock's home in St. Louis earlier in his career. "How many could he [Henderson] steal in one season?" he asked in response to a reporter's question after Rickey had broken his record. "His main asset now is that he's eliminated the fear of failure. He steals second as well as third, like a man with a double-barreled shotgun. If he thinks 200, it's 200."

When the inevitable call came from Cooperstown, and reporters again besieged him, Brock talked about stealing, about technique, about lighting a fuse, and also about something he called "baserunning arrogance":

> [It's] just like pitching arrogance or hitting arrogance.... You are a force and you have to instill you are a force to the opposition. Don Drysdale and Sal Maglie would throw a ball close to the hitter to let you know they were out there. That's pitching arrogance because now he's coming at you. He's just driven you to your very best. And he wants to challenge that.
>
> Baserunning is the same thing, with one exception. The runner gets to first base and stands out there 9 or 10 feet off the base. The question then becomes how do I act, how do I respond? Do I challenge them or do I back away? If you're arrogant, you are presenting a presence that tells the opposition I am ready for the test.

One thing is certain: Lou Brock was always ready for the test. He occupies a unique position in the history of stealing in that he was the bridge between the 1960s and 1970s—two very different eras in the evolution of the stolen base.

In the 1960s, Maury Wills picked up where Luis Aparicio left off, and stealing was just beginning to emerge from its long hibernation. No one knew that record-breaking stolen base totals were looming on the horizon. "When we [Maury Wills and Luis Aparicio] were running, we thought we had reached the limit," Brock said. "We were just building a super highway without speed limits. We were the pioneers, and throughout history, pioneers have had arrows in their backs. Fortunately, I've lived to tell about it."

Wills' pursuit of Ty Cobb's single-season stolen base record focused public interest back on stealing, making baseball fans realize that there was more to the game than just hitting the ball a long way.

Just as Wills began to falter Brock picked up the stolen base baton and ran with abandon. In this respect he served as the perfect lead-in to the "running 1970s," when individual stolen base totals soared and entire teams were stealing hundreds of bases.

Not just once, but twice within four years, Brock riveted national attention on base stealing as he pursued and broke two hallowed records. Brock put the celebrity back into stealing, raising it up on a par with the home run and making it just as exciting for fans to watch a base being stolen as it was to see batted balls reaching the seats.

By the time the Redbird outfielder was chasing Cobb in 1977, however, the stolen base no longer needed much publicity to have baseball fans remember it as an important part of the game. Thanks to Wills and Brock, the 1970s saw the reemergence of the steal as a major offensive force in baseball in a manner that it hadn't been since the heyday of the dead ball era, when "the scientific game" ruled the roost. In the 1970s, baseball literally "ran wild."

9

Running Wild
in the 1970s

In the 1970s the running game and, in particular, the stolen base returned to the diamond with a vengeance. No longer was it just a few lone pioneers like Aparicio, Wills and Brock leading the way. Thanks to newer, more spacious stadiums and artificial surfaces, stealing went from an art practiced by a few players to a skill that no team could do without. In the 1970s, *everyone* was running; a fan who had last watched a game in the 1950s and then hibernated for 20 years might have been excused upon emerging for wondering what in the world was going on down on the playing field, because it surely wasn't baseball the way he remembered it.

Although statisticians may dispute it, the 1970s in baseball really began in 1969. That was the year that Tommy Harper of the American League's expansion Seattle Pilots stole 73 bases. Harper's total was the highest in the A.L. since Ty Cobb swiped 96 in 1915, and it presaged the Stealin' Seventies.

While always a threat to run, Harper's sudden emergence as a top base stealer came out of nowhere. During his previous seven years in the majors the most bases he had ever stolen was 35, with Cincinnati in 1965.

But in spring training with the Pilots in 1969, manager Joe Schultz pulled Harper aside and gave him the green light to steal whenever he could. "You are my Lou Brock," Schultz told him. "So go out there and steal yourself some bases, make yourself some money." (This shows how the value of stealing bases was growing. Just a few years before, suggesting to a player that he could make money by stealing would have been ludicrous.)

Taking Schultz's advice, Harper set the American League on its ear with his flying feet, stealing bases at a incredible clip. Only the fact that he hit a mere .235, with just 126 base hits in 537 at bats, kept him from threatening Wills' single-season stolen base record. (Wills, by contrast, hit .299 with 208 hits in 1962.) As the old adage goes, it's hard to steal first base. Still, Harper's potential as a base stealer seemed unlimited. He had the two most vital ingredients for a theft king: speed and confidence. "In the right situation, I could steal off anybody," he said.

Unfortunately, the right situation never again occurred as often as it did in 1969. The following year, "Tailwind" Tommy suffered a variety of injuries that held his stolen base total down to just 38, which was still good enough for second in the league. The season, however, was not a total loss; by clubbing 31 home runs to go with his 38 steals, Harper joined the elite "30–30" club, whose members included Willie Mays and Henry Aaron.

Harper's legs had one more good year left in them. In 1974, with Boston, Harper's 54 stolen bases not only led the American League, but also broke the immortal Tris Speaker's Red Sox team record. A few years later Harper retired with 408 lifetime steals, and the nagging suspicion that he was more comet than base stealer, streaking briefly and spectacularly across the sky before flaming out.

Harper's terrific 1969 season sounded the starter's pistol for the Runnin' Seventies. In second place behind Tailwind Tommy among the league's top base stealers that year was Bert Campaneris, whose 62 steals would have been good enough to lead the circuit in just about any other year. In fact, even the 37 steals registered by Kansas City's Joe Foy, which ranked him fifth in the American League in 1969, would have made him the league's top base stealer not too many years before. By 1969, however, 37 steals were just barely enough to crack the top five.

This was an omen of things to come. In the 1970s, those who merely dabbled in the science of stealing had to step aside and let the experts take over, or risk getting buried underneath a mountain of stolen sacks. In 1967, for example, the Yankees' Horace Clarke had finished fifth in the league in steals with 21. But by 1969, 21 steals were barely a blip on the stolen base radar screen. The American League was off and running.

During the 1970s, the American League finally achieved parity with its older rival in stolen bases. Whereas throughout the 1950s and 1960s runners in the Senior Circuit consistently stole more bases overall than the American League, in the 1970s the leagues drew virtually even. The National League had more steals in six out of the decade's ten years, while the American League was tops in the remaining four.

Besides the sheer number of bases stolen, the 1970s represented a special milestone in baseball history. For the first time ever, the home run and stolen base were equal partners in a team's offensive attack. No longer did either one or the other dominate; in the 1970s, both the steal and the long ball existed side by side.

For instance, in 1975, 43 N.L. players hit ten or more home runs, and 35 stole ten or more bases. In the American League, 59 players hit ten or more homers, and 49 swiped at least ten bases. This represented a balance that was unprecedented in 20th century baseball.

It had been a long way back for the stolen base, but as the 1970s progressed there was little doubt that the steal had, indeed, returned. In 1973, for the first time since 1918, teams were averaging more than one stolen base per game. Two years later, the California Angels became the first team since the 1918 Pittsburgh Pirates to steal more than 200 bases in a season.

Some of the stolen base totals piled up by the two leagues during the 1970s showed just how far the stolen base had come in only a few years. Considering the persistent identification of baseball with Mom, apple pie and the flag, it's appropriate that the most steal-happy season was the Bicentennial year of 1976, when the two leagues combined for a blistering 3,054 thefts. The A.L.'s 1,690 steals in 1976 was the most accumulated by either league during the decade. Right behind this year was 1977, when the combined total for both leagues was 3,017 steals.

Leading the race around the bases in 1976 were the Oakland A's, who put on the second-greatest single exhibition of base stealing ever seen in baseball. Manager Chuck Tanner had everybody but the bat boy running as the A's raced their way to 341 stolen bases in 1976, setting an A.L. record and falling just 6 steals shy of the major league mark of 347, set by the 1911 New York Giants. Eight A's players stole bases in double figures that year, led by outfielder Bill North's league-leading 75. The other road runners were: Bert Campaneris (54), Don Baylor (52), Claudell Washington (37), Phil Garner (35), Larry Lintz (31), and Matt Alexander (20). Even Sal Bando stole 20 bases that year, or nearly a quarter of his lifetime total of 75.

Tanner obviously decided to fill the power void created by the loss of slugger Reggie Jackson to Baltimore in 1976 with speed as the A's went for their sixth straight A.L. West title, and it almost paid off. Oakland finished second in their division that year, just 2½ games back of the Kansas City Royals (who also had eight players in double figures in steals, led by shortstop Fred Patek with 51). As a team the Royals stole 218 bases, which was second in the league.

(Tanner was one manager who could be counted on not only to have his teams run, but also to run at any time. Once, while managing the Pirates, he received a lot of flak when he had a player steal a base when Pittsburgh was leading 5–0. Several innings later the opposing team tied the score, and Tanner exploded, "Now is it O.K. to run again?")

In the National League, piling up a lot of steals became *de rigueur* for winning baseball; the team that led the league in steals came in either first or second in their division every year from 1970 to 1979. In the Junior Circuit, the results were not quite as definitive, but still impressive: the team that led in steals finished either first, second or last in their division each season.

What was behind the sudden explosion of stealing throughout baseball? Two of the obvious reasons were newer, more spacious stadiums and the increasing use of artificial surfaces.

As baseball swept into a new decade in 1970, it swept out a lot of the "old" remnants that had some people calling it an outdated game from a bygone era. Drab flannel uniforms gave way to colorful knits, clean-shaven faces were replaced by beards and mustaches, and silent, taciturn players were superseded by loud, outspoken personalities.

Another thing that was replaced were the ballparks. Although they had character traits that gave them personalities just like people, these old, cramped stadiums usually located in the hearts of big cities were deemed inadequate for the creature comforts that suburban-bred fans demanded. New parks popped up faster than a lifetime .200 hitter: Busch Stadium in St. Louis (1966), Three Rivers Stadium in Pittsburgh and Riverfront Stadium in Cincinnati (1970), Veterans Stadium in Philadelphia (1971), Royals Stadium in Kansas City (1973), and Olympic Stadium in Montreal and Seattle's Kingdome (1977).

Along the way, it was determined that these new stadiums should be multipurpose, so that they could be used for other events during all those days when the home team wasn't in town. After all, it made no sense having an expensive facility sitting idle for several months, when it could be hosting a rock concert, football game, soccer match, funny car exhibition, or who knows what else instead.

In order to make the stadiums amenable to as many different types of events as possible, they had to be symmetrical; short porches, terraces, and other idiosyncratic touches that had given each baseball park its own individual identity were banished (along with, some might argue, the soul of the game). Each new multiuse facility looked just like another, so that a fan who was dropped down in the middle of the night into one of them would not know if he was in Riverfront, Three Rivers, or Veteran's Stadium.

Since the parks had to be durable to withstand a variety of uses, artificial surface was used in place of grass to cut down on maintenance and reduce the number of rainouts. As previously noted, the synthetic carpet made speed a necessary ingredient for a team and helped bring back stealing.

Artificial surface also had another, often-overlooked impact on stolen bases. With grass and dirt infields, home teams were often able to "creatively" slow down opposing theft artists. Maury Wills, for instance, nearly drowned in the soggy quagmire of Candlestick Park during the 1962 playoff between the Dodgers and the Giants. The artificial surface put an end to such tactics, and made it easier for runners to steal.

"Back before Astroturf, you would have teams watering the base paths down to stop a runner," said Reds catcher Johnny Bench a bit nostalgically in the mid–1970s. "You can't do that anymore. Now you just squeegee the water off."

In response to these new conditions, speed was elevated to the lofty position of offensive importance previously occupied solely by the home run. The advent of deeper power alleys and longer fences in symmetrical parks spelled doom for long ball hitters who had grown fat feasting upon short porches and foul poles within spitting distance. A swift player who could consistently hit balls in the gap and race around the bases was just as important—if not more so—than someone who could occasionally jack one out of the yard. As Tommy Harper noted: "It used to be when a runner got on base he was told, 'stay right there and we'll drive you in.' It took three hits to bring a run in. Now you don't have to get a lot of hits to score, if you get the right guys on base."

But while newer and larger stadiums, plus the growing use of synthetic surfaces, certainly helped bring stealing back to baseball, another often-overlooked factor is the influence of Maury Wills.

By 1970, Wills' highly-publicized feat of stealing 104 bases was eight years old. Youngsters who had watched him turn the baseball world upside down via the stolen base and dreamed of doing it themselves had entered the game, worked their way through the minors, and were making their mark in the majors the same way the Dodger shortstop had—with speed.

Fortunately for them, the baseball landscape had shifted 180 degrees since 1962, and teams were now greeting players of this type with open arms. The "Wills generation" circulated through the big leagues, spreading the gospel of speed as they went.

In many respects, the situation was similar to what happened in baseball at the dawn of the home run era. In 1920, Babe Ruth so dominated the game with his 54 home runs that no one even came close to his performance. The nearest pursuer to Ruth was the Browns' George Sisler, with a mere 19 four-baggers.

By the following year, however, five other big leaguers had cracked the 20 home run plateau. By the middle of the decade, as more and more players imitated the Bambino, 20 home runs became more common. The rest of the game had caught up to (but never surpassed) Ruth.

In a similar fashion, by the 1970s base stealers had caught up to Wills' example. Immediately after Wills had broken Cobb's record there were a few players who stole large numbers of bases, such as Lou Brock and Bert Campaneris. By 1970 and beyond, however, this trickle of players became a flood.

As Hall of Fame second baseman Joe Morgan put it, in his book *A Life in Baseball,* "He [Wills] was a pioneer, a guy who almost single-handedly was responsible for the revolution in playing style that came to the game during the 1960s, and that marked the kind of play the Big Red Machine would perfect during the years that followed."

As the primary circuit in Cincinnati's Big Red Machine, Joe Morgan did indeed epitomize baseball in the 1970s with his explosive mixture of power and speed.

Just like Brock, Morgan did not start out as a base stealer. The stolen base totals that he posted in his first few years with Houston in the mid–1960s were good, but not exceptional: 20 steals in 1965, 11 in 1966, and 29 the following year.

But beginning in 1969, the compact, powerful second sacker ran off a string of nine straight seasons in which he never stole less than 40 bases. Twice—in 1973 and 1975—he swiped a personal-best 67 bases. When he retired after the 1984 season, Morgan's 689 lifetime steals placed him eighth on the all-time list. Despite the high ranking, Morgan never led the National League in steals. (He spent all but the last of his 22 years in the majors in the National League.) In the late 1960s and early 1970s, Brock was the perennial league leader. Later, others such as Davey Lopes and Omar Moreno blocked Morgan from the top spot.

Ironically, it was an injury that convinced Morgan to hone his stealing skills. Early in 1968, he tore the mediate cruciate ligaments in his left knee, and was out for the season. With nothing but time on his hands while he recuperated, Morgan went to every Astros home game. It was there that he realized the one part of his game that was lacking was stealing bases.

So Morgan became a man with a mission. From his seat in the Astrodome he studied opposing teams when they came into Houston, learning the habits of infielders, pitchers, and catchers. He often gained valuable insights into a pitcher's behavior, such as when he noticed that Dodger hurler Don Drysdale bent his knee in an odd manner before throwing to first.

After a full season of study, Morgan was armed with an encyclopedic knowledge about virtually every opposing player in the league. In the process, he had become an expert in the art of base stealing, particularly regarding timing. As he related in *A Life in Baseball*: "The telltale movement was a red light or green light when it came to stealing. When I returned to play, I thereafter always stole on the 'green light-red light' signal I got from reading a pitcher's first movement. Lefties were easier to read because they faced me, but right-handers also gave themselves away in their first movement—if I could see it clearly."

When he returned to action in 1969, Morgan put his "red light-green light" concept into effect and stole 49 bases that season. One summer's worth of observation was about to turn into ten years' worth of agony for National League pitchers and catchers.

Morgan came into his own as a base stealer when he was traded to Cincinnati late in 1971. Just like the Brock trade, there were those in Cincinnati who initially felt that the Reds had given up too much (slugger Lee May and Pete Rose–clone Tommy Helms) to get Morgan. But once the former Astro got comfortable with his new teammates, the true wealth of his talents was revealed. In 1972 he hit .292 with 58 stolen bases (second in the league) and a league-leading 122 runs scored. His play helped spark the Reds into the World Series, where they lost a bitterly fought seven-game contest with the Oakland A's. Despite the defeat, Morgan's superlative play in 1972 silenced his critics. With Morgan now firmly in place, the Big Red Machine was ready to steamroll the opposition.

The Reds were the ideal '70s team. They had the power, pitching, defense and, especially, the speed required to play the type of baseball dictated by new, larger stadiums and artificial surfaces. As Morgan pointed out: "The wide reaches of Riverfront [Cincinnati's home field] and other new National League parks allowed us to take full advantage of our talents. We were the team, more than any other, that put an end to station-to-station baseball, that slow-as-molasses game where runners advanced a base at a time depending almost exclusively on what the guy at bat did."

In reality, station-to-station baseball was breathing its last by that time anyway; Morgan and company just put the last few spike marks into the body. But there is no doubt that the Reds of the 1970s played a running, gambling style of baseball that hadn't been seen for generations.

In fact, sometimes the Reds played a style that had *never* been seen before, such as in a 1973 game against the Phillies. Morgan not only stole third on the front end of a double steal, but stole home as well when the second baseman hesitated with the ball.

Since there wasn't a rule addressing two stolen bases on one pitch, one of the steals was declared a fielder's choice. Baseball subsequently devised the "Morgan Rule," which stated that a player cannot be credited with more than one stolen base on a single play. Morgan and the Reds were taking the steal to places it had never been before.

In 1975, with Morgan again leading the way with 67 steals, the Reds team had a stolen base success ratio of 82 percent. This remains the best team stolen base percentage in baseball history.

Morgan continued to drive the Big Red Machine throughout the 1970s. Along the way, the power-packed second baseman won two Most Valuable Player awards, set several records, and was considered one of the finest second basemen ever to play the game.

Inevitably, however, time eroded Morgan's skills. His final year in baseball was 1984, when he played for the Oakland A's. One day he gathered a group of several young, fast A's players and tried to teach them the finer points of stealing, including the "red light–green light" system. As he was talking, however, he noticed that several of the players were gazing off into the stands, eyeing good-looking women, laughing, and generally acting like they wanted to be anywhere but there. Morgan's disappointment over their poor attitude was still palpable years later. In his book he wrote, "It was like they were in a high school class they didn't want to be in. That was enough for me. As far as I was concerned, school was out, the semester was over."

With the eye of an expert and the wisdom of a world-class base stealer, Morgan also spoke in his book about other base bandits: "Henderson and others like Vince Coleman, like a lot of speedy guys today, know how to steal bases but they are not base stealers—as Maury Wills and Lou Brock were. Wills and Brock would have been embarrassed to be bunted over in a crucial situation, costing the team a valuable out. So would I. When I learned to steal bases, I had also had drummed into my head by Nellie Fox and others that you only stole bases to help your team win."

When the Big Red Machine was at full power during the 1970s, it staged some memorable battles with the Los Angeles Dodgers for N.L. West supremacy. To match Morgan, the Dodgers also had a standout base stealer in swift infielder Davey Lopes.

In 1975, Lopes stole 77 bases in just his third full season to pace the National League. He also set a record (since broken) of 38 consecutive successful steals. Lopes followed that up with 63 thefts in 1976, which again led the league. When he dropped to 47 steals the following year, however, Lopes didn't even make the list of the top five N.L. base stealers—a graphic indication of how quickly individual stolen base totals were climbing.

Lopes was atypical of most 1970s base stealers. Instead of having just a few good years and then fading quickly, Lopes remained a prolific base thief throughout his 16 year career. Although he never again led the league, from 1977 to 1979 he averaged 45 steals per year. He then averaged 23 steals from 1980 through 1983, even though he was creeping up on 40 years old.

Then, in defiance of Father Time, at age 40 Lopes swiped 47 in just 99 games in 1985 with the Chicago Cubs. The next year he stole 25 more bases. When he retired in 1987, Lopes had accumulated 557 total steals.

By 1975, stealing and aggressive baserunning had become so widespread throughout baseball that it spawned a new innovation: the designated runner. That year, the Class A Midwest League became the first circuit in professional baseball to institute the designated runner (DR) for an entire season. According to the rule, the manager had to name the DR on his lineup card prior to the game. Once the contest started, the DR couldn't be used more than three times in one game and not more than once per inning, except as a substitute for the same player. Any player for whom the DR substituted remained in the game.

The DR was the ultimate baseball specialist: he could neither bat nor play the field. He could, however, be replaced if injured. Unfortunately, he could not replace himself if the entire DR experiment failed—which it did. The DR never made it out of the Midwest League.

The DR was the ultimate manifestation of the creature that Charles O. Finley of the Oakland A's had cobbled together the previous year, when he had tried, with baling wire, spit and glue, to turn world-class sprinter Herb Washington into major league baseball's first full-time pinch runner.

Of everything that happened during the Stealin' Seventies, nothing personifies baseball's emphasis on speed more than Washington. There were two weeks remaining in spring training in 1974 when Finley unveiled his latest creation. "It is my personal opinion that Herb Washington will be directly responsible for winning at least 10 games during the season," said Finley at a press conference announcing the signing of Washington.

This wasn't the first time that Charlie O. had sought to feed his need for speed. A few years earlier he had signed the so-called Panamanian Express, Allan Lewis, with the same hope that Lewis' flying feet would win ball games. Unfortunately, Lewis' penchant for doing things such as trying to score from second without touching third doomed that experiment to failure.

Lewis, however, was more like a real player in that he hit and played the outfield (without great success in either case). Washington, however, was simply meant to run. With almost no knowledge of baseball, that was all he *could* do on the diamond.

Washington remained with the A's throughout the entire 1974 campaign, including the post-season, which culminated with the team winning their third straight World Series. Overall, he appeared in 92 games, stole 29 bases, and scored 29 runs. He was also caught stealing 16 times. He neither batted nor played the field.

As far as personally winning 10 games, however, Washington didn't come close to Finley's prediction. Even A's skipper Alvin Dark had to admit that the best Washington had done was "help" win eight games during the season, which is like saying the bullpen catcher "helped" win some games by warming up the right relief pitcher.

Washington was the ultimate baseball charity case; since he never attempted to steal third or home, all he could do was reach second base and wait for assistance before coming home. Several times he was caught stealing in critical situations, and several other times he didn't try to steal when he was inserted into the game for that purpose, which pretty much defeated the idea of the entire experiment.

In the postseason the experiment turned truly ugly. In the divisional championship against the Orioles Washington was caught both times he tried to steal. His tribulations against Mike Marshall in the World Series were recounted in the first chapter of this book.

Obviously needing to put more effort into learning the game, Washington showed where his heart lay by passing up an opportunity to play fall or winter ball in 1974 and instead pursuing his track career. When he returned to the A's for the 1975 season everyone seemed to realize that the great experiment was a failure. In just 13 games for Oakland he stole two bases. Then Herb Washington left baseball.

Base stealing, however, continued hot and heavy even without Charlie O.'s designated runner. By the mid–1970s stealing was becoming so prevalent that, according to Davey Lopes, desperate defenses were using a new trick to slow down speedsters: the friendly first baseman. It seemed that whenever Lopes got on, the first baseman would attempt to engage him in animated conversation. All of this was done, said Lopes, with the intention of disrupting the base thief's concentration: "A base runner who wants to be successful can't be side-tracked even for a split second. Concentration is [the] next most important item [for a base stealer]. This often explains why runners are more successful some days than they are others. Certain times you come to the park with other things on your mind and you tend to daydream. You aren't going to be effective those times."

Dick Allen, who was accused of a lot of things in his time but never of being loquacious, was apparently one of the worst offenders in this regard.

"He would inquire about everything," Lopes said. "When I took my lead, he even would ask, 'Are you going on this pitch?'"

One day, Allen was chatting away with Lopes when Davey abruptly took off and swiped second. The next time Lopes got on, Allen turned to him and said, "Don't ever leave me in the middle of a conversation again."

In 1976, in the midst of the great Bicentennial explosion of stolen bases, Leonard Koppett asked six big league managers why stealing had returned in such force to the majors. Some of their answers were to be expected, such as the emergence of bigger ball parks, along with more players emphasizing speed as part of their game. But the skippers also came up with two other interesting reasons to explain the stolen base stampede. The first was that expansion had diluted not only the pitching, but the catching as well. Thus the number of good catchers who could keep base stealers at bay was at a minimum. The second reason was that most young pitchers received little or no training in how to hold runners on, and base stealers were taking advantage of them.

Two runners who did indeed take advantage of pitchers were both members of the Pittsburgh Pirates' famed "Lightning and Lumber Company." The lumber was often supplied by power-hitting first baseman Willie Stargell; the other part of the equation came from two speedsters at shortstop and in the outfield named Frank Taveras and Omar Moreno. Together, the trio made the Pirates a formidable team in the mid-to-late 1970s.

Both Taveras and Moreno epitomized the majority of base stealers in the 1970s. They exploded onto the scene, quickly piled up scores of steals, and then faded away.

But while Taveras and Moreno burned on the bases, they burned brightly. In May of 1977, Johnny Bench complained of having to face the Pirates' jackrabbits. "I remember when you didn't have to warm up before you went out against the Pirates," he said wistfully. "They've stolen more bases so far this year than they used to steal in a season."

Bench was right. In 1973, the Pirates played as if they had shackles around their ankles, stealing just 23 bases the entire season. But just four years later, when Bench made his remarks, Pittsburgh had swiped more than 50 bases in 24 games, and were on their way to a league-leading 260 steals.

Both of the Bucs' base bandits seemed to come out of nowhere.

Taveras, for instance, suddenly shot to prominence in 1976 with 58 steals, after swiping just 30 total bases in his previous two seasons with Pittsburgh. In 1977 the shortstop hit his peak, stealing 70 bases to lead the league. After that his stolen bases declined each season, until he retired in 1982 after a part-time role with Montreal yielded just a .161 batting average and 4 steals.

For pure speed, however, few players in the late 1970s could touch Omar Moreno. The Panamanian-born outfielder was the perfect artificial turf ballplayer; possessing little power (he never slugged above .382 in his career), all Moreno had to do was slap the ball onto the carpet and then run like hell.

Few base stealers in the history of the game had as much promise as the lightning-quick Moreno, who averaged 74 steals from 1977 to 1980 and seemed almost certain to break Brock's single season record of 118 once he completely learned his craft. In 1977, his first full season, Moreno stole 53 bases. He followed that up with years of 71 and 77 steals, both of which led the league.

In 1980 he reached his peak, stealing 96 sacks (which, ironically, did *not* lead the league, thanks to Ron LeFlore's 97 steals with Montreal). Just like Tommy Harper in 1969, Moreno stole bushels of bases without the benefit of a strong year at the plate; his 96 steals came on just 168 base hits in 676 at bats, and a .249 batting average overall. Who knows how many more bases he could have stolen with a few dozen more hits?

In those puny batting numbers was the key to Moreno's swift demise as both a ballplayer and a base stealer. When he listened to Bucs hitting instructor Harry "the Hat" Walker and chopped the ball onto the ground, Moreno was able to use both the artificial surface and his speed to greatest advantage. All too often, however, Moreno tried to act more like Reggie Jackson than Ty Cobb, and swung from the heels rather than going for the base hit. As a result, he struck out over 100 times in 6 of his 12 big league seasons. In the process, he acquired the nickname of "Omar the Outmaker."

As Moreno's hitting declined, so did his stolen base totals. From 96 steals he dropped to 39 the following year, rallied briefly to swipe 60 sacks in 1982, and then really hit bottom. He left Pittsburgh as a free agent after the 1982 season and, without the benefit of the artificial surface, became just a journeyman player, the years of glory gone. After stealing just 17 bases and hitting .234 for Atlanta in 1986 Moreno called it quits. Over the course of his career, Moreno stole 487 bases, but, as with Harper, there was always the feeling that his potential as a base stealer remained largely untapped.

Not to be outdone, the American League also had some players in the 1970s who burned up the base paths for a few years, only to flame out far too early. The most prominent of these was the Detroit Tigers' Ron LeFlore.

At one point LeFlore was considered the fastest man in baseball—high praise in an era when baseball was filled with more roadrunners than a Warner Bros. cartoon. On the base paths, the muscular, solid outfielder was an absolute blur; he stole 294 bases in just six seasons with the Tigers.

LeFlore's life was the stuff of Hollywood, and indeed, eventually it was the subject of both a book and a movie. In April 1970, after being convicted of assault with intent to commit armed robbery, he was sent to the State Prison of Southern Michigan in Jackson for a term of five to fifteen years. One year later, while in prison, he played baseball for the first time. Two years later, he was working out for Detroit Tiger manager Billy Martin and other team officials. Just about 12 months after the workout, he became the Tigers' starting center fielder. Few more remarkable journeys have been made in the history of sports.

As he admitted in his book *Breakout*, LeFlore was a raw, fundamentally barren player when he first came up to the Tigers, unable to hit a breaking ball and turning even routine fly balls into adventures. Yet one thing that never failed him was his breakneck speed. In 59 games for the Tigers in 1974, LeFlore batted .260 and stole 23 bases.

For the Tigers, this was tantamount to the second coming of Ty Cobb. In 1972, the Tigers had been more like snails, stealing just 17 bases for the entire season. The following year was an improvement—although not much of one—as the aging team wheezed its way to a whopping 28 steals. Unschooled as he was, LeFlore's speed brought a much-needed new dimension to the Tigers.

Realizing that his speed was the one thing that would not

abandon him, LeFlore worked to make himself a better base runner. He enlisted both Maury Wills and Lou Brock to help sharpen his base stealing skills. Brock was particularly helpful, telling LeFlore to watch each pitcher until he discovered which part of the hurler's body moved first when he began to throw to the plate. During a game LeFlore tried it and stole a base. He was still patting himself on the back about how much he was learning when he was picked off second base.

LeFlore worked hard at both his running and his hitting. Unlike some of the other Punch-and-Judy hitter-base stealers of the decade, LeFlore became a solid batter. He consistently hit near or over the .300 mark with Detroit, fashioning hitting streaks of 30 and 27 games. His base stealing also improved dramatically. He swiped 58 bags in 1976, and 68 two years later to lead the league.

LeFlore never took a big lead, preferring instead to use his muscular body like a bulldozer to sweep infielders out of his path. "Nobody can intimidate me, but I can intimidate them," he said. "I'm stocky and I run hard. I don't do no fancy hook slides. I make a ruckus."

Then, in 1979, after hitting .300 and stealing 78 bases (second in the league to Willie Wilson of Kansas City), the Tigers unexpectedly traded LeFlore to Montreal. Seventeen years later, in a 1996 article in *The Detroit News*, the outfielder was still bitter about the deal. "I've never had it explained," he said. "Supposedly, it was because I was going to be a free agent. I guess Sparky [Tigers manager Sparky Anderson] didn't like my personality. He had a strong personality. I had a strong personality."

Although he swiped a career-best 97 bases in 1980 for the Expos to lead the National League, LeFlore's batting average dropped to .257. The following year he was traded to the Chicago White Sox, but instead of leading to a new beginning the deal turned out to be the end for this player whose inspirational story had stirred millions. With the White Sox, LeFlore became a part-time player; his batting average dropped, and his overall performance suffered. After stealing just 36 and 28 bases in 1981 and 1982, LeFlore retired. He stole 455 bases in his brief, nine year career—an average of 50 per season. Again, as with Moreno, one has to wonder how many stolen base records LeFlore would have set if his full potential had been realized.

No discussion of 1970s base stealers would be complete without mentioning perhaps the most unusual thief of them all: Mickey Rivers. Dubbed "Mick the Quick" for his blazing speed, Rivers probably burned out the quickest of all the comets that streaked across the baseball sky in the Stealin' Seventies.

Although he began with the California Angels in 1970, Rivers didn't have his first big year in steals until 1974, when he swiped 30. The following year, however, Rivers and the entire Angels squad ran as if something were chasing them. The team stole 220 bases, the most in the American League, with Rivers leading the way with a league-high 70. The Angels became the first team to steal 200 or more bases in a season since the 1918 Pittsburgh Pirates.

Like Yogi Berra, Rivers was a master of the malapropism, and his off-handed remarks often kept his teammates in stitches. Once, when discussing his goals for an upcoming season, he said he'd "like to hit .300, score 100 runs and stay injury-prone." Another time, when teammate Reggie Jackson said that he had an I.Q. of 160, Rivers responded, "Out of what, 1,000?" He also led the league in pinning unusual nicknames on people; two of his favorites were "Gozzlehead" and "Warplehead."

The year following his 70 steals (1976) found Rivers playing for the Yankees. Although he was an important part of the team's three straight pennants and two world championships (1976–1978), his base stealing magic vanished almost overnight. He stole 43, 22, and 25 bases over the next three years, disappointing totals for someone with his speed and ability. By 1979, when he was shipped to Texas, "Mick the Quick" was barely a base stealing threat.

But this was the way of base stealing in the 1970s: an unknown player would suddenly and dramatically steal a ton of bases, receive a tidal wave of publicity that anointed him as the "next" Cobb, Brock, or Wills, and then fade from the scene almost overnight, only to be replaced by the new "next" Cobb, Brock or Wills.

Ron LeFlore hit on part of the problem with many of the flash-in-the-pan base stealers once, when discussing stealing. "A lot of guys steal on raw speed alone," LeFlore pointed out. "You can't do that all the time. Guys come into the league, and no one knows them, and they're really running fast. Then the pitchers get to know them, and they can't get those good jumps anymore. You've got to work at it. You've got to be a good reader of pitchers. You've got to know which situations to run in."

As the 1970s gave way to the next decade, most people believed it more and more unlikely that there would ever be another base stealer on the magnitude of a Brock, Cobb or Wills. Speed and base stealing were too entrenched, too much a part of the game, for any single player to stay atop the throne as King of Thieves for too long. Most people, however, hadn't reckoned with a young man out in Oakland named Rickey Henderson.

10

Speed Demons of the 1980s

By 1980, stealing was once again an important part of the offensive strategy of many teams. In the aftermath of the Stealin' Seventies, baseball abounded in jackrabbit base stealers; virtually every team had at least one speed specialist, whose job was to get on base, steal, and disrupt the defense. Baseball, it seemed, had learned its lesson: after leaving stealing behind to dally with the home run floozie, the game had realized its mistake and come running back to the stolen base with open arms. The result was a more wide-open, exciting, multi-dimensional game.

Simply because there were so many fleet players, it seemed unlikely that anyone would ever again dominate either league in stolen bases, in the manner of a Cobb, Aparicio, or Brock. The competition was just too difficult. Then along came Rickey Henderson, and that theory was quickly abandoned.

The 1980s brought many changes. On the plus side, the Philadelphia Phillies finally won the first world championship in that organization's long, frustration-filled history, beating the Kansas City Royals in the 1980 World Series. While stars of the 1970s, such as Pete Rose and Nolan Ryan, remained stars in the new decade, new players, led by the Dodgers' electrifying pitcher Fernando Valenzuela, continued the perpetual renewing process that is the very lifeblood of baseball.

In a negative vein, the 1980s were a time of strife and stress in the national pastime, a decade when words like "strike" took on an entirely different meaning, and "substance abuse" became as associated with baseball as runs, hits and errors. As a result the game suffered, getting hit hard in the one place in which it had been strong for years: its image.

On the diamond, for many teams, the 1980s were merely a continuation of the 1970s; running and stealing remained a primary part of their offense. As managers sought more ways to utilize their team's speed, plays like the run-and-hit, double steal, and suicide squeeze became more prevalent. Rube Foster would have been proud.

While the frequency of stealing remained high in both leagues, the 1980s brought a return of N.L. base stealing dominance. Unlike the 1970s, when both leagues had run at virtually the same pace, in the 1980s it was no contest: N.L. players stole more bases than their A.L. counterparts every year of the decade but the last, when the American League squeaked out a 58 base advantage.

What makes the discrepancy in steals between the two leagues surprising is that throughout the 1980s, the National League operated with 12 teams, while the American League had 14. (The American League added Toronto and Seattle in 1977.) But even with two fewer teams, the N.L.'s margin of victory over the American League in stolen bases was often as high as several hundred per season.

The 1980s also brought to a sudden halt the idea that stealing was a prerequisite for winning baseball. Whereas the N.L. team that led the league in steals finished first or second in its division every year during the '70s, in the '80s it was a far different story: the leader in steals finished first in the division just three years (1982, 1985, 1987). Each time it was the St. Louis Cardinals, who had succeeded the Cincinnati Reds as the prototypical synthetic surface team.

In the American League the bond between stealing and winning baseball was virtually nonexistent; the team leading the circuit in thefts finished first in their division just once (the 1980 Kansas City Royals).

Quite possibly the fact that stealing and winning baseball were no longer synonymous reflects how widespread the stolen base had become by this time. No longer a shocking or surprising tactic, stealing was by the 1980s an accepted tactic. Teams stole early and often, and even the most lead-footed clubs compiled yearly theft totals in the 60s, 70s and 80s. Thus, since almost every team was stealing to some degree, it was no longer the hallmark solely of winning clubs.

As previously noted, the 1970s were a time when base stealers burst onto the scene with white-hot intensity, only to flame out after a few years. Most fans might have thought that the same pattern would continue in the 1980s; teams were still recruiting speed demons, and it seemed as if there were always young, fast, base stealing phenoms to replace those who had faded away.

Initially, some people might have put Rickey Henderson in that category. The Oakland A's outfielder electrified the baseball world in 1980 by stealing 100 bases in his first full season. At the tender age of 22, Henderson obviously had the potential to become one of the greatest base stealers of all time. But it takes more than potential and speed to be a great base stealer. As Tommy Harper once noted in *Sports Illustrated:* "99.99 percent of base stealers lose their desire to be great base stealers after a while. They're different from hitters. They tire of every part of their body hurting every day."

This was what baseball fans had to be wondering about Henderson after his sensational 1980 season: Did he have the *desire* to become a great base stealer? By the time the 1980s were over, there was no doubt about Rickey Henderson's desire.

Blessed with extraordinary speed, Henderson learned in the minor leagues how to harness his gift. In his book *Off Base: Confessions of a Thief,* he credited Tom Trebelhorn, his manager with two minor league teams (and who later managed the A.L.'s Milwaukee Brewers) with teaching him how to steal.

"Treb taught me so much about stealing," Henderson said. "He used to drag me out to the park at one o'clock before night games just to teach me how to steal bases. He'd stand on the mound and imitate the pitcher, giving me every move in the book."

The combination of Trebelhorn and Henderson was the perfect marriage of a good teacher and a willing student. Proving himself to be a quick study, Henderson swiped 95 bases in 1977 while with Modesto to lead the California League in his first full year in professional ball. He also tied a record by stealing seven bases in one game. His speed was such a crowd-pleaser that the club arranged for him to run against a racehorse as a publicity gimmick. (Henderson lost by a stride.)

Henderson's electrifying minor league performance quickly caught the attention of the parent club in Oakland. Although the A's of the late 1970s were just a few years removed from winning five straight division championships and three World Series, they were a completely different team. Free agent defections exacerbated by owner Charlie Finley's penny-pinching had deprived the club of its blue chip talent. The A's lost more than 90 games from 1977 to 1979, and the fans responded by avoiding the ballpark. Attendance plummeted from over 1 million in 1975 to slightly more than 300,000 in 1979. Faced with a sea of empty seats, there was no way the A's were going to let an exciting young player like Henderson languish in the minors too long. Sure enough, after another strong season in 1978, he was called up to the A's on June 23, 1979.

In his first game, Henderson went 2–4 and also, appropriately enough, stole a base. Altogether, he played in 89 games for the A's, hitting .274 and leading the club with 33 steals. That year, the Royals' Willie Wilson led the American League with 83 stolen bases, beating out Detroit's Ron LeFlore by five. Henderson's 33 steals did not even rank among the top five in the league. With all the running going on, baseball fans might well have overlooked a young outfielder who swiped "only" 33 bases for a last place team.

But in 1980, it was impossible to overlook Rickey Henderson. The speedy youngster stole an incredible 100 bases, shattering Ty Cobb's American League record of 96. Henderson became the first American League player, and just the third in baseball history (after Wills and Brock), to reach the century mark in steals. Although just a young man, Henderson was already in elite company.

Rickey's partner in crime was Oakland manager Billy Martin. Although he didn't give Henderson an automatic green light, Martin helped his speedy outfielder by astutely picking the proper pitches—more often than not a breaking ball—for him to run on. Martin's uncanny ability to decipher when an off-speed pitch was coming and Henderson's raw speed made an unbeatable combination.

In Henderson, Martin had finally found the speedy, base-stealing machine that he had always wanted, an instinctive player who understood baseball's subtle nuances and could wreak havoc on the other team by his mere presence on the bases. Martin poured all of his formidable base stealing knowledge into the eager young outfielder. "He taught me how to read a pitcher, to get as far away from the base as I could," Henderson remembered in the Martin biography *The Last Yankee*. "He taught me how to go on a pitcher's windup, the point where he reaches the top of his stretch, before he comes set, tells you when you can go—people don't normally think of that, it's much too risky, but you can see it if you study them enough. Billy at first made me take the sign from him, but then he said, 'When you catch on to what I'm doing, then I'm going to turn it over to you and you'll have the green light.' That's what he did."

Martin turned Henderson loose on the bases, in part, because he knew that his young A's team wasn't a powerhouse; they were feisty and scrappy, with lots of speed and good starting pitching, but had little power and virtually no bullpen. Always a proponent of aggressive baseball, it was hardly a leap of faith for Martin to unleash his greyhound outfielder in an effort to win. "Billy knew the team wasn't loaded, so he tried everything to win games," Henderson said.

Martin worked with the other A's as well. He taught them all of his base stealing tricks, such as the advantage of stealing on a 3–0 count (it often draws a surprised and wild throw from the catcher). He showed them how to pull off an almost guaranteed steal of home with runners on first and third, in which the man on first breaks as if trying to steal second, then falls. If the runner falls close enough to the first baseman so that he instinctively applies the tag, but just far enough away so that the fielder has to stretch out while doing so, the first baseman can't recover in time to make an accurate throw home to get the lead runner.

Martin's work paid off handsomely. The A's, who finished last in 1979 with a miserable 54–108 record, bounced all the way up to second in the A.L. West in 1980 with a mark of 83–79. The team stole 175 bases to rank second behind Kansas City's 185. The A's remarkable resurgence and Henderson's landmark 100 steals brought the fans flocking back to Oakland. Attendance surged up to 842,259 in 1980.

But Henderson wasn't the only one burning up the bases in 1980. That year, National League players stole 1,839 bases. There was so much stealing in the Senior Circuit that the 96 steals recorded by Pittsburgh's Omar Moreno didn't even lead the league! That honor went to former Detroit outfielder Ron LeFlore, who paced the National League with 97 thefts in his first (and only) year in Montreal.

American League runners, while a bit less active with 1,455 steals, still had the game's leading thief in Henderson, plus a pretty good runner-up in Willie Wilson, who swiped 79 bases to rank second.

Overall in 1980, just 2 out of the 12 N.L. teams failed to steal 100 bases, and one of them, the Chicago Cubs, came close with 93 steals. In the American League, 6 of the 14 teams stole 100 bases, and two others swiped 90 or more. Baseball was indeed on the move in 1980.

The following year, however, that movement screeched to a grinding halt on June 12, when the players' union went out on strike. By the time baseball resumed almost two months later, 714 games had been lost. To try and restore some semblance of order and continuity, baseball instituted a split-season schedule.

Continuing their journey back to respectability under Martin, the A's won the first half in the A.L. West. In the post-season, they defeated the second-half winners the Royals in the inter-divisional series before succumbing to the New York Yankees in the league championship series. Henderson stole 56 bases in 108 games to lead the American League for the second year in a row.

But 1981 was significant for Henderson for another reason. After a game between the A's and Red Sox, Lou Brock came into the Oakland clubhouse to talk to the outfielder. According to Henderson, baseball's recently retired, all-time leading base stealer told him that if anyone was going to break his record, it would be Rickey.

"At the time I didn't know if I believed him," said Henderson. "I didn't doubt myself, but it was such a monumental task. But just like that, I had a goal. Just like that, I saw it was possible."

Intrigued, Henderson spent three days with Brock in St. Louis during the off-season, getting a crash course in the finer points of base stealing. One of the lessons that the wise old master taught his willing pupil was the value of confidence. "One thing we talked about was that you can have no fear of failure if you're going to steal a lot of bases," Brock later revealed. "You have to have a certain arrogance. You have to have utter confidence. You've got to figure that you'll steal four out of five times. And if they catch you, well, then they owe you four."

Henderson pondered Brock's words throughout the winter. Then, on the first day of spring training in 1982, Martin added fuel to the competitive fire already raging inside of his outfielder. "Rickey, we're going to break the record this year," Martin said, and Henderson immediately knew that he meant Brock's single season mark of 118 stolen bases. To show his confidence in Henderson, Martin loosened the reins somewhat by letting him run more on his own, although he still didn't give Rickey an automatic green light.

However, Henderson soon proved that he didn't need one. He burst from the starting gate in 1982 like Man O' War coming down the stretch, swiping 22 bases in April and another 27 in May. Stealing 49 bases in two months is like swimming the English Channel in one hour; it's bound to attract the attention of the sporting world. Before long, speculation was rampant about whether the Oakland speedster could break Brock's record.

Henderson did nothing to cool the feverish excitement. He continued stealing at a dizzying clip, roaring through the months like a runaway train. On August 2, he notched number 100, and there was no need for speculation any longer. With two months left in the season, it was obvious that Brock's mark was going to fall.

But while Henderson was running wild on the bases, his team was sinking in the standings. Martin's magic was gone; a sore-armed pitching staff and a lack of timely hitting doomed the A's hopes, and they were never a factor in the pennant race. Henderson's race for the record was all Oakland fans had to cheer about that year. Even though the team finished fifth, nearly two million fans flocked to the park to see Rickey, setting an Oakland attendance record in the process.

Unfortunately, despite extraordinary machinations by Martin (described in chapter one), the hometown fans did not get to see Henderson break the record. Late in August, the team departed on a road trip with Henderson one shy of tying the mark. On August 26,

1982, he tied Brock in Milwaukee. The following night, he swiped number 119 against the Brewers.

Once again, just as with Wills and then Brock, a base stealing mark that many had thought would survive for decades had been easily eclipsed. With baseball's renewed emphasis on stealing, it seemed as if stolen base records were being made only to be broken. Cobb's single season mark had stood for 47 years, Wills' record for 12 years, and Brock's mark for just 8. No matter how many bases Henderson stole that year, it didn't seem like it would be enough to keep the record safe.

Not that Henderson didn't try to put the record out of reach. At the end of the season, the Oakland outfielder had racked up 130 stolen bases, or just a little less than one steal for each of the 149 games in which he played. Maybe it wasn't an ironclad guarantee that the record would survive for some time, but it was the next best thing. Henderson's spring training quest had been fulfilled in grand style. (He also set another record by being caught stealing 42 times.)

In 1983, Henderson once again cracked the century mark in steals, racking up 108. The A's, however, continued to flounder, despite new manager Steve Boros. (Martin had left to take another seat on George Steinbrenner's managerial merry-go-round in New York.) In 1984 Henderson's 66 steals led the league for the fifth straight year, but the A's remained a sub-par team.

In 1985 Henderson was traded to the New York Yankees. For the Bronx Bombers, this was their second attempt to add speed to their lineup in the 1980s. In 1982, the usually lumbering Yankees added swift outfielders Ken Griffey and Dave Collins to the mix, and decreed that the new game in the Bronx would be speed, speed, and more speed. Unfortunately, they neglected to mention that another new game would be managers, managers, and more managers. At season's end, the Yanks had gone through three managers, had stolen a mere 69 bases to finish ninth in the league in steals (as compared to 47 in 57 fewer games the previous year), and wound up a dismal 16 games out of first place.

With Henderson they had the real deal as far as speed was concerned, and he immediately paid dividends. In his first season in pinstripes, not only did Henderson lead the league in stolen bases with

80, but he also smacked 24 home runs to become the first "20–50" player in baseball history. As an added bonus, Henderson's steals helped the historically ponderous Yankees lead the league in stolen bases for the first time since 1938.

But while this was a promising beginning for his Yankee career, Henderson's four and one-half years in New York were bittersweet. While arguably the most exciting player on a team packed with stars such as Dave Winfield and Don Mattingly, Henderson was sometimes condemned for "dogging it" and for making too much out of small injuries.

In 1987, Henderson came under intense criticism when he remained out for a long time with what was first thought to be just a sprain, but was later diagnosed as a torn hamstring. As the Yankees spiraled out of first place without him, Henderson was again accused of babying minor aches and pains. The atmosphere between Yankee management and Henderson became permanently poisoned. Because of this injury, Henderson failed to lead the American League in steals for the first time in eight years.

In 1988 Henderson bounced back to have another stellar year, hitting .305 with 93 steals. But his comeback in stolen bases was forced to take a back seat to the Jose Canseco show that played all year in Henderson's old stomping grounds of Oakland. Canseco, a slugger who had shown flashes of speed, put it all together in 1988 when he hit 42 home runs and stole 40 bases to become baseball's first "40–40" player. Although Henderson's 93 steals were more than double his nearest competitor (Detroit's Gary Pettis), the eyes of baseball were focused on Canseco and his quest for 40 steals.

Ironically, when Canseco casually announced in spring training that his 1988 goals included 40 homers and 40 steals, he didn't realize that he was citing a feat unprecedented in baseball history. "I figured five or six players must have done it," he said.

No way, Jose; the closest anyone had ever come to "40–40" was Bobby Bonds, who stole 43 bases and hit 39 homers in 1973 for the Giants. For Canseco, a player with just 31 steals to his credit in a little over two seasons of major league ball, to announce that he was going to be the charter member of the 40–40 club was like Eddie Arcaro saying that he was going to outdunk Wilt Chamberlain.

Undaunted, Canseco doggedly pursued his goal throughout the season, and by September the impossible dream was within reach. On September 18 he hit his fortieth home run against Kansas City Royals ace Bret Saberhagen to achieve half of his objective. The stolen base mark, however, proved more elusive, and as the season wound down to a handful of games, he was still several steals short.

(Watching all the hoopla over Canseco's attempt at 40–40, Mickey Mantle cracked, "If I'd known it was going to be such a big deal, I'd have done it a long time ago.")

Finally, on September 23 against the Milwaukee Brewers, Canseco stole numbers 39 and 40, and the record was his. The last base, however, didn't come without a fight. With one steal already to his credit, Canseco bunted for a base hit in the fifth inning. As the crowd urged him on, Canseco decided to steal on the first pitch to the plate. But, when the opportunity came, the pressure stopped him in his tracks.

"I thought, 'Steal, steal, steal,'" Canseco later said. "And my legs just froze." Fortunately, on the next pitch Canseco calmed himself down, convinced his legs to obey, and thus entered the record book as the sole member of the "40–40" club.

Afterwards, A's coach Bob Watson told Canseco that people were going to expect him to play at that exalted level every year.

"No problem," said the confident Canseco, and he wasn't the only one who felt that way. There were those who considered him a prime candidate to become the first 50–50 player in the game.

But Canseco had spoken too soon. The following year, injuries limited him to just 65 games, in which he hit 17 homers and stole just 6 bases. While his numbers rebounded in subsequent seasons, he never again approached his 1988 performance, and his superstar status diminished over the years.

Rickey Henderson's star, however, has continued to shine brightly. Traded back to Oakland midway through the 1989 season, Henderson showed that there was still plenty of life left in his legs. In May 1990, he broke Ty Cobb's A.L. record for most lifetime steals. That year, after a monster season in which he hit .325 with 28 homers and 65 stolen bases, he was named the A.L.'s Most Valuable Player.

Henderson has always played well when the spotlight is on him, which is why his post-season performances have always been superb. He almost single-handedly defeated the Toronto Blue Jays in the 1989 American League Championship Series, hitting .400 with two home runs, eight runs scored and eight stolen bases. In both the 1989 and 1990 World Series he put on superb offensive exhibitions, hitting and stealing with abandon.

The pinnacle of Henderson's career came on May 1, 1991, when he broke another of Lou Brock's records by stealing his 939th base to become the game's all-time stolen base leader. Fittingly, it came against the Yankees, whom Henderson dearly wanted to pay back for what he considered their mistreatment of him. "I knew it would be a nice present for George Steinbrenner if I could steal the big base against my old team," he wrote, tongue firmly in cheek.

The road to that record-shattering steal had been rocky for Henderson. Although he began 1991 just two behind Brock, Henderson stole only one base before landing on the disabled list with a thigh injury. All the hoopla that had been planned to celebrate the big event was put on hold, and Brock, who had been following Henderson from city to city so as to be present for the big event, went home.

Ultimately Henderson recovered, Brock came back, and the stage was set for baseball history—as well as controversy.

Shyness has never been one of Henderson's flaws. For instance, as he closed in on Brock's record, Henderson printed a stack of souvenir certificates showing a superimposed photograph of himself and Brock stealing a base together. The certificate read, "I was there when Rickey Henderson broke Lou Brock's all-time stolen base record of 938 with steal number 939."

But the real problems erupted after Henderson had stolen the historic base. At the close of a short speech he made on the field after the milestone steal, Henderson said: "Lou Brock was the symbol of great base stealing. But today, I'm the greatest of all time."

A wave of negative publicity engulfed Henderson for that comment, particularly after Nolan Ryan also made baseball history later that same day by throwing his seventh no-hitter. With the media focused squarely on both men, people couldn't help but compare the soft-spoken, modest Ryan with the outspoken, cocky Henderson. It was a comparison in which the A's outfielder came out a poor second.

Yet in fairness, Henderson's closing remark was taken out of context. His entire speech was far more generous. He thanked numerous people, including the Haas family (owners of the Oakland A's) and the fans and city of Oakland. He also paid tribute to the late Billy Martin, calling him "a great friend." But in today's sound-bite world, the only portion of the speech that made the evening news was "I'm the greatest."

Henderson, however, didn't seem bothered in the least by the uproar his remark caused. He makes no excuses for his attitude. He has always done things his way, and this has been good enough not only to make him the best base stealer in baseball history, but to bring him a host of other records and honors as well. Rickey is going to be Rickey, and if people don't like it, well, too bad. He made this quite clear in his book, when he noted how some people wanted him to be more humble when he broke Brock's lifetime steals record: "I guess I should have faked it, broken down in tears and told the world how modest I actually am. Well, that ain't me."

It sure isn't. But yet, without that cockiness, Henderson might never have attained all that he has in baseball. He is the baddest base thief on the planet, and he walks with the confidence that that knowledge brings. It is the same arrogance so vital to a champion base stealer that Lou Brock often spoke about, only packaged and displayed in a different manner. Yet the result, be it Brock or Henderson, is the same: a supremely talented, once-in-a lifetime baseball player who has left an indelible impression on the game. "I don't care who they are [pitchers or catchers]," Henderson said, displaying some of that famous cockiness. "You better make two perfect throws or I'll get you every time."

Throughout his career Henderson has lived and died by the stolen base, and he doesn't want anyone deriding its value to a team. "People have mathematically broken down the success and failure of stolen bases," he wrote, "saying every steal equates to three-tenths of a run and every time a runner is caught he loses six-tenths of a run. That means a runner must steal more than twice as many bases as he's caught to register a positive run production. The theory might make sense mathematically, but I don't buy any of it." He went on to list the benefits of stealing that numbers don't indicate—distracting the pitcher, disrupting the infield, and moving base runners into scoring position without a hit. It is here, he feels, within these shadings of the game that never show up in a box score, that the value of stealing is truly measured.

Henderson has set his stolen base records despite his admission that he's not the fastest runner in baseball. He named Willie Wilson, Bo Jackson, Barry Bonds, Willie McGee, and Vince Coleman as players who were all faster than he was in his prime. But according to Henderson, what separated him from those players was Brock's baserunning arrogance. "All the way through time," Henderson said in *Off Base*, "it was the same thing. Cobb, Jackie Robinson, Maury Wills, Lou Brock, myself—all great base stealers have to possess a certain amount of arrogance to be successful, a me-against-the-world attitude."

Although Henderson has the same temperament as those other greats, he doesn't have the same technique. The most obvious difference is the headfirst slide, which has become a Henderson trademark. Despite widespread feeling that the headfirst slide is more dangerous, Henderson uses it because he feels that it not only protects his legs, but gets him to the bag faster. "The main thing is to get a good jump, a good start, getting a good push off on those first couple of steps," Henderson said. "You may have speed that may be only a little bit better than average, but if you get that good jump on the pitcher you'll be a successful base stealer."

Another difference between Henderson and most of the other Kings of Thievery is how they initially broke for the next base. Brock and Wills used the crossover step, which meant that their first step was their left foot crossing over their right. Henderson, however, uses the push method, meaning that his first step is with his right foot, followed by an extra-long step with his left. He credits the push step with giving him the incredible explosiveness off the base and rapid acceleration that has enabled him to rewrite the record book.

"[Rickey Henderson is] 31 years old, rich, famous, great—and he never lost the thrill of competing," Tommy Harper once noted.

Henderson is indeed competitive. When Vince Coleman first came up and was stealing 100 bases every season, Henderson's pride in his own base stealing accomplishments came bubbling to the surface through his Mr. Cool demeanor. "I wouldn't like it if Coleman or someone else breaks my record," he stated flatly.

That love of competition has kept Henderson running, even as age and injury have eroded his physical skills. In the 1990s Henderson became the epitome of the well-traveled veteran, playing with Oakland, Toronto, Oakland again, San Diego, and Anaheim, to whom he was traded late in the 1997 season.

Along the way, his stolen base totals have inevitably dropped—although they are still very respectable, especially for a player rapidly approaching age 40 whose body has undergone two decades of intense physical abuse. In 1996 with San Diego he stole 37 bases, and the following year, with the Padres and Angels, he racked up another 45 steals. At the beginning of the 1998 season, although clearly in the twilight of his career, Henderson seemed ready, willing and able to continue adding to his lifetime stolen base total of 1,186, in an effort to place the record beyond mortal reach. "I don't think my stolen base record will ever be broken," Henderson wrote in *Off Base*. "If I'm healthy and play for twenty years, then, oh man, I can guarantee nobody will ever touch my record. When I'm done playing, I hope to have at least 1,500 steals. Even if someone steals seventy bases a year for twenty years, he wouldn't match that record."

Each year that Henderson plays, he adds to that record—making it more and more unlikely that anyone will ever beat the Man of Steal at his own game.

Although Henderson has reason to be confident that his all-time stolen base record will never be approached, he must have had a few anxious moments the first time he saw Vince Coleman streaking around the bases.

In 1983, just one season after Henderson had swiped 130 bases, Coleman stole an unbelievable 145 sacks for Macon to set the all-time professional record. Two years later, Coleman exploded out of the blocks in sensational fashion in his debut season with the St. Louis Cardinals. The lightning-quick outfielder set a rookie record by stealing 110 bases, while sparking the Redbirds to the N.L. East Division Championship. Unfortunately, a freak injury suffered in the National League Championship Series against the Dodgers (an automatic tarp rolled over his leg, injuring his ankle) sidelined Coleman for the

World Series. Some blamed Coleman's absence as the reason the Cards lost to the Royals in seven games that year.

Coleman was a high-octane runner blessed with phenomenal speed. When he followed up his rookie campaign by swiping over 100 bases in the next two seasons (107 in 1986 and 109 in 1987, to become the first player ever to steal 100 bases three years in a row) it stamped him as the most legitimate challenger to Rickey Henderson ever to emerge.

But Coleman suffered the fate of many other young base stealers for whom great things had been predicted. In 1988 his stolen base total dropped to 81, followed by a further decline to 65 the following year. Still, he reached 400 steals faster than any player in history, and since he was still youthful, it seemed certain that there would an honored spot for him in the all-time stealing hall of fame.

Then in December 1990, Coleman made a serious career error by signing with the New York Mets as a free agent. Like Omar Moreno, Coleman was an ideal turf player who was much less effective on grass and dirt. Once he traded the carpeted confines of Busch Stadium for Shea Stadium's natural surface, Coleman's game declined dramatically. Dogged by injuries as well, Coleman's stolen base totals during his years with the Mets (1991–1993) were a disappointing 37, 24, and 38.

In 1994 Coleman was traded to the Kansas City Royals, and celebrated his return to a synthetic surface by stealing 50 bases to finish second in the American League to Kenny Lofton. He also tied a league record for the fewest times caught stealing with 50 or more stolen bases (eight).

Coleman had one more good season in 1995, when he swiped 42 bags while splitting time between Kansas City and Seattle. Then he became a journeyman ballplayer, drifting from one team to another. At the beginning of 1998, Coleman's career was in limbo.

Coleman entered 1998 with 752 lifetime steals, which ranked him sixth on the all-time stolen base list. He holds the record for the most consecutive stolen bases without being caught (50, from September 18, 1988, to July 26, 1989) and shares several other marks. Yet after his sensational debut in the 1980s, with three consecutive years of stealing more than 100 bases, it's difficult to believe that he has never seriously challenged Henderson's single season mark of 130, nor that he seems likely to finish among the top two or three on the all-time list.

For a time, especially in the beginning of the '80s, it seemed as if Tim "Rock" Raines was also going to threaten Henderson's record. The muscular outfielder dominated the National League in stolen bases in the early 1980s, until Vince Coleman came along. Even after this, Raines remained a consistent base-stealing threat. From 1981 until 1992, he demonstrated both his skill and durability by averaging 60 stolen bases per year.

Raines gained immediate notoriety as a rookie with the Montreal Expos in 1981. In a season cut to 88 games by the players' strike, he stole a league-leading 71 bases to set a rookie record. It was widely believed that if it hadn't been for the strike, Raines would have broken Brock's single-season stolen base record that year.

The Montreal speedster followed up his sensational first season by leading the National League in steals for the next three years in a row with totals of 78, 90 (his career high) and 75. Even when Coleman took over the top spot among N.L. base stealers, Raines continued pilfering bases at a brisk clip, swiping 70 in both 1985 and 1986.

"I love speed," said Dick Williams, Raines' manager. "Speed makes a lot of things happen. Hitters go into slumps and so do pitchers. But the great thing about speed is that you have it every day. You can count on it."

Williams could certainly count on Raines. In his prime, the outfielder was simply a blur on the bases, possessing almost unbelievable speed. Pitcher Rick Rhoden once jokingly accused him of cheating, because Raines ran the 100 in a blinding 9.2 seconds, and, Rhoden contended, "in the rules [it says] that a player is supposed to be human."

"Nobody taught me how to steal," Raines said. "I relied on speed. That's how it happened. The older I got, the better I got. I depend on a good jump and, of course, my speed. My first two steps are quick. That's the key. I study all the pitchers. I watch them stretch and try to figure out when they're going to the plate."

Interestingly enough, in his prime Raines never considered

himself strictly a base stealer. He told *Sports Illustrated* in 1986 that he was merely a "situational runner," who only stole when his team needed it. "If I went out just to steal," Raines said, in a statement that undoubtedly sent N.L. catchers scurrying for the "Help Wanted" ads, "I could steal 150 or 170 bases."

As the 1998 baseball season dawned, Raines was the all-time stolen base percentage leader among players with at least 400 attempts, safely stealing 85.1 percent of bases attempted. He also held the American League record for most consecutive steals, swiping 40 bases without getting caught between July 22, 1993, and September 9, 1995.

With all that Raines has accomplished on the bases, his stick work is sometimes overlooked, although he is an excellent hitter with flashes of power. In 1983, with 71 RBIs and 90 stolen bases, he became only the fifth player in history and first since Ty Cobb in 1915 to have 70 RBIs and 70 steals. Ten years later, when he cracked his one hundredth lifetime home run while with the White Sox, Raines became just the fourth player to have 100 homers, 100 triples, 1,000 runs scored, 2,000 hits, and 500 stolen bases. The other three members of this select club are Honus Wagner, Lou Brock and Ty Cobb.

Inevitably, age and injuries took their toll on Raines, and by the time he joined the Yankees in 1996 he was stealing just a handful of bases each season. Still, in 1998, Tim Raines stole his eight hundredth lifetime base, joining Rickey Henderson, Lou Brock, and Ty Cobb as the only players in baseball ever to have 800 steals to their credit.

Henderson, Coleman and Raines dominated stealing in the 1980s. Of course there were other excellent base bandits during the decade, like the almost unbelievably fast Willie Wilson, Willie McGee, Otis Nixon, and Paul Molitor. But it was the "feets" of the big three against which all the rest of the 1980s base stealers were measured.

By 1990, however, the advancing years and an inevitable decline in physical ability had caught up to Henderson, Raines, and Coleman. The icons of the stolen base in the 1980s were starting to slip. Would anyone assume their legacy in the 1990s?

Robinson
speaker
Simmons
Gehrig
Ruth
Frisch (R)
Cochrane
Wagner

Dorgan
Stadium
San Giant

11

Today's Game

In 1986, manager Steve Boros of the San Diego Padres said: "The science against stealing has evolved radically in the last four or five years. That has made it tougher than ever to steal. Pitchers have quicker deliveries, step off and quick pitch, hold the ball. Catchers pitch out much more often. Now you've got pitching coaches with stopwatches timing pitchers' deliveries, while other coaches are timing catchers' throws to second base."

At that time, it didn't seem as if any of what Boros was talking about was having much effect on base stealing. After all, Rickey Henderson, Tim Raines, Vince Coleman and others were running wild, base stealing records were being shattered with regularity, and it seemed as if little short of a moat and barbed wire would be able to stop them, or others like them in the future. The likelihood of new techniques by pitchers and catchers being able to clamp down on base stealers seemed very remote indeed.

However, just a few short years later, in the 1990s, Boros seemed more like a prophet than a baseball manager.

For the first time in several decades, no new base stealer *extraordinaire* emerged in the 1990s to rivet public attention on the running game, and on his own feats in particular. Although players such as Kenny Lofton, Marquis Grissom and Chuck Knoblauch all racked up impressive steal totals, no individual player personified the stolen base in the 1990s as Maury Wills had in the 1960s, Lou Brock in the 1970s, and Rickey Henderson in the 1980s. The face of base stealing, so easy to identify in previous decades, had become blurry and indistinct.

While teams still routinely swiped bases in the 1990s, stolen base totals in general were down throughout baseball, both on a team and individual basis. It was almost as if, after all the record-breaking, sensational individual efforts that had occurred in base stealing during the previous three decades, the stolen base had reached its limits. Like a rubber band, the accomplishments of Wills, Henderson, Brock and others had stretched stealing far beyond what was ever thought possible; in the '90s, the rubber band was slowly contracting and assuming a more normal shape.

Early in the decade, stealing was still dominated by players from the 1980s. In the American League, Rickey Henderson topped all runners with 65 steals in 1990 and 58 in 1991, but these numbers were well below his glory years of 90 and 100 steals. In May 1991, the spotlight fell on Henderson for the final time, when he broke Brock's record for lifetime thefts. Since then, although he has continued stealing bases, public attention has shifted away from the Man of Steal.

In the National League, Vince Coleman led all base stealers with 77 thefts in 1990, the sixth and last time he would be King of Thieves. By the following year Coleman was playing for the New York Mets and watching his career spiral into oblivion. Tim Raines, the other major base stealer in the 1980s, was also stealing less.

Early in the decade, several players emerged who initially seemed as if they were going to be the 1990s answer to Henderson, Raines, and Coleman. Subsequent events, however, would prove otherwise.

In 1992, Cleveland Indians first-year outfielder Kenny Lofton emerged as one of a new generation of base stealers by swiping 66 bases in only 78 attempts, for an incredible success ratio of 85 percent. He also shattered the A.L. rookie record for steals, which had been set at 50 by John Cangelosi of the White Sox in 1986. Lofton was the first rookie to lead the American League in steals since Luis Aparicio in 1956.

In the National League, Marquis Grissom of the Montreal Expos initially mirrored Lofton's efforts. Grissom paced the circuit in steals two years in a row, swiping 76 in 1991 and 78 the following year. Like Lofton, Grissom also seemed poised to become one of the premier theft artists of the decade.

But after this promising start, Grissom's base stealing declined. He has been with several teams in both the American League and National League since his days with Montreal and has not led either league in steals since 1992.

Various players claimed the National League stolen base title after Grissom, but no one has made fans forget Lou Brock. Indeed, in 1994, Houston's Craig Biggio led the National League in steals with just 39—an extremely low total, even taking into account the players' strike that short-circuited the season in mid–August. After all, it had not been that long ago that Rickey Henderson had 100 steals by early August.

In the American League, however, Lofton proved to be more of a throwback to baseball's recent running past. He led the American League in steals for five straight seasons (1992–1996), including a personal best 75 in 1996. The only other player to win five A.L. stolen base crowns in his first five major league seasons was Luis Aparicio.

In 1997 Lofton was traded to Atlanta; there, plagued by injuries, he stole just 27 bases. After the season ended, the fleet outfielder returned to Cleveland as a free agent for the 1998 season, and undoubtedly hoped to return to his running ways.

Yet, for all that Lofton has accomplished, his base stealing has not gripped the fans by their shirt collars and pulled their heads up in astonishment the way that the exploits of Henderson, Brock, Coleman and others did. The promise of danger, of hidden menace, of total chaos erupting at any moment, which always hovers around the great base stealers like an invisible cloud crackling with energy, seems largely to be absent in Lofton's case. Perhaps this is because the teams that Lofton has played for usually have been strong enough that they don't need him to try to create something all by himself. There's no need for him to scatter infielders like ten pins when the next batter might hit one out. Cleveland General Manager John Hart made this point prior to the 1996 season: "Kenny is a smart baserunner. He really only runs when we need it. A lot of times, we don't need him to steal bases—not with all the home-run hitters we have. I really do think that Kenny could steal 100 bases if we need him to. But on our club, it doesn't make much sense."

Maybe it's the changing nature of the game that has lessened Lofton's fear factor. Prior to the 1998 season, he had stolen 352 bases, which was more than any player in the 1990s. Yet that figure pales before those racked up just a few years before. For instance, in just three *years* in the 1980s (1985–1987), Vince Coleman stole 326 bases. It's highly likely that Lofton would have put up similar stolen base numbers if he had played in the more running-oriented 1970s or 1980s. Yet despite the fact that he has the speed and the skill, Lofton has not even come close to challenging the feats of Henderson, Coleman and others.

Maybe the problem that Lofton, or any other speed merchant who comes along in the future, has to face is that the *thrill* of stealing is gone because the *need* for stealing is gone. Brock, Henderson, Coleman, Raines, and LeFlore ran at unexpected times, not just to pump up individual statistics but to get something started. They were the catalysts; they were the ones who got their ball clubs going. Lofton and others in the 1990s run only when they need to; the kamikaze atmosphere that formerly existed with the steal is largely absent.

Despite the presence of Lofton and other excellent base stealers, stealing declined throughout the 1990s from the heady days of the 1970s and 1980s. In the National League, the total number of steals dropped from 1,787 in 1990 to 1,560 in 1992. In 1993, the league added two teams (Florida and Colorado) to bring their total up to 14, just like the American League. Even with 14 teams, however, N.L. clubs did not steal as many bases from 1993 through 1996 as they did with just 12 teams in 1990.

The stolen base fared little better in the American League during the same period. In 1995, the 14 A.L. clubs combined to swipe just 1330 bases—the lowest amount since 1984 (not counting the strike-truncated 1994 season). Although this figure bounced up by over 100 bases in 1996, the American League, like its sister league, seemed to be turning its back on the stolen base.

What has happened in the 1990s to cool down stealing throughout baseball? One explanation may be that, without the presence of a publicity-generating, base stealing "celebrity" such as Wills, Brock, or Henderson, the stolen base has simply dropped off the radar screens of some managers. Without reading about and watching one of these marquee players stealing bases and wreaking offensive havoc, it's easy to forget how much can be accomplished by the running game.

Another reason that stealing has lost some emphasis in the '90s is that the offenses of many clubs are more balanced. Throughout the twentieth century, the offensive emphasis in baseball has swung wildly between the stolen base and the home run. It's possible that in the last decade of the century, something of an equilibrium between the two has finally been reached.

Another factor mitigating the steal has been the return of the old-fashioned ballpark and grass. A backlash against the sterile, all-purpose, artificial surface stadiums of the 1970s—the very factors that breathed new life into the running game—resulted in a rebirth of ball parks with personality and natural playing surfaces, such as Baltimore's Camden Yards. The new parks have a 1920s feel, and are more attuned to the needs of hitters than of base stealers. Since fans have enthusiastically embraced these "new/old" parks, it is certain that more of them will be built in the future, and that hitters, and not base stealers, will be the ones to benefit.

Still another reason for the decline in stealing in the 1990s is a lack of good pitching. Continued expansion has watered down major league pitching so much that teams are turning to almost anyone who can throw strikes and isn't terrified at the prospect of someone like Ken Griffey, Jr. or Mark McGwire glaring at him with malice in their hearts from a mere 60 feet, 6 inches away.

In 1996 hitting reached a crescendo, as the 28 major league clubs combined to set a new record of 4,962 home runs. Not just one, but three teams—Baltimore, Seattle, and Oakland—hit more than 240 home runs to break the single-season mark set by the 1961 New York Yankees. Just as in the 1920s, when home runs surge, steals recede, although the more balanced offenses of the '90s have kept the stolen base from completely disappearing.

"Pitching has been extremely bad," said Pittsburgh pitching coach Ray Miller in 1994, talking about why stolen bases were down. "If a pitcher has nothing, you're not going to give him an out."

On the other hand, pitchers have helped their own cause against the Hendersons of the world by developing and perfecting the slide step—a method of delivering the pitch to home that is faster and quicker than normal. "I'd never heard of the slide step before 1988. Now everyone has one," said Angels second baseman Harold Reynolds in 1994. "It's tough for a base runner to get a beat on a pitcher's rhythm. You have to wait in the count, and by that time the ball has been hit."

Some players even credit the slide step with killing any chances that a base stealer will ever again reach the century mark. "The days of the 100-steal man are over," declared Otis Nixon of the Red Sox. "Sixty or seventy will lead the league."

Along with the slide step, by the mid–1990s, pitchers had also become much better at holding base runners on. Young hurlers, having grown up watching Henderson, Raines, and others make the lives of pitchers and catchers absolutely miserable, were well schooled in the art of keeping base stealers close to the bag by the time they arrived in the majors. "Every manager tells his players, if they can't hold runners on, they won't be here," Miller said in 1994. "When I came to the National League in '86, if a pitcher was slow to the plate, everyone ran." According to Miller, he watched a tape of a game from 1988 and timed the pitchers, and found that some took as long as 1.9 to 2.1 seconds to deliver the ball to the plate. The slide step has cut that down drastically, to where even 1.5 seconds is now considered slow. "Every team in the league can throw someone at you with a 1.1 or a 1.2," he said. "If a guy's that quick, why run?"

In 1995, catcher Mike LaValliere of the Chicago White Sox had another theory about the stealing slowdown. He disagreed with all the talk of slide steps, quicker deliveries to home plate, and pitchers doing a better job of holding runners on. Instead, LaValliere quipped, the base stealing drop-off resulted from catcher–shoe manufacturer collusion. "All the catchers got together in the off-season and worked a deal with the shoe companies," he said. "We had every player's spikes cut down slightly, so no one is quite as fast."

Whatever the explanation, there is no doubt that stealing has taken a downturn in the 1990s—and it doesn't seem likely that it will rebound anytime soon.

As the opening of the 1999 season neared, there was little reason to believe that stealing was going to recapture its fading popularity. No new, young speed merchants were poised to threaten Henderson's seasonal record of 130 steals and reap the publicity that would come with such an effort.

No milestones seemed likely to be reached in the lifetime steals category either. Tim Raines, whose 795 career thefts ranked fifth at the start of the 1998 season, was the only active player with even a remote chance of moving into the upper echelon on the all-time stolen base list. However, Raines is in the twilight of his career and trails Ty Cobb, who is the next player ahead of him, by nearly 100 steals. It will take an extraordinary effort by Raines to surpass Cobb.

Thus the possibility of some big, splashy event to refocus public attention on the stolen base seems slim. Does this mean that stealing is destined to sink back into the lead-footed ooze of the 1930s, 1940s, and 1950s, when players and teams ran so infrequently that pitchers practically forgot how to hold runners on and fans could go whole seasons without ever seeing the home team swipe a base?

Not likely. Small market teams that struggle to compete financially and continue to lose premium players and home run hitters in salary disputes will need to turn somewhere to generate offense. While a running game will not totally compensate for a lack of power hitting by superstars, it at least gives young, hungry players the chance to show that they belong in the big leagues. An offense based around the stolen base, the hit-and-run, and the suicide squeeze will not only pick up some of the slack caused by the absence of the home run, but will generate excitement and bring fans to the park to watch these young bucks zip around the bases.

Another thing that will help stealing survive is the extremely diverse mixture of players in baseball today. As more and more players enter the game due to expansion, it is obvious that some of them will have to steal rather than slug their way into the major leagues. Each new expansion team not only needs players for its major league club, but for its minor league affiliates as well. The more professional baseball players there are, the more likely it is that some of them will use speed and baserunning skills rather than slugging to forge a major league career.

In the end, the stolen base is too valuable a weapon, too useful a tactic, to let slip away as completely as it once did. The game suffers too much when it becomes one-dimensional. The best baseball combines all the elements that have made it great over the years: power, pitching, defense, and speed. When the game is hitting on all four of those cylinders, when each of those elements is meshing like the gears of a well-oiled machine, no other sport can match baseball for sheer excitement.

Ultimately, baseball, like all sports, thrives on the visceral thrill— the feeling of pure exultation that wells up inside us when the skills of a superb athlete are put on public display for our enjoyment. When a base runner suddenly breaks for the bag, pitting his speed and skill against the skill of the pitcher and catcher, it is one of the most thrilling and exciting plays in baseball. As we wait for the call, a thousand thoughts flash through our minds: Is the runner safe? Is he out? Has the umpire made the right call? Did he pick a good time to go? Did the fielder make a clean tag? Was the catcher's throw on the money? Could the pitcher have done more to hold the runner on? Has he taken us out of a big inning, or set us up for one? In those few seconds of heart-pounding uncertainty lie some of the best moments that baseball has to offer.

"The runner loose on the paths, daring the defense to stop him, is the most spectacular sight of all," wrote Ty Cobb in 1961. The same holds true today—and will hold true as long as baseball is played.

12

A Gallery of Thieves (and Would-Be Bandits)

There have been many notable base stealers throughout the history of baseball whose base path exploits have been by and large forgotten. What follows is a sampling of some of the greats and near-greats who thrilled crowds and helped establish stealing as the hallmark of scientific, yet aggressive, baseball.

Benny Kauff

Benny Kauff had the potential to be one of the greatest base stealers of all time. Unfortunately, potential never turned into reality.

The son of an Ohio coal miner, Kauff burst into prominence in 1914 with the Indianapolis Hoosiers of the Federal League. Just 24 years old, Kauff had a dream season, leading the league in batting average (.370), hits (211), doubles (44), stolen bases (75), runs (120), and total bases (305). The following year Kauff again led the Federal League in several offensive categories, including steals (55).

Great things were predicted for the young ball player. *Sporting Life* declared him the "premier slugger, fielder and base stealer in the league," adding that he was "being called the second Ty Cobb."

Benny Kauff seemed like a certain superstar when he joined the National League, but he never fulfilled his potential (courtesy of National Baseball Hall of Fame Library, Cooperstown, New York).

The brash Kauff did nothing to discourage this type of comparison. "I'll make Cobb look like a bush leaguer if I can play for the [New York] Giants," he boasted, during a contract dispute between the Federal and National leagues over his services.

Kauff's vainglorious preening prompted a sportswriter to write:

> Though I hate to pull the chatter,
> I admit that I'm some batter;
> If I play I'll make a sucker out of Cobb:
> I'm a one-man batting rally,
> And I knock 'em down the alley,
> I'm modest little Benny-on-the-job.

In 1916 the Federal League folded and Kauff joined the New York Giants in the National League. During the next two seasons he put up numbers that reminded no one of Ty Cobb—or even the Federal League Benny Kauff, for that matter—hitting .264 and .308 while stealing 40 and 30 bases, respectively. After an injury limited his playing time in 1918, his last full year with the Giants in 1919 resulted in a .277 average and 21 steals.

The ending of Kauff's story is a sad one. In 1920 he was arrested and indicted for being involved with car thieves. Although acquitted, Kauff was banned from baseball by new commissioner Kenesaw Mountain Landis, who was on a mission to restore the game's image.

Landis said that Kauff's presence on a baseball diamond would "burden patrons of the game with grave apprehension as to its integrity." The crusty jurist also claimed that the acquittal "smelled to the high heaven, and was one of the worst miscarriages of justice ever to come to my attention." Although Kauff sued Landis for reinstatement following his acquittal, he lost, and never played again.

Curt Welch

The man who made the legendary "$15,000 Slide" in the deciding game of the 1886 World Series was one of the premier base stealers of his era, but a passion for alcohol ended his career prematurely and sent him to an early grave.

Welch's ballplaying skills rescued him from working in a factory.

In 1883, at age 21, he played center field with Toledo in the Northwestern Association. When the franchise joined the American Association the following year, Welch found himself in the major leagues. Although his batting average was a puny .224, the base stealer was signed by the St. Louis Browns when Toledo folded after the 1884 season.

With the Browns, Welch quickly became a star. His fielding skills were legendary—supposedly he could judge the distance that a fly ball would travel by merely hearing the crack of the bat—and he led all American Association outfielders in putouts during his three seasons with St. Louis.

At the plate, although he never hit over .282, Welch was an offensive force. As well as being a superb sacrifice bunter, he was also an expert at getting hit by pitches. (In fact, Welch initially got on base in the tenth inning of the last game of the 1886 series when he was hit by a pitch. After the White Sox convinced the umpire that Welch had made no effort to get out of the way, the Browns outfielder returned to the batter's box and singled.)

Once on base, Welch used his superior speed to run wild. He averaged 56 stolen bases over seven seasons, including a career-best 95 in 1888. That year his salary was $3,300, the highest ever paid to an outfielder up to that time.

Welch was so popular with the St. Louis fans that Browns owner Chris Von der Ahe once reportedly turned down $10,000 for him. But although he could overtake fly balls, he could not outrun the debilitating effects of alcohol, which destroyed his skills and caused several teams to give up on him.

In August of 1892, now just a shadow of his former self, Welch was released by Baltimore of the National League. He joined Cincinnati, only to be suspended for "boozing." By 1896 he was dead of "consumption" at the youthful age of 34.

Clyde Milan

Nicknamed "Deerfoot" because of his speed, Washington Senators outfielder Clyde Milan had the misfortune of playing in the same era as Ty Cobb, and so today most of his base stealing exploits have been obscured by the glare of the Georgia Peach's brilliance.

Clyde Milan stole 88 bases for the Washington Senators in 1912 (courtesy of National Baseball Hall of Fame Library, Cooperstown, New York).

Milan came up to the Senators in 1907. For the first few years he showed only flashes of base stealing ability, swiping 29 bases in 1908 and just 10 the following year.

But in 1910 Milan blossomed into a legitimate stolen base threat, finishing fifth in the American League with 44 steals. After notching 58 thefts in 1911, Milan reached his zenith the following year, when he led the American League with 88 steals. In 1913 the fleet-footed Tennessean's 75 steals again paced the circuit. Although his totals fell off after that, he remained a stolen base threat until he retired in 1922 with 495 lifetime steals.

In a 1913 newspaper story, Milan attributed his vast improvement as a base stealer to finally realizing that "a fellow had to do a lot of things besides run wild to be a good base runner."

"When I broke in I thought all a man with speed had to do was get on in some way and then throw in the speed clutch," Milan said. However, he found out to his chagrin that this was not true: "I watched with disgust other players much slower than me steal with ease on the same catcher that had thrown me out."

Determined to improve, Milan began studying pitchers' movements, and uncovered a wealth of useful information. "I pay particular attention to the feet and the shoulder of the man pitching," he said. "There are few pitchers who do not give away their intentions of pitching or throwing to first by some peculiar movement."

Milan's crowd-pleasing stealing and baserunning made him one of the Senators' most popular players. In his day Milan was as well known as Cobb, but today his name has been lost amid the pages of baseball history.

Shortly before his death in 1953, the man also called "Zeb" and "Wildhog" talked about the lack of stealing in 1950s baseball: "Back when I was stealing a lot, I was always trying to beat out Cobb, Eddie Collins, Tris Speaker, Ray Chapman, Freddie Maisel and those guys every year. All were great, and we had a regular duel as we went for the records. It's different now. There's no competition. The desire just isn't there."

Pepper Martin

John Leonard Roosevelt Martin of Oklahoma was not the fastest runner in the world, nor was he the most prolific base stealer. But by stealing in an era when the stolen base was in decline, and by picking baseball's biggest stage—the World Series—to do it, he became famous as one of the leading base thieves of his day.

Pepper Martin racing helter-skelter to a base (courtesy of National Baseball Hall of Fame Library, Cooperstown, New York).

After breaking in with the St. Louis Cardinals in 1928, Martin was up and down with the parent club until 1931, when he became the regular third baseman. That year the hyperactive Martin, described as "the only man who could march at a dog trot," sparked the Cardinals to the pennant by hitting .300 and stealing 16 bases, which in those homer-happy times was good enough to rank third in the National League.

Impressive though those numbers were, Martin was just getting warmed up. In the 1931 World Series against Connie Mack's power-house Philadelphia A's, Martin was a one-man wrecking crew. He hit .500 (12 for 24), stole five bases, and scored five runs in helping the Cardinals beat the favored A's in seven games. His performance earned him the immortal nickname "The Wild Hoss of the Osage."

What was even more amazing about Martin's base stealing performance was that he did it against Mickey Cochrane, one of the great catchers in the game. Martin ran Cochrane so ragged that at one point, seeing Martin walking up to the plate yet again, the exasperated catcher said, "Don't you ever make out?"

Pepper's mastery of Cochrane was so complete that the New York Baseball Writers wrote a song parody about it later that year to the tune of "Goodbye Sweetheart":

> Goodbye Mickey, this is Pepper Martin,
> I'm on first base, soon I will be startin'.
> Down to second, I'll fly like a bird.
> Then on my word, I think I'll steal third.
> I'm sayin' goodbye Mickey, tie your glove and mask on.
> If your jock strap's loose, put another clasp on.
> The way I feel, there's nothing I won't steal,
> So goodbye Mickey, goodbye.

Martin's World Series performance was so dominating that H.I. Phillips wrote in the *New York Sun* that he had gone to Philadelphia to "see a World Series played between the A's and one John Leonard Martin of Oklahoma."

Martin led the National League in steals three times (1933, 1934 and 1936). Although he recorded just 146 steals during his career, it was more *how* he stole rather than *how many* he stole that wowed the crowd. The Wild Hoss came into a base headfirst, one hand out-stretched for the bag, sending dust everywhere as his chin plowed a furrow in the dirt. (Since he never wore a jockstrap, and sometimes didn't even wear underwear, his chin wasn't the only thing that sometimes plowed the dirt.)

"He ran the bases in a manner so heedless of his physical safety," said one writer, "that he had the fans screaming with excitement.... He slid into bases on his chest, smearing the dirt on himself and his uniform, spurting it high along the base lines, risking a broken nose, a split skull, cracked ribs..."

Martin's kamikaze style set him apart during an era when aggressive base runners were a vanishing breed. Leo Durocher once said that Martin was the only player he ever worried about on the field. In a time when baseball was ruled by the home run, Martin's frenetic baserunning and free-wheeling attitude were a welcome change of pace.

Martin was one of the leaders of the Cardinals' riotous Gashouse Gang and was frequently in the middle of the team's zany antics. Once, when the temperature soared to 110 degrees during a game, he and Dizzy Dean built a fire in front of the dugout, then sat in front of it wrapped in blankets, like a couple of tribal chiefs. Another time, he and Rip Collins disguised themselves as electricians and burst into a hotel banquet in Philadelphia, where they proceeded to stage a mock fight before letting the audience in on the joke.

Martin was also never at a loss for words. After his bravura performance in the 1931 World Series, baseball commissioner Kenesaw Mountain Landis congratulated him, saying, "I wish I could trade places with you, young man." Without missing a beat Martin replied, "Give me your $50,000, Judge, and take my $5,000 and it's a deal."

Once, when asked how he could run so fast, Martin answered, "In Oklahoma, once you start running out there, there's nothing to stop you." Those last five words are a fitting epitaph for the irrepressible Wild Hoss of the Osage.

Ben Chapman

Dubbed the "Birmingham Bullet" because of his blazing speed, Ben Chapman seemed destined for a long, successful big league career. Unfortunately, his own temper and prejudices got in the way.

Born in Nashville on Christmas Day but raised in Alabama, Chapman displayed his speed in the minors in 1928 and 1929, stealing 30 bases with Asheville in the South Atlantic League and 26 with St. Paul in the American Association.

In 1930 he was brought up to the New York Yankees, where he hit .316 and stole 14 bases. The following year he hit his stride, stealing 61 bases to easily lead both leagues (Frankie Frisch paced the National League with 28) while batting .315.

The young outfielder seemed on the verge of super-stardom. In February, 1932, a glowing newspaper article labeled Chapman the "Meteor of the Base Paths." The story claimed that his baserunning "was one of the outstanding features of 1931," and that he "raised his way to fame on fast-flying feet when he proved himself to be far and away the greatest base stealer in baseball."

Those were heady words indeed, and Yankee manager Joe McCarthy added to the accolades when he said that the Birmingham Bullet "has everything that goes to make the good ballplayer—youth, perfect health and physique, ambition and eagerness, speed and judgment, style and genius. If he doesn't reach the top he will have only himself to blame."

McCarthy's words proved eerily prophetic. Although he led the American League in steals three more times, Chapman never again came close to the 61 he garnered in 1931. (His second best year saw him steal 38 bases in 1932.) In 1934, McCarthy blamed Chapman's plummeting stolen base numbers on the fact that pitchers began watching him more intently after his banner 1931 season.

By that time, however, the Birmingham Bullet was firing blanks in the Big Apple. The same fiery disposition that drove him to steal with reckless abandon was also his undoing, particularly his tendency to launch anti–Semitic tirades at Jewish Yankee fans. Finally, 36 games into the 1936 season, the Yanks sent him to the Senators, supposedly after being confronted by petitions from fans demanding Chapman's removal (although his holdout earlier that year didn't exactly endear him to management).

In 1937 Chapman was fined $50 and suspended for three days for threatening to punch umpire John Quinn. That year, he swiped 35 bases to lead the league for the fourth and final time. He finished his career with 287 stolen bases.

In later years Chapman's baserunning excellence would be forgotten. What would be remembered was his intolerant racial attitudes, especially his ferocious verbal abuse of Jackie Robinson in

Ben Chapman was nicknamed the Birmingham Bullet because of his speed (courtesy National Baseball Hall of Fame Library, Cooperstown, New York).

1947, when Chapman was managing the Phillies and Robinson was in his first season with the Dodgers.

George Case

According to a 1943 newspaper article, Washington Senators outfielder George Washington Case was "first in speed, first in burglary, and last in the hearts of American League catchers." Like Pepper Martin and Ben Chapman before him, Case stood out during an era when good base stealers were few and far between.

Born in Trenton, New Jersey, Case came up to the Senators for a cup of coffee in 1937, playing in just 22 games, hitting .289 and stealing two bases. That cup of coffee, however, quickly turned into a full-course meal: Two years later Case, now a regular, pilfered 51 sacks to lead the American League, a total that beat the *combined* amount of the top three National League base stealers.

Thus began Case's unprecedented reign of terror on American League pitchers and catchers. For five years in a row (1939–1943) the speedster led the league in steals, something that not even the great Cobb had ever done. Case reached his peak in 1943, stealing 61 bases. Even the year his streak was finally broken by Snuffy Stirnweiss of the Yankees, who stole 55 bases in 1944 to lead the American League, Case still finished second with 49 steals.

Case was such an exceptional base thief that his stolen base totals sometimes doubled and even tripled those of the National League leader. In 1939, Case's fifty-one steals were exactly three times as many as Lee Handley's and Stan Hack's seventeen. In 1943, when Case had 61 steals, Brooklyn's Arky Vaughan led the National League with just 20.

Case was considered the fastest player in baseball; some even said he was the fastest ever to play the game. Clyde Milan declared Case "faster than Ty Cobb, Eddie Collins, [and] Max Carey." Senators owner Clark Griffith thought that Case was the swiftest player he had ever seen, and predicted that he would ultimately beat Cobb's single-season record of 96 stolen bases.

To settle the issue of how fast Case was, he was timed running the bases by officials of the Amateur Athletic Union. The outfielder, in full flannel uniform, heavy wool socks and spiked shoes, circled the bases in a record 13.5 seconds, breaking the old mark of 13.8 seconds set by Hans Lobert in 1910.

Like Milan before him, Case was one of the Senators' most popular players. One fan was so smitten with the Senators' outfielder with the "super-charged shoes" that he named a racehorse after him. The equine George Case won several races at New Jersey's Garden State Park and also sired some foals. One can only imagine the look on the face of the ballplayer's brother-in-law when he visited the track one day and read in the program that two of the horses were "sired by George Case."

Case's career was short; he played just 11 years, all but one of them (1946, with Cleveland) with the Senators. During that brief time, however, he amassed 349 total steals and led the American League six times in thefts.

In 1961, the former stolen base champ bemoaned the depths to which the art of stealing had fallen at that time. "The pitchers [today] seldom throw over to first. When I used to get on, the pitcher and first baseman would be playing catch. And another thing I've noticed nowadays—the catchers don't call for pitchouts the way they used to do. A catcher like Birdie Tebbetts would call for two pitchouts in a row against me and sometimes as many as three straight." Then he added wistfully: "Brother, I'd like to be playing now. I'd be stealing a lot more than I did 20 years ago."

One of the reasons that Case left the game early (he was just 32 years old when he retired) was the physical toll that stealing took on him. In 1945, Case told writer Shirley Povich that he had to wear a special girdle to ease the strain on his aching body. "It protects my sore thighs and I've got a special rubber stocking for my left knee. It's great stuff to be a baserunning champion, but I have to dress the part, and that's no fun."

Later, after Case retired, his son explained that his father quit when he did because his body was worn out. "Scar tissue had developed on his spine," said the boy. Case reportedly lived in pain for the rest of his life—a sad reminder of the price that attaining a championship level in any sport can extract from a person.

Jim Busby

What is a guy with only 97 lifetime stolen bases doing in a book about stealing? The answer is that during baseball's cement shoes era, also known as the 1950s, Busby was one of the few American Leaguers stealing bases. Along with Minnie Minoso, Jim Rivera, Jackie Jensen and Luis Aparicio, Busby dominated stealing in the American League throughout much of the decade.

Great base stealers were a rare breed in the early 1950s, especially in the American League. In 1951, when Busby stole 26 bases (a career best) to finish second behind Minoso, several New York Yankees couldn't say enough nice things about him.

Pitcher Vic Raschi rated Busby higher than Jackie Robinson on the bases. "Busby's break baffles the pitchers. It challenges the catchers," said Raschi. Mound-mate Allie Reynolds concurred, saying that Busby was even better than George Case. "No comparison," said Reynolds. "Busby has it over Case by a good margin. Jimmy gets to the bag faster."

Catcher Yogi Berra, who had his problems with Busby on the bases, said that the outfielder "moves back and forth [on the bases] with nonchalance and then, WHUSH! He's off!"

Indeed, Busby bothered the Yankees so much that Berra, shortstop Phil Rizzuto, and center fielder Joe DiMaggio worked out a trick play in which Berra would deliberately overthrow second when Busby was trying to steal. Then DiMaggio, who had been sneaking in close to back up the play, was supposed to pick up the ball and fire it to third to nail Busby, who was hopefully on his way there because of the overthrow. Unfortunately, the play never worked because, according to Rizzuto, "DiMaggio was tired."

"Anyway, it was very well thought out," the Scooter assured sports writer Dan Daniel.

So confident was Busby of his speed that in 1953, when he was with Washington, he offered to race Mickey Mantle or anyone else for the title of "Fastest Man in the American League" at the All-Star Game, as long as $1,000 was paid to the winner. Although Mantle was willing, manager Casey Stengel quashed the idea. That doesn't mean, however, that the race never happened. In his book *Billyball*, Billy Martin wrote that Mantle and Busby did indeed race during the 1953 season, when the Yankees came to Washington. According to Martin, Busby, who had been a high school sprinter, set up starting blocks to get a quick jump, and went through numerous warm-up routines while Mantle just stood around watching him. Then, when the gun went off, Busby burst out in front by ten yards. Martin wrote: "Then, all of a sudden, here comes Mantle … Buzz-z-z-z! He went by Busby like a train. His last fifteen strides were just unbelievable."

Thus was settled the question of who was the fastest man in the American League.

Bob Dillinger

Few base thieves have been as aptly named as Bob Dillinger, who paced the American League in steals for three straight seasons and then dropped out of the major leagues almost overnight.

During a time when stealing was as popular as pickles on ice cream, the bespectacled Dillinger set the St. Louis Browns' farm system on fire with his speed. He swiped 67 bases to lead the Western League in 1939, and followed that by stealing another 67 the next year to pace the Middle Atlantic Circuit. Dillinger was so fast that he lost a race against Olympic track star Jesse Owens by just a few feet.

The sad-sack Browns, who rarely saw light in their gloomy second-division existence, knew a hot prospect when they saw one, and were eager to bring Dillinger up to the majors. World War II, however, interrupted their plans, and instead Dillinger joined Uncle Sam's team. Finally, in 1946 the third baseman made it to the parent club for half the season, hitting .280 with eight steals in 83 games.

In 1947 Dillinger blossomed into the player that the Browns were hoping for, hitting .294 and leading the American League with 34 steals. The total was extremely high for that era and stamped Dillinger as a most wanted man on the bases. He led the league again the next two years by pilfering 28 and 20 bases.

Dillinger was such a highly regarded player that in 1950, the notoriously tight-fisted Connie Mack parted with $100,000 to obtain him for the Philadelphia A's. Great things were predicted for Dillinger in the City of Brotherly Love; one article even said that Dillinger "undoubtedly will be the A's best base stealer since Eddie Collins."

Besides being a sensational hitter and spectacular fielder, George Sisler was also an excellent base stealer (courtesy of National Baseball Hall of Fame Library, Cooperstown, New York).

Unfortunately, things very quickly went sour for Dillinger in Philadelphia. By July, even though he was hitting .309, Dillinger had stolen only a handful of bases, and the spark he was supposed to give the A's had flickered out. On July 14, with the team floundering, Mack sold Dillinger to Pittsburgh for $35,000. Although he hit .301 for the season, the former flash stole just nine bases.

Remarkably, Dillinger played just one more year in the major leagues. In 1951 he split time between the Pirates and the White Sox, hitting .292 and stealing a mere five bases. After that he dropped out of the big leagues for good, his six-year career over despite his speed and a lifetime .306 batting average.

Dillinger's abrupt departure from the majors was puzzling; it seemed like there should have been some team willing to take a chance on a speedy .300 hitter. One possible explanation for the lack of interest in Dillinger came from Browns executive Bill DeWitt. He claimed that the third baseman's eyesight was not good, particularly on balls hit to his left, and that this affected his fielding. According to DeWitt, the other Browns players would ride Dillinger about missing balls and he would respond, "How can I get 'em when I can't see 'em?" (Of course, how Dillinger was consistently able to hit .300 if his eyes were so bad remains unknown.)

Another explanation came in a 1952 article that appeared after Dillinger was sold to the Pacific Coast League by the White Sox. The crux of the story was that Dillinger had lost his desire to play major league ball. A baseball official was quoted as saying that Dillinger had "more natural ability than almost any player in the game today, yet he just puts out so much and no more."

The story supported this argument by also quoting Dillinger, who supposedly once told a Browns executive that "If I knew any other way of making this much money, I sure wouldn't put on this monkey suit every day." Monkey suit or not, Dillinger performed more like a cheetah during his brief major league tenure.

George Sisler

"He could do everything. He could hit, hit with power, field, run and throw."

So said Ty Cobb—a man to whom praise of any type did not

come easy—about George Sisler, who many think might have been the best first baseman of all-time.

One of the many things that Sisler could do well was run. In fact, for such a ferocious hitter (Sisler's batting average for his first eight seasons was an astronomical .367), the St. Louis Browns' star could really turn on the jets. Gorgeous George, as he was known, led the American League in stolen bases four times between 1918 and 1927, peaking with a high of 51 steals in 1922. From 1916 through 1922, Sisler averaged 38 stolen bases per season. During that same period Cobb averaged 32 steals per year and Max Carey, the premier base bandit in the National League, averaged 46. Somehow, Sisler also found time to steal home 20 times for the Browns.

Sheer speed was responsible for many of Sisler's stolen bases. He was considered one of the fastest runners in the American League, even faster than Cobb. In a 1916 newspaper story, when asked if he was faster than the Georgia Peach, Sisler responded, "You men in the press box ought to know, for Ty and I just play while you see."

In 1922, Gorgeous George had what some consider to be the greatest single season ever. He hit .420, lashed 246 hits, scored 134 runs, hammered 18 triples, and stole 51 bases—all league-leading totals. Sisler's all-around excellence helped the Browns come within an eyelash of beating out the New York Yankees for the American League pennant.

As if his hitting weren't enough to rave about, Sisler was also a consummate fielder. He was called the Spalding Guide player because his picture was used in that publication to illustrate excellence at first base. For years the story was told that Gorgeous George once fielded a grounder and flipped the ball toward first base, where he had expected the pitcher to be covering. Seeing that the hurler was still rooted to the mound, Sisler leaped to the bag and caught his own toss.

Unfortunately, a severe sinus infection afflicted Sisler after his sensational 1922 season, and he was never the same player afterward (although he was still quite good).

Could Sisler really do it all, or was this just another case of "old-timer superioritis"? As proof of the former, in 1915 Sisler pitched against the legendary Walter Johnson—and won, 2–1.

Gorgeous George indeed; he sounds more like Superman!

Rod Carew

Like George Sisler, Rod Carew is remembered as a sensational hitter, not a base stealer. Indeed, there is much to recall about Carew's performance at the plate: he hit .300 or better for 15 straight seasons, won six American League batting titles, collected over 3,000 hits, and compiled a lifetime batting average of .328.

All of this sensational stick work masked another of Carew's abilities: base stealing. Over the course of his 19 year career Carew swiped 353 bags. His best year was 1976, when he stole 49 bases.

But what made Carew unique among base thieves was his uncanny ability to steal home. He did it 17 times during his career, including a record-tying seven in 1969 when he was with the Minnesota Twins. Billy Martin, who would later be a major influence on Rickey Henderson, was managing the Twins that year, and it was Martin who came up with the idea of having Carew focus on stealing home.

Carew recalled the situation for Art Rust, Jr., in Rust's book *Legends: Conversations with Baseball Greats*:

> That [the seven steals of home] was set up by Billy Martin. We worked on it in spring training, because Billy came up to me and said, "Rod, some days, you know the hitters might not be hitting, so we're going to work on something—to see if we can steal some runs." And he worked with me as far as timing the pitchers, the wind-up over at third base, getting the good short walk leading off the bag, and breaking—showing me when I should break when the pitcher's getting ready to deliver. So I had a sign with the hitters. They knew that once I flashed that sign, they were not supposed to swing. They were supposed to try to block the catcher out for me so that I could slide under safely.

In another book, a biography of Billy Martin by David Falkner entitled *The Last Yankee*, Carew paid tribute to his late manager. "I used to think about stealing bases in terms of speed, in terms of my legs," he said. "Billy taught me that you steal with your head. In stealing home, you watch the pitcher, you take your lead in a certain way, you get into the minds of the pitcher and catcher, you watch what they do. You don't have to be particularly fast to take advantage."

Ironically, just like Pete Reiser, who always claimed that he was robbed of an eighth steal of home by a bad call, Carew also said that an umpire's error cost him a chance at eight. According to Carew, during a game in Seattle in 1969 he stole home for the eighth time. However, he was called out, despite the fact that the ball was underneath the catcher rather than in his glove.

Davey Lopes once said of stealing home, "That's for amateurs. That isn't for guys who make their living stealing." Lopes may have been right, and Carew certainly made his living at the dish, and not on the bases. Yet, of all the bases to steal, home is the most difficult. Not only is the runner literally trying to outrace a pitch to the plate, but there's also the added risk of serious injury from crashing into the catcher and his protective equipment. Of course, if the batter doesn't know that the runner is coming, and swings away, there's the possibility that the runner could wind up eating with a straw for weeks if the ball is hit right at him.

In 1980, Carew listed the ingredients needed for a successful steal of home: a pitcher who uses a windup and holds the ball in his glove, the ability to get a walking lead, and, most importantly, the element of surprise. "No matter how often you've gone, the opposition never seems to expect it," he said. "A lot of times, the pitcher will get caught offstride and throw the ball away when a good throw would have caught you."

Getting caught certainly didn't happen too often to Rod Carew. Among post–World War II players, only Jackie Robinson stole home more times (19) than Carew.

Minnie Minoso

Saturnino Orestes Armas "Minnie" Minoso was the prototype of a new style of ballplayer just emerging in the early 1950s, one that was the total opposite of the slow-footed slugger populating many a major league roster. By combining power, the ability to hit to all fields, speed, and excellent defense (he won four Gold Gloves), Minoso was the vanguard of a new generation of multidimensional ballplayers such as Willie Mays, Hank Aaron, and Ernie Banks.

Minoso got his start in organized ball with the New York Cubans in the Negro League. Upon coming to the White Sox in 1951 in a trade with Cleveland, the happy-go-lucky Cuban blossomed into a star. He led the American League in steals in his first three years in Chicago, swiping 31, 22, and 25 bases. During this same period (1951–1953), no other American League player had more than 44 steals. The fleet outfielder averaged 20 steals per season from 1951 to 1957, and was always among the top five in stolen bases in the American League.

Like Jackie Robinson, Minoso's speed put intense pressure on the opposing team. "Minoso always upsets the infield," said Yankee shortstop Phil Rizzuto. "You know you have to field the ball cleanly and rush your throws when he's at bat or on base. He just doesn't give you any chance to relax, mentally or physically. He gives you the jitters."

Minoso, who was exceedingly superstitious, occasionally gave himself the jitters as well. One day, after going hitless against the Red Sox, he showered with his uniform on to wash away the bad luck that had cursed his batting. The very next game he went 4–4. Immediately afterward, eight of his White Sox teammates jumped into the shower with *their* uniforms on.

Minoso's plate-crowding batting stance made him a frequent target of inside pitches. He got hit by pitches 192 times in his career, ranking seventh on the all-time list for that dubious achievement. Fortunately, his good nature defused many situations that could have turned ugly. Once, when it was suggested that prejudice was the real reason he was getting plunked so often, he jokingly asked to be painted white.

When he stole his two hundredth base in 1963 while with the Washington Senators, Minoso became only the twelfth player in the last 35 years to reach that total. He finished his career with 205 steals.

Willie Mays

It seems almost unfair. Here was a man who could hit, throw, run, and field with abilities, as the old *Superman* TV show used to say, "far beyond those of mortal men." On top of that, he was also a league-leading base stealer. Couldn't he be bad—or at least just average—at anything?

To anyone who ever saw him play, the obvious answer to that question is "no." Nothing that Willie Howard Mays ever did on the diamond was average, and that included stealing.

Although today his base stealing has been overshadowed by his all-around greatness, Mays led the National League in steals four straight years (1956–1959), swiping 40, 38, 31, and 27, respectively. While these numbers seem puny in comparison to those of the 1970s and 1980s, for the 1950s these were virtually Cobbian totals. Indeed, there were some years in which Mays' dominance in base stealing was similar to that of the Tiger outfielder. In 1956, for example, his 40 steals almost doubled the 21 thefts of his nearest rival, Brooklyn's Jim Gilliam.

Mays' sensational 1956 season—36 homers, 40 steals—made him just the second member in baseball history of the "30–30" club (30 steals and 30 home runs). (The only other player to do it previously was Ken Williams of the 1922 St. Louis Browns, who hit 39 homers and stole 37 bases.) In 1960 Mays joined another of the game's most exclusive groups by becoming the first player to hit more than 200 home runs and steal more than 200 bases.

By 1960, however, there was a new base stealing whiz in town named Maury Wills. Mays, perhaps sensing that the skinny Dodger shortstop was about to become the new base-stealing bully on the block, eased the throttle back and finished the season with 25 steals.

Two years later, Wills set the baseball world on its ear by swiping 104 bases. With his days as Thief of Bags obviously over in the face of that type of performance, Mays spoke about stealing. "I could steal fifty bases or more if I wanted to," he said. "But there are other things on the ball field I have to do and stealing bases burns up too much energy."

True to his word, Mays continued to do "the other things on the ball field" extremely well throughout his career. His base stealing, however, trailed off considerably. Whereas he had averaged 27 steals per years from 1955 through 1962, the years between 1963 and 1970 saw him average just eight steals per season. He finished his career with 338 lifetime stolen bases, and the knowledge, that, for a time in the late 1950s, there wasn't a more complete player in baseball than Willie Howard Mays.

In Praise of the Speed-Challenged

Let's face it: to steal a base, you have to be fast. Not so fast that you leave scorch marks on the infield when you run, but fast enough so that when you attempt to steal, you have a reasonable expectation of making it to the base before the next game begins.

Unfortunately, some players *don't* have that expectation. To them, "speed" will always mean something that they do in their cars, and "stealing" is something only performed by robbers. Formerly, they'd just be called "slow." But, in the spirit of today's politically-correct atmosphere, let's instead dub them "speed-challenged." Their ranks include Gus Triandos, Russ Nixon and Cecil Fielder.

Gus Triandos

It was once said that a calendar was used to time Gus Triandos' speed. That wasn't true; his speed was actually measured against the growth of a blade of grass. During his 13 year career, the lumbering catcher attempted to steal just one base—and was successful.

Initially the property of the New York Yankees, Triandos was actually once described, in an article on the team's young players, as being "fairly fast on the base paths." Triandos cleverly kept this speed under wraps until 1958, when he unleashed it to steal the one and only base of his career—ironically, against the Yankees, who had traded him to Baltimore late in 1954. He finished his career with one steal in one attempt.

Russ Nixon

At least Triandos stole one base. Russ Nixon didn't steal any. Like Triandos, Nixon was a catcher to whom the idea of stealing a base was as foreign as the notion of Ty Cobb saying, "Beg pardon, old chap," when he came slashing into a base with spikes high. Nixon played 906 games in his 12 year career and never stole a single sack. This was the pinnacle of stealing futility until Cecil Fielder came along, and inched the record away from him.

Cecil Fielder

In the second game of the 1996 season, New York Yankee slugger Cecil Fielder stole second base. What made this remarkable was that it was the first base Fielder had stolen in nearly 1,100 games. "I could hear him coming. I was dumbfounded. I didn't know how to act," explained umpire Tim Tschida. Although his consecutive no-steal streak was broken, Fielder remains the only player to play in 1,000 games without stealing a base.

Appendix:
League-Leading Base Stealers

American Association

American League

1912 C. Milan, Washington 88
1913 C. Milan, Washington 75
1914 F. Maisel, New York 74
1915 T. Cobb, Detroit... 96
1916 T. Cobb, Detroit... 68
1917 T. Cobb, Detroit... 55
1918 G. Sisler, St. Louis 45
1919 E. Collins, Chicago.. 33
1920 S. Rice, Washington 63
1921 G. Sisler, St. Louis 35
1922 G. Sisler, St. Louis 51
1923 E. Collins, Chicago.. 49
1924 E. Collins, Chicago.. 42
1925 J. Mostil, Chicago... 43
1926 J. Mostil, Chicago... 35
1927 G. Sisler, St. Louis 27
1928 B. Meyer, Boston 30
1929 C. Gehringer, Detroit.. 27
1930 M. McManus, Detroit 23
1931 B. Chapman, New York 61
1932 B. Chapman, New York 38
1933 B. Chapman, New York 27
1934 B. Werber, Boston 40
1935 B. Werber, Boston 29
1936 L. Lary, St. Louis... 37
1937 B. Werber, St. Louis, and
      B. Chapman, Washington/Boston 35
1938 F. Crosetti, New York 27
1939 G. Case, Washington 51
1940 G. Case, Washington 35
1941 G. Case, Washington 33
1942 G. Case, Washington 44
1943 G. Case, Washington 61
1944 G. Stirnweiss, New York...................................... 55
1945 G. Stirnweiss, New York...................................... 33
1946 G. Case, Cleveland 28
1947 B. Dillinger, St. Louis....................................... 34
1948 B. Dillinger, St. Louis....................................... 28
1949 B. Dillinger, St. Louis....................................... 20
1950 D. DiMaggio, Boston 15
1951 M. Minoso, Cleveland/Chicago 31
1952 M. Minoso, Chicago.. 22
1953 M. Minoso, Chicago.. 25
1954 J. Jensen, Boston.. 22

1955	J. Rivera, Chicago	25
1956	L. Aparicio, Chicago	21
1957	L. Aparicio, Chicago	28
1958	L. Aparicio, Chicago	29
1959	L. Aparicio, Chicago	56
1960	L. Aparicio, Chicago	51
1961	L. Aparicio, Chicago	53
1962	L. Aparicio, Chicago	31
1963	L. Aparicio, Baltimore	40
1964	L. Aparicio, Baltimore	57
1965	B. Campaneris, Kansas City	51
1966	B. Campaneris, Kansas City	52
1967	B. Campaneris, Kansas City	55
1968	B. Campaneris, Oakland	62
1969	T. Harper, Seattle	73
1970	B. Campaneris, Oakland	42
1971	A. Otis, Kansas City	52
1972	B. Campaneris, Oakland	52
1973	T. Harper, Boston	54
1974	B. North, Oakland	54
1975	M. Rivers, California	70
1976	B. North, Oakland	75
1977	F. Patek, Kansas City	53
1978	R. LeFlore, Detroit	68
1979	W. Wilson, Kansas City	83
1980	R. Henderson, Oakland	100
1981	R. Henderson, Oakland	56
1982	R. Henderson, Oakland	130
1983	R. Henderson, Oakland	108
1984	R. Henderson, Oakland	66
1985	R. Henderson, New York	80
1986	R. Henderson, New York	87
1987	H. Reynolds, Seattle	60
1988	R. Henderson, New York	93
1989	R. Henderson, New York/Oakland	77
1990	R. Henderson, Oakland	65
1991	R. Henderson, Oakland	58
1992	K. Lofton, Cleveland	66
1993	K. Lofton, Cleveland	70
1994	K. Lofton, Cleveland	60
1995	K. Lofton, Cleveland	54
1996	K. Lofton, Cleveland	75
1997	B. Hunter, Detroit	74
1998	R. Henderson, Oakland	66

Federal League

1914	B. Kauff, Indiana	75
1915	B. Kauff, Brooklyn	55

National League

1887	M. Ward, New York	111
1888	D. Hoy, Washington	82
1889	J. Fogarty, Philadelphia	99
1890	B. Hamilton, Philadelphia	102
1891	B. Hamilton, Philadelphia	111
1892	M. Ward, Brooklyn.	88
1893	T. Brown, Louisville	66
1894	B. Hamilton, Philadelphia	99
1895	B. Hamilton, Philadelphia	97
1896	J. Kelley, Baltimore.	87
1897	B. Lange, Chicago.	73
1898	E. Delahanty, Philadelphia.	58
1899	J. Sheckard, Baltimore	77
1900	J. Barrett, Cincinnati	46
1901	H. Wagner, Pittsburgh	48
1902	H. Wagner, Pittsburgh	43
1903	J. Sheckard, Brooklyn, and F. Chance, Chicago.	67
1904	H. Wagner, Pittsburgh	53
1905	B. Maloney, Chicago, and A. Devlin, New York.	59
1906	F. Chance, Chicago.	57
1907	H. Wagner, Pittsburgh	61
1908	H. Wagner, Pittsburgh	53
1909	B. Bescher, Cincinnati	54
1910	B. Bescher, Cincinnati	70
1911	B. Bescher, Cincinnati	81
1912	B. Bescher, Cincinnati	67
1913	M. Carey, Pittsburgh	61
1914	G. Burns, New York	62
1915	M. Carey, Pittsburgh	36
1916	M. Carey, Pittsburgh	63
1917	M. Carey, Pittsburgh	46
1918	M. Carey, Pittsburgh	58
1919	G. Burns, New York	40
1920	M. Carey, Pittsburgh	52
1921	F. Frisch, New York.	49
1922	M. Carey, Pittsburgh	51
1923	M. Carey, Pittsburgh	51

1924	M. Carey, Pittsburgh	49
1925	M. Carey, Pittsburgh	46
1926	K. Cuyler, Pittsburgh	35
1927	F. Frisch, St. Louis	48
1928	K. Cuyler, Chicago	37
1929	K. Cuyler, Chicago	43
1930	K. Cuyler, Chicago	37
1931	F. Frisch, St. Louis	28
1932	C. Klein, Philadelphia	20
1933	P. Martin, St. Louis	26
1934	P. Martin, St. Louis	23
1935	A. Galan, Chicago	22
1936	P. Martin, St. Louis	23
1937	A. Galan, Chicago	23
1938	S. Hack, Chicago	16
1939	S. Hack, Chicago, and L. Handley, Pittsburgh	17
1940	L. Frey, Cincinnati	22
1941	D. Murtaugh, Philadelphia	18
1942	P. Reiser, Brooklyn	20
1943	A. Vaughan, Brooklyn	20
1944	J. Barrett, Pittsburgh	28
1945	R. Schoendienst, St. Louis	26
1946	P. Reiser, Brooklyn	34
1947	J. Robinson, Brooklyn	29
1948	R. Ashburn, Philadelphia	32
1949	J. Robinson, Brooklyn	37
1950	S. Jethroe, Boston	35
1951	S. Jethroe, Boston	35
1952	P. W. Reese, Brooklyn	30
1953	B. Bruton, Milwaukee	26
1954	B. Bruton, Milwaukee	34
1955	B. Bruton, Milwaukee	25
1956	W. Mays, New York	40
1957	W. Mays, New York	38
1958	W. Mays, New York	31
1959	W. Mays, New York	27
1960	M. Wills, Los Angeles	50
1961	M. Wills, Los Angeles	35
1962	M. Wills, Los Angeles	104
1963	M. Wills, Los Angeles	40
1964	M. Wills, Los Angeles	53
1965	M. Wills, Los Angeles	94
1966	L. Brock, St. Louis	74
1967	L. Brock, St. Louis	52

1968	L. Brock, St. Louis	62
1969	L. Brock, St. Louis	53
1970	B. Tolan, Cincinnati	57
1971	L. Brock, St. Louis	64
1972	L. Brock, St. Louis	63
1973	L. Brock, St. Louis	70
1974	L. Brock, St. Louis	118
1975	D. Lopes, Los Angeles	77
1976	D. Lopes, Los Angeles	63
1977	F. Taveras, Pittsburgh	70
1978	O. Moreno, Pittsburgh	71
1979	O. Moreno, Pittsburgh	77
1980	R. LeFlore, Montreal	97
1981	T. Raines, Montreal	71
1982	T. Raines, Montreal	78
1983	T. Raines, Montreal	90
1984	T. Raines, Montreal	75
1985	V. Coleman, St. Louis	110
1986	V. Coleman, St. Louis	107
1987	V. Coleman, St. Louis	109
1988	V. Coleman, St. Louis	81
1989	V. Coleman, St. Louis	65
1990	V. Coleman, St. Louis	77
1991	M. Grissom, Montreal	76
1992	M. Grissom, Montreal	78
1993	C. Carr, Florida	58
1994	C. Biggio, Houston	39
1995	Q. Veras, Florida	56
1996	E. Young, Colorado	53
1997	T. Womack, Pittsburgh	60
1998	T. Womack, Pittsburgh	58

Players League

| 1890 | H. Stovey, Boston | 97 |

Teams with the Most League-Leading Base Stealers

American League

| Chicago | 17 |
| Oakland | 12 |

Detroit 10
New York 10
Cleveland 9
St. Louis 9
Washington 9
Boston 6
Kansas City 3
Philadelphia 3
Baltimore 2
Seattle 2
California 1

National League

Pittsburgh 22
St. Louis 20
Chicago 11
New York 9
Philadelphia 9
Brooklyn 8
Los Angeles 8
Cincinnati 7
Montreal 7
Milwaukee 3
Baltimore 2
Boston 2
Florida 2
Colorado 1
Houston 1
Louisville 1
Washington 1

TEAM STOLEN BASE LEADERS

American League

Anaheim Angels 1975 . . . . 70 by Mickey Rivers
Baltimore Orioles 1964 . . . . 57 by Luis Aparicio
Boston Red Sox 1973 . . . . 54 by Tommy Harper
Chicago White Sox 1983 . . . . 77 by Rudy Law
Cleveland Indians 1996 . . . . 75 by Kenny Lofton
Detroit Tigers 1915 . . . . 96 by Ty Cobb

Kansas City A's 1967 . . . . 55 by Bert Campaneris
Kansas City Royals 1979 . . . . 83 by Willie Wilson
Milwaukee Brewers 1992 . . . . 54 by Pat Listach
Minnesota Twins 1997 . . . . 62 by Chuck Knoblauch
New York Yankees 1988 . . . . 93 by Rickey Henderson
Oakland A's 1982 . . . . 130 by Rickey Henderson
Philadelphia A's 1910 . . . . 81 by Eddie Collins
St. Louis Browns 1922 . . . . 51 by George Sisler
Seattle Mariners 1987 . . . . 60 by Harold Reynolds
Seattle Pilots 1969 . . . . 73 by Tommy Harper
Texas Rangers 1978 . . . . 52 by Bump Wills
Toronto Blue Jays 1984 . . . . 60 by Dave Collins
Washington Senators (Original Club) 1912 . . . . 88 by Clyde Milan
Washington Senators (Expansion Club) 1970 . . . . 29 by Ed Stroud

National League

Atlanta Braves 1991 . . . . 72 by Otis Nixon
Boston Braves 1896 . . . . 93 by Billy Hamilton
Brooklyn Dodgers 1892 . . . . 94 by Monte Ward
Chicago Cubs 1896 . . . . 100 by Bill Lange
Cincinnati Reds 1891 . . . . 93 by Arlie Latham
Colorado Rockies 1996 . . . . 53 by Eric Young
Florida Marlins 1993 . . . . 58 by Chuck Carr
Houston Astros 1988 . . . . 65 by Gerald Young
Los Angeles Dodgers 1962 . . . . 104 by Maury Wills
Milwaukee Braves 1954 . . . . 34 by Billy Bruton
Montreal Expos 1980 . . . . 97 by Ron LeFlore
New York Giants 1887 . . . . 111 by Monte Ward
New York Mets 1982 . . . . 58 by Mookie Wilson
Philadelphia Phillies 1891 . . . . 115 by Billy Hamilton
Pittsburgh Pirates 1980 . . . . 96 by Omar Moreno
St. Louis Cardinals 1974 . . . . 118 by Lou Brock
San Diego Padres 1984 . . . . 70 by Alan Wiggins
San Francisco Giants 1979 . . . . 58 by Bill North

Bibliography

The sheer volume of books on baseball is simply staggering. While I'm certain that I have missed many works that could have been of infinite help to me, the following books were certainly extremely useful.

Another indispensable reference source was the National Baseball Library and Archives at the National Baseball Hall of Fame and Museum, Inc., in Cooperstown, New York. Files from the library on virtually every player mentioned in detail in this book were studied in the preparation of this manuscript. The information contained within these files, some of which has been used for this book, is invaluable.

Aaseng, Nathan. *Jose Canseco: Baseball's 40–40 Man*. Minneapolis: Lerner, 1989.

Bankes, James. *The Pittsburgh Crawfords: The Lives and Times of Black Baseball's Most Exciting Team*. Dubuque, Iowa: Wm. C. Brown, 1991.

Bauleke, Ann. *Rickey Henderson: Record Stealer*. Minneapolis: Lerner, 1991.

Bjarkman, Peter C. *Top 10 Baseball Base Stealers*. Springfield, New Jersey: Enslow Publishers, 1995.

Burke, Larry. *The Baseball Chronicles*. New York: Smithmark, 1995.

Cataneo, David. *Baseball Legends and Lore*. New York: Barnes & Noble, 1997.

Chadwick, Bruce. *When the Game Was Black and White*. New York: Abbeville Press, 1992.

Charlton, Jim. *The Who, What, When, Where, Why and How of Baseball*. New York: Barnes & Noble, 1995.

Clark, Dick, and Larry Lester, eds. *The Negro Leagues Book*. Cleveland, Ohio: The Society for American Baseball Research, 1994.

Curran, William. *Big Sticks*. New York: William Morrow, 1990.

Davids, L. Robert. *Insider's Baseball*. New York: Scribner's Sons, 1983.

DeValeria, Dennis, and Jeanne Burke DeValeria. *Honus Wagner*. New York: Henry Holt, 1995.

DiMaggio, Joe. *Baseball for Everyone*. New York: Whittlesey House, McGraw-Hill, 1948.

Falkner, David. *The Last Yankee*. New York: Simon & Schuster, 1992.

Falls, Joe. *The Detroit Tigers*. New York: Walker, 1989.

Fitzgerald, Ed. *The American League*. New York: Grosset & Dunlap, 1963.

Gutman, Dan. *Baseball Babylon*. New York: Penguin Books, 1992.

_____. *Baseball's Biggest Bloopers*. New York: Viking, 1993.

Henderson, Rickey. *Off Base: Confessions of a Thief*. New York: HarperCollins, 1992.

Holway, John B. *Black Diamonds*. New York: Stadium Books, 1991.

_____. *Blackball Stars*. Westport, Conn.: Meckler Books, 1988.

Hynd, Noel. *The Giants of the Polo Grounds*. New York: Doubleday, 1988.

James, Bill. *The Historical Baseball Abstract*. New York: Villard, 1988.

Kerrane, Kevin, and Richard Grossinger, eds. *Baseball Diamonds*. Garden City, New York: Anchor Press/Doubleday, 1980.

Knapp, Ron. *From Prison to the Major Leagues*. New York: Julian Messner, 1980.

LeFlore, Ron, with Jim Hawkins. *Breakout: From Prison to the Big Leagues*. New York: Harper & Row, 1978.

Martin, Billy, & Phil Pepe. *BillyBall*. Garden City, New York: Doubleday, 1987.

Nash, Bruce, and Allan Zullo. *Believe It Or Else*. New York: Dell, 1992.

The New York Times Book of Baseball History. New York: Quadrangle/The New York Times, 1975.

150 Years of Baseball. Lincolnwood, Ill.: Publications International, 1989.

O'Neil, Buck. *I Was Right on Time*. New York: Simon & Schuster, 1996.

Ritter, Lawrence S. *The Glory of Their Times*. New York: Macmillan, 1966.

Robinson, Ray. *Speed Kings of the Base Paths*. New York: G.P. Putnam's Sons, 1964.

Rogosin, Donn. *Invisible Men*. New York: Atheneum, 1983.

Rust, Art, Jr. *Legends: Conversations with Baseball Greats*. New York: McGraw-Hill, 1989.

Seymour, Harold. *Baseball: The Early Years*. New York: Oxford University Press, 1960.

_____. *Baseball: The Golden Age*. New York: Oxford University Press, 1971.

Wallace, Joseph. *The Baseball Anthology*. New York: Harry N. Abrams, 1994.

Waggoner, Glen, Kathleen Moloney and Hugh Howard. *Baseball by the Rules*. New York: Prentice Hall, 1987.

Ward, Geoffrey C., and Ken Burns. *Baseball: An Illustrated History*. New York: Alfred A. Knopf, 1994.

Wills, Maury, and Mike Celizic. *On the Run*. New York: Carroll & Graf, 1991.

Index